AN INTRODUCTION TO CATHOLICISM

The Vatican. The Inquisition. Contraception. Celibacy. Apparitions and miracles. Plots and scandals. The Catholic Church is seldom out of the news. But what do its one billion adherents really believe, and how do they put their beliefs into practice in worship, in the family, and in society?

This down-to-earth account goes back to the early Christian creeds to uncover the roots of modern Catholic thinking. It avoids getting bogged down in theological technicalities and throws light on aspects of the Church's institutional structure and liturgical practice that even Catholics can find baffling: Why go to confession? How are people made saints? What is "infallible" about the pope? Topics addressed include:

- scripture and tradition;
- sacraments and prayer;
- popular piety;
- personal and social morality;
- reform, mission, and interreligious dialogue.

Lawrence Cunningham, a theologian, prize-winning writer, and university teacher, provides an overview of Catholicism today which will be indispensable for undergraduates and lay study groups.

LAWRENCE S. CUNNINGHAM is John A. O'Brien Professor of Theology at the University of Notre Dame. His scholarly interests are in the areas of systematic theology and culture, Christian spirituality, and the history of Christian spirituality. His most recent book is *A Brief History of Saints*. He has edited or written twenty other books and is co-editor of the academic monograph series "Studies in Theology and Spirituality." He has won three awards for his teaching and has been honored four times by the Catholic Press Association for his writing.

AN INTRODUCTION TO CATHOLICISM

LAWRENCE S. CUNNINGHAM

CAMBRIDGE
UNIVERSITY PRESS

CAMBRIDGE UNIVERSITY PRESS

Cambridge, New York, Melbourne, Madrid, Cape Town, Singapore, São Paulo, Delhi

Cambridge University Press

The Edinburgh Building, Cambridge CB2 8RU, UK

Published in the United States of America by Cambridge University Press, New York

www.cambridge.org

Information on this title: www.cambridge.org/9780521608558

First published 2009

Printed in the United States of America by Edwards Brothers Incorporated

A catalogue record for this publication is available from the British Library

ISBN 978-0-521-84607-3 hardback
ISBN 978-0-521-60855-8 paperback

Contents

v

Illustrations

Preface

When the editors of Cambridge University Press asked me to contribute a volume on Roman Catholicism for a series of books they were publishing on the religious traditions of Christianity I was both honored to have been asked and pleased to accept. Having worked on the book for some time, I now note ruefully that it was a task far more complicated than I had first imagined. To write about Catholicism encompassing its history, practice(s), and beliefs within the manageable framework of a single volume is not easy especially if the book is not to be a dreary litany of persons and ideas and a catalog of devotional practices, customs, and movements. Take a common term such as "Vatican" – a word that is often identified with Roman Catholicism. Vatican can refer to a specific place in Rome with a history that predates Christianity; it is the site of the purported burial place of the Apostle Peter; it is the location of a major basilica over the tomb of Saint Peter whose history goes back to the early fourth century; it has been the home of the popes since the late Middle Ages. Beyond those markers, it is also a shorthand term for the official administrative body assisting the pope (as in "The Vatican said yesterday . . ."), and those offices are often misidentified with the Vatican City State which is a sovereign state established in 1929 after the successful negotiations with the Italian government in a formal treaty known at the Lateran Treaty.

The polyvalent sense of the word "Vatican" is only one instance of a whole set of terms and images which have behind them a long history upon which meanings, nuances, and refinements have accrued. Were some fourth-century Catholics somehow allowed to come back to life and enter a contemporary Catholic Church or read a contemporary catechism, they would find much that would puzzle them and other things with which they would have some acquaintance. They would be amazed that their co-religionists honor seven sacraments, regard the pope as infallible, recite a rote set of prayers called the rosary, and allow only an unmarried clergy, and they would have no sense at all of what the words "cardinal," "transubstantiation," "papal encyclical," etc., mean. In fact, many Catholics today, only dimly aware of the history of their tradition, would be amazed that their fourth-century co-religionists would be amazed.

These religious ancestors of ours, however, would be quite comfortable with the idea of a bishop or priest presiding at the liturgy; they would recognize the readings from scripture; they would understand the offering and communion of bread and wine as signs of the real presence of Christ, and they would know that priests become priests by the laying on of hands; furthermore, they would know that one does not communicate without first having been baptized, and they would know the elements of the recited creed and recognize the general formulation of that creed.

One of the main burdens of this volume will be to explain how Catholic belief and practice evolved over the centuries. This is not primarily a history of Catholicism, but history will play a large part in my attempt to describe how the essential core of Catholic belief and practice encompasses both a fidelity to essentials – what we call the Apostolic Tradition – and a way of adding to and celebrating a deeper understanding of what that tradition is and how it is lived. This work, then, is neither a book of technical theology nor of pure history. It is a work that attempts to blend the two along with an account of worship, popular devotions, and, of course, how Catholics understand both personal and social morality.

I puzzled long and hard over how much technical theology should be included in this book and finally decided to treat theological issues, especially controversial ones, rather lightly. This neglect is not done from indifference since I earn my bread and butter by studying these matters. The reason behind that decision is easy to explain: Fundamental theological doctrines have behind them such a long and complicated history that it is not easy to describe them without endless qualifications, definitions, and caveats. That God grants us divine favor is easy enough to assert but how that favor, technically known as "grace," has been understood is the subject of many weighty volumes and not a few contentious disputes. That it is God who saves us through Jesus Christ is a fundamental truth in Christianity, but the dynamics of being saved really merit a separate treatment of monograph length. My default mode was, where appropriate, to assert such beliefs without tracking out their justification or the history of their understanding.

In a similar fashion, it struck me as important to take note of popular piety and common usages in the Catholic tradition simply because they are part of the public perception of the Church: For example, Catholics say the rosary; Catholics make pilgrimages to shrines. Such practices are not of the essence, but, when properly understood, they do cast some light on the Catholic experience. They are traditions but not the Tradition.

In order to wrestle my account into some kind of order, this book will use thematic chapters. There are eleven of them. The number may seem a bit odd, but, as a long-time classroom teacher, it struck me that eleven might account for the number of weeks in a term (at least on this side of the Atlantic) with time enough for examinations and a week of vacation in term. My target audience is not my academic peers but for reasonably literate inquirers. For that reason, footnotes are sparse but suggested readings are appended to each chapter to aid the more inquisitive reader. The brief twelfth chapter is mainly bibliographical, and it also is modest – citing, for the most part, reference works in English. Each chapter also has a boxed figure to study in a bit more depth a specific topic only lightly touched on in the text. The chapters will also have shorter boxes on a tinted background so as to free the main text from too much factual clutter.

Acknowledgments

This book benefited directly and indirectly from the wisdom of many people. Much of what is asserted in these pages was first delivered orally in the classroom over the past thirty years. For fear of neglecting to name all of them, let me, in the first instance, express my gratitude globally to my colleagues in the Department of Theology at the University of Notre Dame both for being willing to help me with my many queries and for providing such a nurturing community within which to work. A special word of thanks goes to my next-door neighbor in the department, Cyril O'Regan, and my chairman, John Cavadini.

I have also been instructed by time spent in short-term teaching appointments at Spring Hill College in Mobile, Alabama; Saint John's University in Collegeville, Minnesota; and the College of Saint Elizabeth in Convent Station, New Jersey. From those visits I have garnered much about the diversity of Catholic life. The Cistercian monastic communities of the Abbey of Gethsemani and Santa Rita Abbey have at times afforded me the leisure and quiet that make thinking possible, so, to their superiors, Dom Damien Thompson and Mother Miriam Pollard, I owe a debt of thanks. I wish to recognize my wife Cecilia and my two daughters, Sarah Mary and Julia Clare, for making my life so wonderful while urging me on with the gentle query about how the book is going. Finally, let me offer many thanks to Kate Brett of Cambridge University Press for taking me on as an author and for her understanding patience as I finished the book.

I would like to dedicate this work to the students of my university, past, present and future who study, work, and pray under the shadow of Notre Dame.

CHAPTER I

The many meanings of Catholicism

INTRODUCTION

It is common for many people to understand the word "Catholicism" to mean a particular denomination as distinguished, say, from Protestantism or Orthodoxy, within the larger world of Christianity. Thus, for example, Catholics say the rosary, revere the pope, go to mass on Sunday, and have a clergy that does not marry, and those characteristics, among many other things, distinguish Catholics from Protestants. Catholics are also said to reflect certain ethnic backgrounds: The Irish are Catholics but the Scots are Presbyterian; Italians are Catholics but Norwegians are Lutheran. In some places, Catholics are identified by class. In the USA a century ago, Catholics were considered mainly but not exclusively working class while some mainline Protestants were identified with the managerial class. In England, until very recently, that was also the case. These and similar stereotypes are very much a part of the popular culture, but they are stereotypes nonetheless. People are divided by denominational difference, and they frequently understand themselves through their inherited religious upbringing: To be Irish is to be Catholic. This popular conception of Catholicism, understood as a sociological category, is true of most large religious traditions. To belong to any or other religious tradition depends very much on where one lives and how one perceives oneself relative to the larger culture.

In that general sense, then, Catholicism can be considered as one Christian denomination among many but identifiable as having its own distinct culture, character, and sometimes dependent on ancestry and geographical location. Catholicism, then, not to put too fine a point on it, can be understood as a recognizable social grouping. This sociological understanding is not the way in which we wish to present Catholicism in this volume although, to be sure, we will have to pay attention to Catholicism's social manifestation in the world while also being alert to its cultural character. This volume is not a book about the social description of Catholicism but about Catholic belief and practice. It is also an "insider's view" in that the presentation is made by someone who is a member of the Catholic Church.

We should also note in passing – and this will be discussed further in this chapter – that within Catholicism there is more than one tradition (for example, there are Roman and Byzantine Catholics – all part of the Catholic Church). This distinction needs to be pointed out because words such as "Catholic," "Orthodox," and "Protestant" are abstractions. Presbyterians are not Lutherans, and Russian Orthodoxy is not the exact same thing as Greek Orthodoxy.

The burden of this present chapter is to get behind the bewilderingly complex phenomenon of Catholicism to ask not how to describe all of the parts that make up the structure, belief system, and worship of the Catholic Church – we will attend to such matters later in this work – but to ask a far more fundamental question: What does it mean historically, sociologically, and theologically when we use the word "catholic"?

To answer that question will demand that we pay attention to how the word "catholic" was first used in the Christian vocabulary, how it developed in the history of Christianity, and, further, how the word is understood from within the Church which calls itself "Catholic." This is not as easy as it at first might seem since many people who are not denominationally Catholic still profess a belief that the Church is catholic when they recite the historic creeds about their belief in the "one, holy, catholic, and apostolic church."

When we have done the preliminary historical work we can then further stipulate what the essential characteristics of catholicity are as Catholics understand them. In this chapter, then, we will trace out the evolution of the word "catholic" and how it is understood from within the Catholic tradition, and we will inquire into its theological significance. Once having done that, it will then become possible to reflect on the development of Catholic belief and practice. It is within that context that we will be able to explore fully the statement in the historic creeds which says that we believe in the "one, holy, catholic, and apostolic church" and how that creedal phrase is understood by those who identify themselves as being Catholics.

It should also be said, again at the outset, that what follows is an account written from *within* the Roman Catholic tradition. It is very much a simplified account, which may be read differently from other perspectives. Some may very well quarrel with some assertions made in this work. In other words: This is a Catholic account of Catholicism and a somewhat traditionally unapologetic one at that. No one understands better than the writer that many will quarrel with the understanding of Catholicism presented here (including some fellow Catholics!), but readers must be tolerant as we lay out the Catholic self-understanding even if not all would accept the premises that stand in the background of this understanding.

THE HISTORY OF A WORD

The word "catholic" comes from two Greek words, *kath holou,* which means something like "of the whole." When we use the word "catholic" in nonreligious discourse (for example, "Her tastes in literature were very catholic"), we mean some something like "broad," "far ranging," and the like. In that sense, the opposite of "catholic" is "narrow" or "limited." The word "catholic" is not found in the New Testament. It does occur, as we shall see, very early in Christian history. To understand the word, we need to make a preliminary observation about the primitive growth of Christianity.

The word that we usually find translated as "church" in the New Testament (and the term is used most commonly by Saint Paul) comes from the Greek word *ekklesia* (from which we derive the word "ecclesiastical"), which means an "assembly," "community," or "congregation." When Saint Paul, who makes most use of the term *ekklesia,* uses the word, he is referring to those groups of early believers who assembled in community for common worship and instruction. The word *ekklesia* did not mean a structure or building but the community itself. Indeed, Paul clearly distinguishes the assembly from the place where it met in a phrase which is to be found in his postscript to his letter to the Romans where he wishes to have greetings to be sent to Prisca and Aquila and "also the Church (*ekklesia*) which meets in their house (*oikos*)" (Rom. 16:4). It is worth noting that in that same section of his letter Paul refers not only to "church" in the singular but also in the plural: "Greet one another with a holy kiss. All the Churches of Christ greet you" (Rom. 16:16). We can truly speak, as does Paul himself in his letters, of the Christian assembly and Christian assemblies.

We can then think of the earliest stages of Christianity as a loosely organized network of small communities in various parts of the Mediterranean world keeping linked to each other by traveling apostles, evangelists, and other missionaries as well as by circulating letters like those of Paul's letter to the Churches of Galatia, Corinth, or Philippi.

Thus, at the end of his letter to the Corinthian Christians, Paul mentions in passing the "churches of Galatia" (1 Cor. 16:1) and the Churches of Asia (1 Cor. 16:19). If there was a center hub of this network, it would have to be Jerusalem, the place where Jesus lived out his earthly life and the place where the Apostles of Jesus began their public lives. Christianity radiated from Jerusalem, but even Jerusalem was not the center of Christianity in any strict organizational sense.

It is within the context of this wide-ranging network of small Christian communities that the word "catholic" first appears. It is generally agreed that the first Christian to use the word "catholic" was a Christian convert named Ignatius (?35–107), who was the leader of the Church in Antioch, even though he may have been born in Syria. Condemned to death by Emperor Trajan, he was to be transported from his city to Rome, under guard, to die in the arena, which, in fact, occurred around the year 107. Ignatius lived in the period that closed the Age of the Apostles. He wrote seven letters to various churches while making his journey. In a letter to the Church in Smyrna (in present-day Turkey), he writes, "Where the bishop appears, let to the people be, just as where Christ is, there is the Catholic Church." The obvious sense of that passage is that the word "catholic" was to be understood as the whole church as opposed to this or that particular congregation: the whole or entire as opposed to the part. Ignatius, in short, was thinking of the entire body of Christians as opposed to any particular community that was part of that whole. Thus, in the first instance, the word "catholic" meant the whole (body of Christian believers) as opposed to this or that particular community of Christians. It was not then a description of a denomination but an adjective to describe a collectivity, i.e. the Christian community globally understood as opposed to this or that particular community. The word "catholic" enters the Christian vocabulary simply as a way of describing the whole or entirety of the Christian body of believers as opposed to its particular instantiation in this or that particular place.

Before the end of the second century, the word "catholic" began to mean the witness and teaching of this whole or "catholic" church as opposed to the claims of dissident groups. This new understanding begins to sharpen the notion of catholicity. That is the sense in which Irenaeus of Lyons (?130–200) in France uses the term. Irenaeus came from Asia Minor (probably Smyrna) but settled in what is present-day France in the city of Lyons after having studied and worked in Rome. Ordained a priest, he became Bishop of that city around the year 178. In a famous work written to confute those who held erroneous ideas about Christianity, he assumed the unity of one world church of Christianity which held one faith and one preaching:

the Church, although scattered over the whole world, diligently observes [this faith], as if it occupied but one house and believes as if it had but one mind and preaches and teaches as if it had one mouth. And although there are many dialects in the world, the meaning of the tradition is one and the same. For the same faith is held and handed down by the Churches established in the Germanies, the Spains, among the Celtic tribes, in the East, in Lybia, and in the central portions of the world. But as the sun, the creation of God, is one and the same in all the world, so is the light of the preaching of the truth, which shines on all who desire to come to the knowledge of the truth. (*Adversus haereses*, I: 10, 1–2)

Two things are to be noted about that passage. First, Irenaeus clearly distinguishes churches (plural) and the Church (singular). It is in that latter sense in which the word "catholic" is to be understood (i.e. the worldwide church). Second, and more importantly, Irenaeus now adds another qualification to the words "Catholic Church" (i.e. the entire church): It is in that Catholic Church where one finds the faith handed down by the Apostles of Christ.

In that added meaning, Irenaeus now develops a meaning of the word "catholic" which was to become very common, that is, the term "catholic" now means those who hold to the authentic faith of the Apostles who were entrusted with the teaching of Jesus. Thus, "catholic" became a synonym for the word "orthodox." The word "orthodox" has two meanings: (1) right or correct belief and (2) right or correct worship. Thus, Catholic and Orthodox became the term used to indicate the "great church" as opposed to this or that heretical sect or schismatic group who dared to call itself "Christian." Writing in the middle of the third century, the bishop (and eventual martyr) Cyprian (d.258) of Carthage in Roman North Africa uses an extended metaphor to make the point:

The Church also is one, each part of which is held by each one for the whole. As there are many rays of the sun, but one light; and many branches of a tree but one trunk based on its tenacious roots; and since from one spring flows many streams even if many seemed diffused because of the liberality of the overflowing abundance preserved in the source. (*De unitate ecclesiae*, Chapter 5)

From the fourth century on, then, the word "catholic" meant the "true" Church (often times called the "Great Church") as opposed to schismatic or heretical groups.

A very interesting distinction between schismatic groups and the Catholic Church can be seen in the martyrdom account of the priest

Pionius and his companions during the persecution of Emperor Decius around AD 250. When Pionius was brought before the tribunal the following exchange took place:

What is your name?
Pionius.
Are you a Christian?
Yes.
What church do you belong to?
The Catholic Church; with Christ there is no other.

What makes that exchange so interesting is that when Pionius was finally condemned to death, he was burned at the stake with a follower of the schismatic sect founded by Marcion in the mid-second century in Rome. What is clear about this text is that Pionius clearly distinguished the Catholic Church from other sectarian movements then current in the world.[1]

The clearest expression of the notion that catholicity is to be taken as the universal consensus of belief is to be found in a famous passage from the fifth-century monk theologian Vincent of Lerins (d. *c*.450). He expressed it this way:

In the Catholic Church itself, every care must be taken to hold fast to what has been believed everywhere, always and by all. This is truly and properly 'catholic' as indicated by the force and etymology of the name itself which comprises everything truly universal. This general rule will be truly applied if we follow the principles of universality, antiquity, and consent. (*Commonitorium*, Chapter 2)

Vincent goes on to say that by universality he means the faith that the Church professes all over the world. By antiquity, he means that the faith is not in dissonance with what the Church professed as far back as can be determined, and, similarly, consent means that "we adopt the definitions and propositions of all, or almost all, the bishops and doctors" (*Commonitorium*, Chapter 2). Vincent, then, understands catholicity to mean the universally held truths handed down by apostolic authority as it is perceived in the whole of Christianity.

At this early stage of Christian history, then, catholicity meant two things: (1) the unity of all the local churches in union with each other; and (2) the common faith as it was professed in its worship, creeds, and other

---

[1] The full text of this martyrdom text can be found in *Acts of the Christian Martyrs*, edited by Herbert Musurillo, S.J. (Oxford: Clarendon, 1983), pp. 136–67; my citation abbreviates the exchange.

articulations of the ancient tradition. Thus, when bishops met in a universal (ecumenical) council – the first one was at Nicaea in 325 – they joined together to express their common faith and to express their unity against dissident groups who were not in unity and did not hold to the "catholic" faith.

Here is an explanation of the word "catholic" given by Saint Cyril of Jerusalem to newly baptized converts in the late forth century:

The Church is called Catholic because it is spread out throughout the world, from end to end of the earth; also because it teaches universally and completely all the doctrines which man should know visible and invisible, heavenly and earthly, and also because it subjects to right worship all mankind, all rulers and ruled, lettered and unlettered; further because it treats and heals universally every sort of sin committed by body and soul, and it possesses in itself every conceivable virtue, whether in deeds, words or spiritual gifts of every kind. (*Catechetical Sermon*, No. 18)

For reasons too complex to describe here, the general unity of Christianity understood as the Great Church or the Catholic Church, was broken in the early Middle Ages with the Church of the East and the Church of the West separating. It then became customary, and somewhat confusingly, to describe Eastern Christianity by the term "Orthodox" and Western Christianity as "Catholic" even though each church would insist that it was both orthodox (right believing and right worshiping) and catholic (universal). In popular speech, however, Orthodox and Catholic became a common way of distinguishing the Churches of the East and the West. That distinction is standard today.

A further division in Christianity arose in the sixteenth century in the West when many Christians separated from the Catholic Church. This division, of course, is known familiarly as the Protestant Reformation. With that fissure, the term "Protestant" entered into common usage to describe those various Christian bodies who had separated from the old Catholic Church as a way of "protesting" the older church's deviations from the Gospel. Even later, it became customary to speak of the Catholic Church as the "Roman Catholic Church" because the unity of Catholicism depends on unity with the bishop of Rome, who is also known as the pope. We shall see below that the phrase "Roman Catholic" can be understood in a misleading fashion. It would be more accurate to speak of the Catholic Church at Rome. The term "Roman Catholic" was often used by those in the Church of England (Anglican) who wished to distinguish the Orthodox and Roman Catholic Churches from the Anglican Church. This "branch" theory (i.e. one Catholic Church with three branches of Anglican, Orthodox, and Roman Catholic) has received a mixed reception even within the Anglican Communion.

To sum up: The term "catholic" has a long history behind it but in common usage we today speak of Catholic, Orthodox, and Protestant as generic terms to describe broadly the three great divisions of Christianity. In the rest of this volume, we will understand "Catholic" in the generic way (i.e. as opposed to the Orthodox or Protestant or Anglican Churches) as is commonly used unless stipulated otherwise.

HOW CATHOLICS UNDERSTAND CATHOLICITY

According to the authoritative *Catechism of the Catholic Church* (No. 830), three things constitute the essential marks of the Catholic Church: (1) the complete and full confession of faith as it was preserved from the tradition of the first Apostles; (2) the full sacramental life of worship and liturgy; (3) and the ordained ministry of bishops in apostolic succession who are in union with each other and the bishop of Rome (i.e. the pope). A word should be noted about these three essentials:

1. A complete and full profession of faith: The possession and teaching of everything given by Christ both as recorded in the biblical witness and as that teaching has been articulated in the constant teaching of the Church and enshrined in its creeds. We will expand on this subject in Chapter 5, on the so-called rule of faith.
2. A full sacramental life: In the Catholic Church are those rites ordained by Christ and accepted in the Church to incorporate people into the faith, to nurture their Christian lives in worship, and to make available to them the gift of Christ. This crucial part of catholicity will receive its own chapter also when we describe the liturgical and sacramental character of Catholicism.
3. An ordained ministry in apostolic succession: It is of the Catholic faith that the bishops are the legitimate successors of the Apostles of Jesus Christ. The Catholic Church is present when each bishop in his local church is in communion with all other bishops and that communion is especially bonded through communion with the bishop of Rome, the successor of Peter.

The *Catechism* (No. 832) goes on to say that when those three elements are a reality – where the full Gospel is preached, the sacraments are fully available, and the local bishop is in communion with all other bishops and the bishop of Rome – there is present the Catholic Church. So, the Catholic Church is not just the sum total of all churches: catholicity is fully present in each local church that has possession of those three essential characteristics. Thus, we can speak of the Catholic Church in London, Jakarta, Paris, Dublin, Rome, Los Angeles, etc. In that sense, it is more technically correct, as we already noted, to speak of the Catholic Church at Rome rather than the Roman Catholic Church. In that sense, at least, Catholics insist that the Catholic Church is a *visible* reality – where the three elements are present, there is the Catholic Church.

With those characteristics in mind, we can then add that from the point of view of the Catholic Church another church would be in schism (from the Greek *skisma* – to tear or rent) if it broke the bond of the bishops who are in union with the bishop of Rome, the pope. That is what the Catholic Church has judged the Orthodox Church to have done. It would be (formally) heretical if it denied one or other of the dogmatic teachings of the creedal tradition or denied the legitimacy of some of the sacraments of the Church. In point of fact, as the Catholic Church tries to emphasize points of closeness rather than points of rupture, the Catholic Church attempts to be in dialogue with other Christian bodies to foster greater unity rather than to emphasize divergences.

CATHOLICITY CLOSELY CONSIDERED

A generation ago, the American Jesuit theologian Avery Dulles (now Cardinal Avery Dulles) gave the Martin D'Arcy lectures at Oxford University which were later published under the title *The Catholicity of the Church*. That work remains to this day the best and most comprehensive English-language study of the meanings of catholicity from the perspective of a Catholic thinker. The book is very substantial and need not be fully outlined here. However, a few of its major theses should be noted because they will be studied in more depth later in this present book. Here it will be sufficient to sketch out some of the more pertinent points to add to our understanding of the term "catholic." These elements may be understood as distinguishing characteristics of catholicity.

First, Catholicism roots itself in the biblical belief that the created world comes from God and that God's presence is somehow to be detected in this world without being identified with it. Catholicism, in short, affirms both the transcendence of God (God is not to be identified with the world) and the immanence of God (God is detected through the world). That tension between God's transcendence and God's imminence is made manifest in the Catholic understanding of who Jesus Christ is. It is part of Catholic faith that Jesus is both divine and human – that He is the Word made flesh (see John 1:14) – and, further, that his humanity and divinity are present in one single person. Furthermore, Jesus left a community made up of humans who are at the same time the bearer of the message and power of Jesus. And, further, this community functions as a visible sign through visible signs to manifest and provide of power of Jesus.

The theological notion that the invisible can be mediated through the visible is called the *sacramental* principle, namely, that signs (sacraments) deliver meaning. That is why the Catholic tradition has called creation itself a sacrament: it is a sign of the creator God. The Catholic tradition calls Jesus Christ the Great Sacrament because in his life he shows us God. Christ is a visible sign in the world who grants us the favor (i.e. grace) of God. The Church, likewise, is a sacrament that functions through further sacraments using visible signs, such as water in baptism, bread and wine in the eucharist, etc. This commitment to a strong sense of the power of the visible to mediate the invisible also explains why the Catholic Church is hospitable to ritual, art, sculpture, vestments, etc.

Catholicism, then, in the first place, is characterized as committed to the *sacramental principle.*

Second, the Catholic Church understands itself to be "catholic" in the sense that it wishes the Gospel to be preached universally – to the whole "world." In that sense, the Catholic Church is a missionary enterprise. As an ideal, then, it is contrary to Catholicism to restrict itself to one ethnic class or to one language or to one stratum of society. In that sense, at least, its catholicity is an ideal to be achieved as opposed to an already-arrived-at reality. Since that kind of fullness will come only at the end of history, the Catholic Church must constantly seek out strategies to preach the Gospel in a fashion that all peoples in all their particularities can hear it.

Attempting to teach the Gospel to all nations explains why what seems like the bewildering complexity of institutions, schools, literary texts, music, art, various media, forms of ministry, etc. all dwell within the Church: They are means towards the end of inviting everyone to hear the Good News of Jesus and to embrace its life-giving message.

This aspect of catholicity means that the Catholic Church is both inclusive (everyone is welcome) and expansive or missionary as it attempts to invite all peoples to be a member of the Church. In order to do that, the Catholic Church is concerned to keep two realities in constant tension. On the one hand, it must remain faithful to the Gospel of Jesus Christ, and yet, on the other hand, it must find ways of expressing that gospel so as, simultaneously, the message is not compromised while being understandable.

The process of preaching the Gospel in a pure but understandable fashion is often called *inculturation.* By inculturation, Catholics believe that the essential teaching(s) of Jesus, the essential rites (sacraments), and the essential unity of the Church are to be preserved while expressions of that teaching, those rites, and the manner of unity must take into account the place, time, and culture where the Catholic Church is present. At an observable level, it is clear that the Catholicism of Italy, Ireland, India, etc., might have a different tone and accent, but all of those places sense themselves to be part of the unity of Catholicism itself because their local bishops are in union with each other and with the bishop of Rome.

Finally, the Catholic Church conceives of itself not only in terms of its historical reach to all peoples but it also affirms that the Church is made up of all those who have lived and who are now with God. This doctrine, sometimes called the "Communion of Saints" is often invoked in the prayer of the Catholic Church as it prays in unity with the Mother of Jesus Christ, all the saints, and those who have gone before us in death. The traditional emphasis that Catholicism pays to the veneration of Mary and the saints is rooted in the belief that they may pray before us in the presence of God just as we pray for the needs of each other here on earth. Catholicism is, then, characterized also by its *universality,* both realized and, at the same time, desired. Catholicism would resist the notion of perfectionism by which only pure, undefiled, and totally subservient members count: Catholicism takes seriously the notion that such perfection only occurs at the end of time.

Third, Catholicism puts a supreme value on Tradition. Tradition means a "handing down" and, when used with a capital letter, that Catholics believe that the Gospel and the worship of the Church have been handed down, preserved, and preached from the beginning of the public life of Jesus to the present day. Catholics further believe that this "handing down" has been entrusted primarily to the bishops of the Church who are considered to be the legitimate successors of the Apostles. Thus, Catholicism puts a strong emphasis on the continuity of the Church and the Church's teaching and worship. The *Catechism of the Catholic Church* sums up this conviction about its being built on the witness of the Apostles of Jesus in three brief affirmations (No. 857): (1) The Catholic Church is built on the foundation of the Apostles; (2) with the aid of the Holy Spirit, the Church keeps and hands on the teaching; (3) and continues to be taught, sanctified by the Apostles through their successors, the College of Bishops.

Here we should note that there is a distinction to be made between Tradition and traditions. Tradition with a capital "T" stands for that unchangeable witness and proclamation of the Gospel given to the Apostles and their successors the College of Bishops, while traditions, with a small "t," are those changeable customs, laws, and practices which the Church had adopted over the centuries in order to facilitate and further their mission. Thus, just to cite some examples, the Catholic Church teaches as part of its irreformable Tradition that bishops are successors of the Apostles who are ordained to guide, teach, and sanctify the Church, while the fact that bishops are to be unmarried (that is, celibate) is an ancient tradition which could be changed. There is nothing essential to the Tradition that that would prevent bishops (including the pope) and their priests from being married. Similarly, the Catholic Tradition teaches that Mary is the Mother of God and is to be venerated as such. That doctrine was solemnly taught at the Council of Ephesus in 431 and is the common doctrine of both the Catholic Church and the Orthodox Church. However, traditional practices such as shrines, the saying of the rosary, purported apparitions of the Virgin at Lourdes, Fatima, etc., are not essential to the Catholic Tradition even if such practices may flow from the essential truth of Mary's place in the authentic teaching of the Church about her. That distinction is a crucial one to which we will return in the course of this book.

The Catholic Church is *apostolic* in the sense described above, and its apostolic character guarantees the authenticity of the Tradition of belief and practice. To put it simply: The Tradition of Catholicism is founded on, and continues to exhibit, faith in Jesus Christ and his teaching first handed to the Apostles and present today in their successors.

CATHOLICISM DESCRIBED

By way of summary, we can make the following synthesis of the material discussed earlier in this chapter. Catholicism, understood as a distinct body within the larger Christian world, can be described as having the following essential characteristics:

1. The conviction that it possesses in full the Gospel Message of Jesus Christ as handed down from the first Apostles. Thus, Catholicism asserts itself to be characterized as apostolic.

2. The belief that it possesses the signs and gestures through which the favor of Jesus Christ is mediated to every generation through its sacramental life. Thus, the Catholic Church understands itself to be fully sacramental.

3. The assertion that all of the bishops, successors of the Apostles, must be in union with each other and that the center of that unity resides in the bishop of Rome. That union of bishops with the bishop of Rome (who is familiarly known as the pope) marks the Catholic Church as One.

4. That in the teaching and worship of the Catholic Church one can find the fullness of Christ's teaching and the means to be sanctified in this life by growing more identified with Christ who is the Way, the Truth, and the Life. Furthermore, in each age, people do, in fact, discover Christ and the authentic ways of living in union with Him. In that sense, we describe the Catholic Church as holy even though individual members or particular institutions within the Church may be marred by sin and imperfection.

5. The Catholic Church further confesses that Christ will not abandon the Church nor the Church's capacity to teach authentically and to minister effectively. The guarantee that Christ will be with the Church until the end of history, keeping it and preserving it in truth and holiness, expressed the Catholic Church's conviction of indefectibility. This conviction, however, does not mean that the Church is "perfect" but that it will not be hopelessly compromised or ruined or become fully estranged from the teachings of Jesus first given to the apostolic church.

6. Catholicism insists that its message is destined for all persons regardless of class, race, gender, or social status. It is not to be identified with any particular culture or age or social set. Its mission is to the whole world and to all persons. In that sense, Catholicism is a missionary religion which attempts to speak and teach in diverse ways even though it does so ever mindful of the need to protect its essential unity. That missionary outreach and conviction that teaching and practice is for all nations is to be understood as part of its essential catholicity.

7. Catholicism is fundamentally the making concrete of the Good News of Jesus Christ. Catholicism's entire sense of morality and ethical norms flows from its apostolic teaching. In other words, Catholic morality flows from its understanding of the biblical doctrine of creation and redemption and, of course, the paradigmatic value of the life of Jesus Christ.

ONE FURTHER DISTINCTION

While it is common to identify the Catholic Church with the Roman tradition, that is a mistake. There are other Churches, with distinct liturgical, canonical, and administrative features which are in union with the bishop of Rome but which do have their own distinct profile. There are twenty-one such particular Churches who are in union with the bishop of Rome and, in addition, to the Roman Rite (which is the one most well known to most Catholics), there are nine different rites employed by those particular Churches. They are: the Byzantine Rite (used, for example, by the Ukranian and Ruthenian churches); the Armenian Rite; the Coptic Rite (found mainly in Egypt); the Ethiopian Rite; the Maronite Rite (common in Lebanon); the East Syrian and Chaldean Rite; the Syro-Malabar Rite; the West Syrian Rite; and the Syro-Malankaran Rite.

To further complicate matters, some of these Churches have ties to the bishop of Rome and others, of the same rite, do not (for example, the Copts and Armenian; some in union with the bishop of Rome), while others, such as the Maronites of Lebanon, are all in union with the bishop of Rome. These Churches following these various rites are typically called "Eastern Catholic Rites," but the term is somewhat misleading since the term "Eastern" must include Eastern Europe, while others are found in the Middle East, and still others, like the Syro-Malabars, are from the south of India.

These different rites have their own customs and laws summed up in The Code of Canons of the Eastern Churches, adopted in 1990, which is a revision of more ancient laws. However, the canons in that code only contain laws which are common to all of the Churches while each distinct Church has its own jurisprudence and ancient customs peculiar to its tradition. The Code of Canons is for the Eastern Churches what the 1983 Code of Canon Law is for the Roman Rite Church. The Code of Canons reflects the ancient disciplinary canons adopted in the early centuries by ecumenical councils and regional synods and reflects the thinking of the Second Vatican Council's Decree on Eastern Catholic Churches.

In one crucial sense, despite the complicated history of these various Churches and the vexatious relationship they might have with their Orthodox counterparts (who often refer to them somewhat pejoratively as "Uniates"), these Churches reflect rather dramatically the three pillars of Catholicism. They all teach the faith as it has come down from the apostolic tradition; their liturgical life offers the entire range of sacramental life; and their bishops are in union with all other bishops and with the bishop of Rome.

The Eastern Churches also reflect the diversity within unity, which, ideally, is a model for catholicity. They have different disciplinary canons (for example, their non-monastic priests may marry), a different tradition of theological reflection, a diverse form of spirituality, and their own form of internal organization. Symbolically, they give presence to a metaphor that was often used by the late Pope John Paul II to the effect that the Church should "breathe with two lungs" – Eastern and Western. While today the Roman Church is the largest of the Churches, it is crucial to remember, in the words of the Decree on Eastern Catholic Churches that "these churches are of equal rank, so that none of them is superior to the others because of its rite. They have the same rights and obligations, even with regard to preaching the Gospel in the whole world [see Mark 16:15], under the direction of the Roman Pontiff" (No. 3).

Since many of the Churches mentioned above are in a minority situation in much of the world, it is crucial to recall their presence because they offer a way of understanding the critical distinction between Tradition and traditions. They are Churches with their own integrity, serving, apart from their own intrinsic worth, to remind us that quite frequently we too narrowly construe what it means to be Catholic. Many of these Churches represent very ancient Christian ways of being. It is all too common to forget their profound impact on the Church of Rome, but a correct understanding of them contributes enormously when one tries to gain a sophisticated understanding of the meaning of catholicity.

CATHOLICISM CONTRASTED

It is obvious that Roman Catholicism is a Christian tradition quite distinct from both the world of Eastern Orthodoxy and the many denominations associated with the Protestant Reformation. Later in this volume, we will explain how these divisions and distinctions came about. For now, we can make two broad generalizations.

First, Catholicism accepts Orthodoxy as a historic witness to the Apostolic Church but separated from Catholicism over questions of governance and certain practices and a few theological formulations. The Catholic Church accepts as legitimate both Orthodoxy's episcopate and its priesthood as well as the authenticity of its sacraments and the veracity of its historic creeds. For many complex historical and cultural reasons, Orthodoxy and Catholicism are separated one from the other but, in many ways, are similar in both belief and practice. Essentially, the Catholic Church accepts the Orthodox Church as apostolic, possessed of a full and authentic sacramental system, and faithful guardian of the Tradition. Its separation from Catholicism is a sad fact, but attempts continue to heal that separation by constant dialogue. The relationship of Orthodoxy and Catholicism is one of schism, and, in this age, as well as in the past, sincere attempts are made to heal that breach.

With respect to Protestantism, the situation is far more complicated. Certain churches within the family of the Reformation bear a striking resemblance to Catholicism in terms of their worship and their creedal affirmations while being quite distinct in their self-understanding vis-à-vis Catholicism. As a general rule of thumb, one could say that those Protestant Churches that emphasize a highly structured liturgical life, adherence to the historic creeds, and the retention of the episcopacy (for example, Anglicans and Lutherans) are closer at first glance to Catholicism, while those "low" Churches which have neither an episcopal structure (for example, Presbyterians) nor a strong sense of liturgical worship (for example, Baptists) are more clearly distinct from Catholicism. What most characterizes Protestantism is the large range of quite different church styles, which tend to manifest themselves into different denominations. The net result of that diversity is that it is extremely misleading to contrast Protestantism and Catholicism in any meaningful fashion unless one stipulates what particular strand of the Reformation one is discussing even when it is true that what one can say is that a Protestant is one who is quite consciously not Catholic or Orthodox.

CATHOLICISM FROM THE BOTTOM UP

To this point, our discussion of Catholicism has operated at a certain level of abstraction. It might be useful, to finish this initial exploration of Catholicism, to ask this question: What does the experience of Catholicism look like to a mythical Catholic who might be described as the average "person in the pew"? Such an angle will not take into account religious sisters, monks, missionaries, theologians in their studies, functionaries in the Vatican, and all the others who live within the Church in particular ministries. We focus here on the "ordinary Catholic."

Most ordinary Catholics identify their life as Catholics within the confines of a typical parish or local Catholic community. A parish can be defined as a particular area under the leadership of an ordained priest who serves as its "pastor." That priest functions as an extension of the ministry of the bishop and has his power by a sharing in the orders and juris-diction of the bishop. It is usually there in the local parish that Catholics are baptized, learn about their faith from the pulpit and religious instruction, go to worship on Sunday by attending mass, marry their spouse, and will have their funeral mass conducted. In some parts of the world, they might also receive their primary and secondary education through a parish or regional school sponsored by the local church. Their parish more than likely (but not always) is marked off with specific geographical boundaries.

While many Catholics will identify strongly with their local parish and its priest(s), it would not be uncommon to have a visitation from the local bishop who oversees the diocese within which the parish is located. It is he who has assigned the priests to the parish. The bishop would come to administer the sacrament of Confirmation for those who are soon to reach puberty and may come for other occasions of significance. The priests are extensions of the pastoral role of the bishop.

The bishop, in turn, would make a visit every five years to the Vatican (these visits are called, in Latin, *ad limina* visits (*ad limina* means roughly "to the threshold") to give his report to the Roman authorities about the state of his diocese which is the geographical area over which he has jurisdiction. At a simplified level, one can see that the local parish member is removed by only a few steps from the center of Catholic unity via the parish priest and the pastor's connection to the local bishop who answers to, and is in communion with the pope, the bishop of Rome. In practice, the experience of the Church is felt most intensely at the very local level of the parish.

The parish itself would reflect in its very environment the long history of Catholicism. The focal point of the parish is the altar where mass is celebrated; to the left of the altar would be the pulpit from which the scriptures are proclaimed and the sermons on that proclamation of the readings. Somewhere, the Holy Eucharist will be reserved in a tabernacle, and elsewhere there will be a sacred space with an icon or statue of the Blessed Virgin Mary. The windows will probably contain stained-glass depictions of sacred history or images of the saints. Over the main altar will be a crucifix, which is to say, a cross with the image of the body of Jesus affixed. On the walls there will be (most likely) fourteen tablets, which make up the stations of the cross (the story of the Passion) – a devotional ensemble that dates back to the early modern period. In con-trast, generally, to Protestant churches, the Catholic church will be highly visual and iconic. Apart from the altar and the pulpit, all of the other parts of the church are accretions developed over the centuries, and we will have occasion to speak about their development later in this book.

While the "typical" parish is quite often very local (in some cases, almost tribal) in character, there are many small ways in which the congregation is reminded that it belongs to a larger reality – to the wide world church. It may well be that a parish is made up of one social class or a particular ethnic grouping that seems to make the parish ingrown. Nonetheless, there are ways in which being part of a larger reality is made clear. At each mass, the priest prays for the local bishop and the bishop of Rome, the pope, by name. Letters from the bishop are read from the pulpit. Special collections are periodically taken up for the needs of the Church beyond the local scene. Missionaries come to give a vision of the Church beyond the local confines of the place and to plead for mission support. Either through a parish school or a regional one or through Sunday school, the teachings of the Church and the character of Catholic culture are transmitted.

Our typical parish, of course, presupposes a settled life where people are not very mobile, where the rhythms of life are tied to place, and where generations live within a context of social stability. In the West, at least, this is increasingly not the case. People are increasingly on the move in many parts of the world through immigration, the search for better economic opportunities, the collapse of agricultural smallholdings, and so on. The vast housing complexes (to say nothing of slums, barrios, favelas, etc.) that ring the major cities of most of the world bring new challenges that make the settled parishes of integral geographical locations more problematic and the need for imaginative approaches more pressing. It may well be that the recent emergence of "small Christian communities" provide a new model for the Catholic congregation(s) of the future. As long as the apostolic faith is taught, the sacraments administered, and the communities are in union there, the Catholic Church will be. Those realities are of the essence, while the accumulated ways of being Catholic represented by traditional parishes are only part of the long history of the Catholic Church.

What has been described above – parish, diocese, Rome – is a somewhat idealized and abstract way of linking the local to the universal. In reality, Catholics worship in chapels associated with religious orders, downtown churches that serve a constantly shifting urban population, in small chapels found in hospitals, on university campuses, or erected to serve as extensions of a large parish, through military chaplains, and so on. The essential point is that no matter how particular a place where people congregate to worship, there is an organic connection between that place and its congregation with a bishop who is in union with the bishop of Rome. That highly complex web of interrelationship is what constitutes the Catholic Church as a visible reality.

THE CATHOLIC SUBSTANCE

Some generations ago, the Protestant theologian Paul Tillich distinguished the Catholic substance and the Protestant principle. By "substance," Tillich had in mind the strong emphasis on Tradition in Catholicism while Protestantism's principle was to judge and "protest" the Tradition in fidelity to the Word of God. In today's jargon, we could see that Catholicism emphasizes a principle of "trust," while Protestantism is inclined towards "suspicion."

Recently, some Catholic writers have attempted to describe the main lines of the Catholic substance – the characteristics that most commonly identify Catholicism as catholic. Richard McBrien's *Catholicism* attends to three theological foci which are paramount:

1. The emphasis on sacramentality – material reality is good, coming from the hand of God, redeemed in Jesus Christ, and renewed in the Spirit. Everything that is, is a sign of God's grace in the world.
2. Signs do not only signify but also cause what they signify. Hence, Catholics have a strong sense of mediation. The grace of God is mediated to us through Christ, the Church, the signs which the Church employs, and in the actions and events that occur in the church. Our encounter with God in Christ is always a mediated but real experience.
3. Communion: Even though each of us must live as individuals under God, we are by nature people in communion. Hence, Catholicism sees itself as the People of God: We are a radically social and relational people. Thus, the Church puts a strong emphasis on the communion of all under God. That is why the Church is so central in the overall theological scheme of Catholic thinking.

More recently, in 2003, Fathers Gerald O'Collins and Mario Ferrugia have taken up the same issue and offered their profile of catholicity, *Catholicism: The Story of Catholic Christianity*. Their profile somewhat overlaps with McBrien, but they begin with the centrality of Jesus Christ and his mother, the Virgin Mary. They argue that the long history of Catholicism is centrally concerned with ways of imitating Jesus and showing those ways to others. The way of Jesus for Catholics, however, cannot be understood without the role that Mary plays in the liturgical, devotional, and theological life of Catholicism.

In accord with McBrien, they also single out the central idea of sacramentality – that grace is mediated to us through the good created world. Finally, they argue that Catholicism has always been a faith that emphasizes the both/and: grace and freedom, faith and reason, unity and diversity, local and universal.

Obviously, in both of these descriptions, there are some overlapping and generalizations but the purpose of the exercise is to somehow capture in a few general observations the underlying themes of that complex phenomenon known as Catholicism.

One profound way to approach Catholicism is to listen carefully to the prayers of its worship and, more particularly, to the canon of the Roman Catholic mass which is at the heart of weekly worship. There are four such prayers that may be said on a rotating basis. If we consider the first eucharistic prayer known as the Roman Canon we can get a sense of how the Catholic Church thinks of itself.

The presiding priest speaks in the plural since he speaks in the name of the whole worshiping community. He says that he offers gifts (of bread and wine) in sacrifice "for your holy catholic church." More specifically, he offers those gifts for the current pope and the local bishop who are mentioned by name. He asks God to remember all who are present who are in "union with the whole church." He goes on to "honor" (please note: not "adore") Mary, Joseph, the Apostles and martyrs and all the saints, who are called "your whole family." In other words, this prayer reflects the notion that the Catholic Church includes not only those who are alive today but everyone who has lived in the Christian faith starting with those involved in Christ's incarnation beginning with Mary. In fact, later in the prayer, the priest likens his gifts to those of Old Testament figures such as Abel, Abraham, and the ancient priest Melchisedech. Further on, he remembers all who have died and "sleep in Christ."

This vast panoply constitutes the richest description of the fundamental meaning of catholicity: all who are in Christ from the very beginning until now and until the end of time. That is why we pray to be included in "some share of the fellowship" of the Apostles, martyrs, and saints who have come before us. It is in that rich prayer, and others like it, that catholicity is expressed as a theological reality that goes well beyond any sociological description of a denomination.

Of course, the catholicity described in the Church's own liturgy is a highly refined one. It may seem at variance with the messy realities of the Catholic Church as it is actually observed. It is part of faith that the Church is a mystery not in the sense that it is a puzzle (although it may well be that for some) but in the sense that something hidden lies behind its human manifestation. Catholics believe that to be the case. They often appeal to Saint Paul's metaphor that we are part of a body whose "head is Christ" and, in that sense, the deepest meaning of catholicity pertains to faith.

Box 1 The demographics of contemporary Catholicism

When we look at the world as a whole, it is clear that Catholicism as a visible presence is strong in some parts of the world and weak or practically non-existent in other parts. In Europe, the strength of Catholicism is traditionally found in those places which did not go over to the Protestant Reformation of the sixteenth century: the Mediterranean countries such as Malta, Spain, Portugal, France, and Italy as well as parts of Germany, Austria, Belgium, Poland, Hungary, and Lithuania. Ireland remained, in the main, Catholic, while Great Britain, in the main, did not.

Missionary activity from those countries in the period of the Catholic Reformation and, later, during the colonial period spread Catholicism to the Philippines, and Latin and Central America in the Southern Hemisphere and French-speaking Canada in the Northern Hemisphere. Catholicism grew strong in the USA from the middle of the nineteenth century mainly because of the influx of immigrants. That same activity also spread Catholicism in Africa especially, but not exclusively, in the French-speaking areas of the continent.

Small minorities of Catholics have existed for centuries in those lands where Islam is now the majority religion (Lebanon, historical Palestine, Syria, Iraq, etc.) or through colonial expansion in North Africa in countries such as Algeria and Morocco. In the Far East, there are small Catholic communities both in the Indian subcontinent (Kerala in the south of India has a long Catholic history) as well as in countries such as Thailand, Laos, and in Vietnam, where the Catholic Church represents a significant minority of the population. China has a small minority population of Catholics as does (South) Korea, with an even smaller one in Japan.

Statistics about the overall Catholic population are very hard to come by with any degree of accuracy, but the following are some more or less reliable numbers as of the year 2000:

Africa	130,000,000+
Americas	519,391,000+
Asia	107,302,000
Europe	280,144,200
Oceania	8,202,200
World total	1,045,058,100

Of course, those raw statistics (taken from *Global Catholicism* [Froehle and Gautier 2003]) are only approximate. Nor do they give the growth of Catholicism or its decline over time. Just to cite one example: The Catholic

Box 1 (cont.)

population of Africa grew by 728 percent between 1950 and 2000 while the Catholic population of Europe grew by 55 percent over the period between 1900 and 1950 but only by 32 percent in the period from 1950 to 2000. As recent research has shown, the greatest Catholic growth has occurred in Africa, which has its own significance when compared with the much slower growth, say, in Western Europe (largely due to declining birth rates and secularization). The number of Catholics in Central and South America is in flux thanks in part to the aggressive growth of Protestantism. The impact of these population shifts will be considered in due course. The bottom line is that Catholicism can claim a significant percentage of the world's population, but it is extremely difficult to ascertain just what percentage of the world's population that is. It is also the case that the number of Catholics is disproportionately distributed: Asia holds 61 percent of the world's population but only 10 percent of the world's Catholics, while Latin America constitutes 14 percent of the world's population but nearly 50 percent of the Catholics.

Catholics of a given geographical area might see themselves as a tiny minority (for example, in parts of the Middle East) or as a majority of the population (for example, in Poland or Brazil), but they do not always appreciate that they are part of a much larger whole that constitutes the Catholic Church in its totality. In the USA, for example, one out of every four Americans is a Catholic, with a total of roughly 65 million Catholics in the country. American Catholics, as a consequence, see themselves as a significant presence in the country. It always comes as a bit of a jolt for them to be reminded that American Catholics make up only 6 percent of the total population of Catholics in the world.

FURTHER READING

Buckley, James J., Bauerschmidt, Frederick Christian, and Pomplun, Trent, eds., *The Blackwell Companion to Catholicism* (Oxford: Blackwell, 2007).

Catechism of the Catholic Church (Vatican City: Editrice Vaticana, 1994). This is an authoritative summary of Catholic teaching.

Dulles, Avery, *The Catholicity of the Church* (Oxford: Clarendon, 1985). Seminal work on the notion of catholicity.

Faulk, Edward, *101 Questions & Answers on Eastern Catholic Churches* (New York, N.Y.: Paulist, 2007).

McBrien, Richard, *Catholicism* (San Francisco, Calif.: HarperCollins, 1994). An encyclopedic study.

O'Collins, S. J., Gerald and Farrugia, S. J., Mario, *Catholicism: The Story of Catholic Christianity* (Oxford: Oxford University Press, 2003). Excellent one-volume survey.

Roberson, Ronald, *The Eastern Christian Churches*, revised 6th edn (Rome: Pontifical Oriental Institute, 1999).

CHAPTER 2

Roman Catholicism

INTRODUCTION

Even though, as we saw in the first chapter, the adjective "Roman" added to Catholicism can be misunderstood, it is clear that it is the city of Rome in general and the bishop of Rome, known more familiarly as the "pope," in particular that gives Catholicism its defining character. After all, unity with the bishop of Rome is the linchpin that guarantees the unity of Catholicism. More than anything else, the division of Orthodoxy and Catholicism is best exemplified by the fact that Orthodoxy is not in union with the bishop of Rome, the pope. Both the Orthodox Church and the Byzantine Rite of the Catholic Church use the same liturgy ascribed to Saint John Chrysostom but the difference is that during the liturgy the Byzantines pray for the bishop of Rome and the Orthodox do not. At a more popular level, Catholicism is almost instinctively identified with the papacy. Even the popes themselves, in recent times, have acknowledged that the papacy is a stumbling block for other Christians.[1]

It would be, however, the most naive idea to think that as Christianity developed there was already in place a full-blown papacy as we understand the papacy today. The papacy, with all of its claims of authority and the very central role that it plays in the Catholic Church today, is the result of a very long historical evolution. To understand that history, complex as it is, and to understand the claims made on behalf of the bishop of Rome is to understand the history of Catholicism itself. That approach, of course, is history narrated from "on high," but it is one way to at least grasp the larger contours of Catholicism. This chapter, then, will attempt to give a broad but necessarily abbreviated account of the papacy as an institution. We will leave it to another chapter to tell the story of Catholicism "from below."

---

[1] The late John Paul II said as much in his 1995 encyclical *Ut unum sint.*

23

It is clear that when Saint Paul wrote his Epistle to the Romans he was writing to what he considered to be a single church, if by "church" we understand this to be in Paul's terms of the Christian assembly or congregation, which was to be the recipient of his letter. A closer examination of the situation in Rome, however, indicates that the Christian presence in Rome after Paul's death (he, as well as Saint Peter, are presumed to have died in Rome during Nero's persecution in AD 64) was quite complex and consisted of more than one unified community. Every scrap of historical evidence that we possess, and the scholarship which has examined it, shows that there were competing Christian factions within the city and nothing like a single spokesperson for the Roman Christian *ekklesia*.

It was not until around the middle of the second century that we begin to see the emergence of a monarchical episcopate in Rome – a single authoritative voice that emerged most likely under the pressure of the competing sectarian groups who represented either some form of exaggerated dualism contrasting the God of the Old Testament and of the New, as was the case of Marcion, whom we will meet again in our story, or in the elaborate forms of Gnosticism preached by, among others, Valentinus. It is clear that by the end of the second century there was a single authoritative bishop who oversaw the Roman Church, and, further, his authority derived, in large part, from his claim that he was the legitimate heir of the Apostle Peter, who was the first among the Apostles. Writing in Book III of his treatise against the heretics (*Adversus haereses*) around the year 180, Irenaeus of Lyons, who had lived in Rome, not only appealed to the teachings of the Roman bishops as a sure sign of the authentic apostolic faith but even provided a list of them working back from his friend Bishop Eleutherius (d.189) to the Apostle Peter. There may be problems with the litany of names recounted by Irenaeus, but it is clear that he believed there was a legitimate succession deriving from the Apostle Peter himself – a belief he probably picked up during his own sojourn in Rome.

Irenaeus was clear on two points: The Roman church was founded on the martyred presence of the Apostles Paul and Peter, and Peter's successors had a lineage. Irenaeus concludes that "it is a matter of necessity that every church should agree with this church on account of its preeminent authority, that is, the faithful everywhere, inasmuch as the apostolic tradition has been continuously by those [faithful ones] who exist everywhere" (*Adversus haereses,* III.3.3).

That Peter and Paul had died in Rome and were buried there is an ancient tradition which has some compelling historical evidence behind it. Allusions to their martyrdom and their burial in Rome is remarked upon by early writers going back to the end of the first century. Around the year 200, a Roman writer indicated that he could show the memorials (*trophaea*) of the Apostles to visitors. The authority of the bishop of Rome rested largely on the claim that he was the keeper of those shrines of Peter and Paul and an inheritor of the authority vested in Peter as the one upon whom Christ would found his church (Matt. 16:18) – claim that would be evoked more frequently after the second century. By the third century, the bishops of Rome would intervene by the invocation of their authority as Peter's successors even though the autonomy of local churches outside of Rome would still be maintained.

What most characterized the lives of the popes of the period up until the early fourth century was that they headed a church which was subject to sporadic persecution by the Roman authorities especially in the middle of the third century during the reign of Emperor Decius (250) through the period of the early fourth century. Somewhat surprisingly, despite the periods of persecution, the Church at Rome continued to grow and even prosper. During the middle of the third century, the Church was a substantial owner of real estate and, if figures are reliable, numbered about 50,000 faithful under the care of forty-six priests and seven deacons. The Roman Church had enough of the goods of this world to send aid to less fortunate Christian churches in other parts of the world. Letters from the Roman Church were sent to and read out loud at churches in other parts of the world.

The last great persecution of the Church was inaugurated under the military Emperor Diocletian (even though his wife and daughter may well have been Christians themselves) in 298 as a way of reinvigorating the old pagan religion which the Emperor saw as enshrining the Roman values upon which the Empire rested. The persecution, ferocious and widespread, especially in North Africa and the eastern parts of the Empire, lasted for nearly ten years but did not succeed in halting the spread of Christianity. Shortly after ascending to the imperial throne in 312, Constantine, bowing to the inevitable and somewhat sympathetic to the Christian faith himself, issued an edict of toleration in the city of Milan for the Christian faith.

The Constantinian influence on the shape of Roman Catholicism is difficult to exaggerate. Through imperial generosity, the Church in Rome had the huge Lateran Basilica built to serve, as it does to this day, as the cathedral for the bishop of Rome. He oversaw the building of a basilica over the *tropheum* honoring the burial place of Saint Peter on the Vatican hill across the Tiber. That church would last until the late fifteenth century when it began to be replaced with what is today present Saint Peter's in the Vatican. Constantine's mother, Helena, a devout Christian, lavished monies on the places associated with the life of Jesus in ancient Palestine. She built the original Church of the Holy Sepulchre in Jerusalem.

Since Constantine had built a parallel city named for himself in the East – Constantinople (present-day Istanbul) – he had an equal interest in the Eastern reaches of his empire. When a ferocious dispute broke out over the divinity of Christ that threatened to divide the Church, it was Constantine (and not the pope) who called together a universal (ecumenical) council of the Church at Nicaea in 325 to settle the matter. The pope sent two representatives to that council, but the direct intervention of the Emperor was one symptom of what would become a neuralgic problem for the papacy, namely, how to balance the rights of the Church in relationship to the power of the Empire, which, after all, gave explicit support, both financial and political, to the Church which had now emerged from its persecuted past. The problem would become all the more acute when Emperor Theodosius made Christianity the official religion of the State in 381.

The Pallium

From the late fourth century on, it was customary for the bishop of Rome to wear, over his liturgical vestments, a woolen collar with two pendants, one falling down the back and the other in front. A variation of such pallia may be seen in mosaics in Ravenna which date to the sixth century. By the end of the ninth century, it was common for popes to grant the wearing of the pallium to archbishops at the head of major (metropolitan) dioceses, who wore them while presiding at the liturgy. The pallium was a sign of the unity between the metropolitan bishops and the bishop of Rome when worn by such prelates; the Church understands the pallium, when worn by the pope, as a sign of the fullness of his power as the successor of Saint Peter.

Today, the pallium is made from lambs blessed on the feast of Saint Agnes (January 21) and granted to those who are to receive them on the Feast of Saints Peter and Paul on June 29. It is usual for the new recipient to adopt the pallium on the day when he says his first mass as a newly installed archbishop.

FROM CONSTANTINE TO GREGORY THE GREAT

Constantine left Rome for his new city in 324, leaving, as one of the best historians of the papacy Eamon Duffy has written, the building of Christian Rome to the popes. They undertook the task with enthusiasm. New churches sprang up in the city; popes such as Damasus (d.385) saw Rome as a Christian city with the pope as its head. In his program, his zealous promotion of the cult of the saints and preserver of the papal memory, his ruthless political control over the city, and his implacable detestation of the old paganism, Damasus wished to think of Rome not as springing from the mythical figures of Romulus and Remus but from the two Apostles whose shrines he governed, Saints Peter and Paul. Like his successors, Damasus would send legislative briefs, called decretals, to other churches, especially those who had historic connections to the city of Rome itself.

In this period, however, there were countervailing pressures on the growth of papal prestige. The emperors now lived in the city of Constantinople, and the patriarch there vied for the prestige and status afforded the bishop of Rome. There were also pressures in the West not least of which was the constant threat of incursions of Barbarians coming down from the north. There was not anything like a centralized papacy over the whole Church in this period, but the Churches of the world did have to take into account the primacy of the bishop of Rome because of his claims to be guardian of the tombs of Peter and Paul.

The vexatious issues of the period came into sharp relief in the period of one of the most able of the popes and one of the few who has been afforded by history with the title of "Great": Pope Leo the Great (440–61). Leo, himself a Roman, devoutly believed that the Church, founded on Peter and Paul, was a work of providence that provided a central point for the evangelization of the world. He kept representatives of his office in various parts of the Western world, in Christian North Africa, and even in Greece. He personally went north to negotiate with Attila the Hun to stop his sack of the city, but, when the Vandals did invade Rome and sacked it for weeks in 455, he led the attempts to rebuild the city and its infrastructure.

Perhaps Leo's finest moment came early in his reign. The doctrinal disputes about the nature of Christ's humanity and divinity had wracked the Church from the early fourth century. A series of councils met to discuss and clarify these issues, with one called in 451 at Chalcedon outside Constantinople to which Leo, although not there himself, sent a

long letter (known as the "Tome of Leo") setting out the doctrine of
the two natures and one person in Christ. This letter was adopted by the
bishops and became the bedrock of Catholic orthodoxy about Christ.
The Patriarch of Constantinople said, echoing the claim upon which the
whole power of the papacy rested, "Peter has spoken through Leo."

Leo the Great had worked out a theory about the relationship between
the papacy and the empire at a time when imperial presumptions about
the role of the emperor in the governance of the Church were even more
insistent. The pope, according to Leo, held the power first given to Peter
as a right of inheritance even though, personally, he was not a saint as
great as Peter. It was the role of the successor of Peter to govern the
Church, and, in that governance, it was the successor of Peter and not the
emperor who held the right of governance.

The sixth century saw a series of unremitting invasions, wars, and
despoliations of the Italian peninsula to a degree that, it has been estimated, at the beginning of the century Rome's population had dwindled
to fewer than 50,000 people (there had been 800,000 in Rome at the
beginning of the fifth century). Towards the end of the century, the
population began to rise again, and it was in that period that one of
the most influential popes of the first millennium took office: Gregory the
Great (590–604).

Gregory had been a monk in Rome, who, for a period after his
ordination as a deacon, served the materials needs of Rome, looked over
the vast patrimony of the Church, and, after his election to the papacy,
attempted to hold together the Church by persuasion and through legates
speaking for him in his dealings with both the East as well as North Africa
and the Iberian peninsula. Amid that myriad of administrative duties, he
also found time to write books which were influential well into the
medieval period and beyond. His *Pastoral Care* was a handbook for
Christian ministry, while his sprawling commentary on Job (*Moralia in
Job*) was a fountain of scriptural exegesis, spirituality, and theological
reflection. In his *Dialogues,* Gregory gives us, among other things, about
all that we know of Saint Benedict, the founder of Western monasticism.
His concern for the liturgy of the Church was such that his name is
attached to the standard chant used in the Church, although it is not clear
that Gregorian chant was actually developed by him.

One of the most influential acts of Gregory's papacy was his decision in
596 to send forty monks under the leadership of a monk named
Augustine to England to evangelize the Anglo-Saxons. This was the first
time that a pope dispatched missionaries outside the confines of the

Roman Empire for the purposes of evangelization. He later appointed Augustine as the Archbishop of Canterbury, beginning a line which exists to this day. The mission begun by those first monks would not only mark the shape of British Christianity but also would have an extended influence in other parts of the world in subsequent times. It was the British monk Boniface who would evangelize Germany, and it was Alcuin who would be the intellectual leader of the so-called "Carolingian Renaissance" during the reign of Charlemagne in the ninth century.

The popes, however dire the sociopolitical conditions were in the West, still insisted on their position as heirs of Peter and Paul and as guardians of their legacy. It may have been the Emperor in Constantinople who called the second ecumenical council there in 680–81 to settle matters about the wills of Christ, but the Pope of the time, Agatho, in his letter to the Council made it clear that the Roman Church was still "acknowledged by the whole Catholic Church to be the mother and mistress of all churches and to derive her authority from St. Peter, the prince of the Apostles, to whom Christ committed his whole flock with a promise that his faith should never fall."

GREGORY VII AND CHURCH REFORM

The period between the death of Gregory the Great and the emergence of a strong church reformer in the person of Gregory VII in the eleventh century cannot be even briefly summarized, but some points at least requirement mention. First, the rise of Islam in the seventh century deprived the Christian world of its substantial presence not only in the Middle East but also all over North Africa and into the Iberian Peninsula. Second, the rise of the Frankish Kingdom, first under Pepin and then Charlemagne, revived the idea of a holy Roman emperor in the West and initiated a period of cultural life known as the "Carolingian Renaissance" as well as providing the Church with a strong protector in the West. Third, the relationship of the Church in the East and West finally broke into schism in the middle of the eleventh century, and those broken relationships have not been healed to this day. Finally, in the tenth and early eleventh centuries, Rome in general and the papacy in particular were in a state of profound corruption and decadence. The worst popes in the history of the Catholic Church reigned in the tenth century – some of them degenerates put on the chair of Peter by rapacious aristocratic families who struggled for control of the city. If there was a "Dark Age," tenth-century Rome would certainly qualify.

The monk and Roman deacon Hildebrand was elected pope in 1073, taking the name of Gregory VII, and died in office in 1085. More than any pope before him, Gregory extended the claim of universal jurisdiction over the entire Church. He reserved the name "pope" to himself alone (it was a title used by many bishops before him and is still used variously in the Eastern church), claimed the right to move bishops by decree, and enunciated the famous dictum *Prima sedes a nemine judicatur* – the First See can be judged by no one, i.e. there is no earthly authority above the pope with competency to judge him. In a series of synods, he issued strong decrees against clerical marriage, forbade the buying or selling of clerical offices (simony), and demanded that all bishops make visitations to Rome and that all should make promises of obedience. Through his legates, he forced these regulations on all churches. By forbidding the lay investiture of bishops and abbots (i.e. feudal lords nominating their own candidates for ecclesiastical offices), he came into conflict with the Holy Roman Emperor, Henry IV, who he excommunicated, forcing the Emperor to visit him at Canossa in northern Italy and beg for forgiveness outside his residence. In the battles that arose between emperor and pope (including the election of an anti-pope), he himself ended up in exile from Rome, dying in Salerno where he was buried.

Gregory's reforms were not totally successful, but his lasting import consisted on the reforming impulse he unleashed and, perhaps, more importantly, on his impulse to inflate the claims of universal jurisdiction over the Church in tandem with his strategies to centralize his authority over the bishops of local churches, and, finally, to emphasize the spiritual authority of the Church over that of secular rulers.

THE GREGORIAN REFORMS TO INNOCENT III

While the reform impulses begun by Gregory did not result in a purified Catholicism, it did give energy, at a number of levels, to reform efforts. New or repristinated older religious orders were founded. Between 1123 and 1215, popes called four reforming councils to meet at the Lateran palaces to legislate a whole range of reforms both to correct the more flagrant abuses among all ranks of the clergy and to combat the more conspicuous heretical movements of the day. The college of cardinals, a body slowly developed from the ranks of Roman clergy of suburban bishops, priests, and deacons, manned the increasing bureaucracy of the Church in Rome while other cardinals became legates of the pope to other parts of the world in order to enforce the decrees coming from Rome.

One event that happened at the end of the eleventh century was the call of Pope Urban II in 1095 to mount a crusade to retake the holy places in Jerusalem from the Muslims. The answer to that call – part military crusade and part religious event – was answered from all over Europe. The bearers of the cross – crusaders – marched under the slogan *Deus vult* – "God wills it!" – and initially met with great success in 1099 when Jerusalem was conquered in the midst of a fearful slaughter of the local inhabitants. The crusader kingdom itself would eventually fall, but the great crusade has lingered long in the memory of Islam.

Historians generally agree that the apex of the medieval papacy was that of the reign of Pope Innocent III (1198–1216). He was the nephew of an earlier pope (Clement III) and made it quite plain that he viewed his office to be the spiritual center of the world and not merely of the Catholic Church. His external politics consisted of ferocious fights with a number of monarchs (he excommunicated King John in England) who did not bend to his will but, in terms of the inner life of the Church, he was an indefatigable heir of the reforming intentions of the Gregorian period. He saw the value of and gave support to the new evangelically minded movements such as the Franciscans; he demanded and got efficiency and simplicity from his own curia, encouraged bishops to settle regional matters at their own synods, combated heresy – especially the dualist Albigensians in France – and reformed the finances of the papacy. He underwrote the Fourth Crusade and, when it met defeat, had plans for a fifth one. He presided over the Fourth Lateran Council in 1215 whose decrees had long-lasting effects. It was Lateran IV that stipulated that all Catholics were to confess their sins and to go to holy communion at least once a year as a basic criterion for membership in the Church and, less happily, ordered that Jews and Muslims wear distinctive garb for purposes of identification (and segregation).

In 1216, the energetic pope had traveled north from Rome to settle some political dispute when, unexpectedly, he caught a fever and died. A contemporary chronicler recounted how the pope's body, while it rested in its bier in Perugia, was despoiled of its costly robes by an unruly mob. The most powerful pope of the medieval period was not even able to receive a dignified funeral.

TO THE AVIGNON PAPACY AND GREAT SCHISM

In the century that followed the death of Innocent III there was a rapid succession of popes (four were elected and died in the year 1276 alone) who were pale imitators of Innocent. The tumultuous political situation in Europe and the internecine world of the Roman aristocracy made the election of a pope an arduous task. In 1293–4, a struggle to elect a pope led to a moment of desperation: The cardinals, as a compromise, elected an aged and pious hermit, Pietro del Morrone, who took the name Celestine V. After the election, Celestine found himself, by turns, hopelessly out of his depth in administering the Church and appalled by the corruption of the papal court. He resigned the papacy after less than six months in office but was held a virtual prisoner in a town south of Rome where he died in 1296. While recognized as a saint by the Church, Dante placed him in the anteroom to Hell as one who had made the "great refusal."

His successor, Boniface VIII, in fact, had encouraged the papal resignation. Dante, who loathed him, placed him in Hell in the *Inferno* naming him the "great prince of the Pharisees." Wildly devoted to enriching himself and his family, personally pugnacious and vindictive, he was not without gifts. To him we owe a great deal in the area of the codification of Church law and in the founding of a university in Rome, and he was the first pope to call a jubilee year in Rome (in 1300), which attracted vast hordes of pilgrims as happens even up to our own day. His struggles with the King of France led him to wield the fullness of his papal powers, and he was responsible for one of the most infamous papal bulls in the history of the Church – a bull directed pointedly at the King of France. It is in that famous document that Boniface extends to its highest point the purported power of the papacy where he claimed that the "two swords" (i.e. the temporal and spiritual power) were under the authority of the pope and, further, that outside the Church there is neither remission of sins nor salvation. It was, as it were, the last great assertion of absolute claims made by the papacy on behalf of its universal jurisdiction. In that sense, as a number of scholars have pointed out, Boniface VIII represented the culmination (and the decline) of the medieval papacy. King Philip the Fair of France responded in the spirit of the age: with vitriolic propaganda and a plan to take the pope to France and try him on an array of charges. The pope, however, returned to Rome under a safe passage from his fortress in Anagni and, shortly thereafter in 1303, died from the mistreatment he had received from his would-be captors.

In 1305, the election of Clement V proved to be a decisive and sad period of the Church. French by nationality, he settled in a Dominican priory in the town of Avignon in France to escape the harried state of

Rome. For roughly the next seventy years, a succession of French prelates reigned not in Rome but in Avignon despite pleas from all quarters and from great saints such as Catherine of Siena to return to the City of the Apostles. The period was often called the "Babylonian Captivity of the Church" because the seven decades paralleled the captivity of the Jewish people in Babylon. It was during this time that the modern bureaucracy of the papacy was first put into systematic order for the purpose of overseeing, mainly, the financial affairs of the Church, especially in terms of the contributions expected for the offices of bishop, abbot, and other benefices of the clerical and religious orders. It should be noted in passing that it was at this time, partially under the pressures of the abuses in the Church, that the first rumblings that presaged the Reformation began to appear. The papacy of Gregory XI coincided almost exactly with the public life of the English reformer John Wycliffe (who died in 1384).

THE GREAT SCHISM

The election of Urban VI in Rome in 1378 was unfortunate because his intransigent character and his desire to undermine French influence in the Church led a dissident group of French cardinals to elect an anti-pope and an attempt to have Urban's election rendered null and void. From that time until 1417, every Roman pope had a parallel pope with which to contend. There was genuine consternation about who held the legitimate right to the papacy. On one occasion, to sort matters out, there was even a third claimant elected. The intrigues and confusing history of this half century are beyond even simple description in this book, but the very painful situation did create enormously complicated legal and theological questions which were quite urgent. If both claimants insisted on their legitimacy and neither would cede to the other what body, if any, could judicate who the rightful pope was? An ecumenical council? But an ecumenical council must meet in communion with the pope, and the legitimacy of the pope was the issue at hand. Could a council make a final judgment?

The healing of the schism was finally accomplished at a general council held at Constance in 1415 called by one of the then three papal claimants. After much wrangling, the Council deposed the claimant from Pisa as well as the Avignon claimant and persuaded the Roman claimant to resign. Finally, in 1417, Martin V was elected and effectively ended what had been a terrible situation in the Church. His successor, Eugene IV, amid other pressing cares, held a Church council that met first at Basel, then Ferrara, and finally in Florence and which effectuated a brief lived reunion of the Orthodox and Roman Catholic Church as well as some other Eastern Churches (Copts, Armenians, etc.). These conciliatory efforts were short-lived. Eugene did not live to see the fall of Constantinople to the Ottoman Turks in 1453, ending the long reign of the Byzantine emperors.

RENAISSANCE POPES TO THE REFORMATION

The second half of the fifteenth century saw a series of popes, some good and some truly awful, who used their papal power to enhance the city of Rome in general and the papacy in particular with the fruits of the then-flourishing Italian Renaissance. It was to this period that we owe the development of the Vatican library as well as the flourishing of classical learning, patronage of the arts, and general opulence with which this period was identified. Various attempts were made to mount crusades against the Turks with indifferent success, and most of the popes of the period made sure that their relatives were placed in high office. Sixtus IV (1471–87), to whom we owe the Sistine Chapel and its choir as well as the Vatican archives, will be remembered for having made six of his nephews cardinals. Whatever his extravagances, however, he pales in comparison to the infamous Spanish Borgia pope, Alexander VI, who held the papacy from 1492 to 1503. His reign was characterized, as a recent commentator has written, by gold, women, and family interests. He made his natural son, Cesare, the Lord of the Papal States and his daughter, Lucrezia, practically ran the Vatican when he was absent from the city. It is rumored that he was poisoned while dining with a cardinal. The apex (or, perhaps, the nadir) of the Renaissance papacy can be found in the reign of Julius II (d.1513), who was known as the *papa terribile*. While history remembers him mainly for his patronage of Raphael, Michelangelo, Bramante, and the first plan to tear down the old Saint Peter's in order to build a new one, his own contemporaries remember him as a warrior who donned armor for his wars in the papal states. Bitterly satirized by Erasmus, he did call a reform council (Lateran V), but the reforms which were stipulated lacked any will within the Church to have them carried out. He had ordered a great tomb for himself, and some of Michelangelo's great sculptures (for example, *Moses*) were designed for the purpose although the tomb was never fully erected. Today, popes are elected in the Sistine Chapel under the great ceiling painted by Michelangelo – a commission by Julius, as were the frescos in the Vatican *stanze* done by Raphael.

THE POPES AND THE PROTESTANT REFORMATION

It is reported of Leo X, who succeeded Julius in 1513, that upon his election he said, "now that God has given us the papacy I fully intend to enjoy it." The Florentine son of Lorenzo the Magnificent, he looks out on posterity from the famous portrait painted by Raphael: corpulent, smug, and elegant. A lover of the fine things of this world, he is best remembered in history for two things that are, in fact, intimately connected: the preaching of an indulgence all over Europe to raise monies for the building of the new Saint Peter's basilica and the excommunication of an obscure German Augustinian friar named Martin Luther who was vehemently opposed to the preaching of the indulgence in general and the attendant abuses connected with the preaching in particular. A papal bull condemning forty-some propositions of Luther was published in 1520, but, when Luther burned the bull in public in 1521, he was excommunicated. It is not clear that Leo ever understood the seriousness of what he had done.

The only Dutchman ever elected to the papacy, Adrian (or Hadrian) VI, lasted only one year in the papacy (1522–3). The Roman people, accustomed to the lavish spending Italian popes, hated his economies and his puritan temper, while he himself was faced with the twin problems of the ever-spreading reform movement in the north and the menace of the Turks in the East. It is said that when he died the Roman populace hailed his Jewish physician as the "Savior of the Roman People" (*Salvator Populi Romani)* and marched to his home in the Roman ghetto with garlands in a torchlight procession.

The subsequent popes began to take seriously the now obvious split of the Church triggered by Luther's rebellion. Despite the fact that most of them still offered their patronage to the artists of the period (for example, Michelangelo painted his famous *The Last Judgment* for the Sistine Chapel, and work on the new Saint Peter's went on apace), efforts were made to counteract the effects of the Reformation both by internal reform and by energies supplied by the rise of new religious orders which became instruments of that reform. Paul III (1534–49) was a crucial figure in this reform movement. Not only did he support the foundation of the Society of Jesus (the Jesuits) as a leading arm of reform but he called an ecumenical council which met for the first time in the northern city of Trent (in 1545) and would meet intermittently from then until 1563 when Pius IV would bring it to a final conclusion after it had been held in abeyance for nearly a decade.

The doctrinal and disciplinary work of the Council of Trent would be the reference point for Catholicism well into modern times. Pope Pius V (1566–72) would add a capstone to the reforming decrees of Trent by publishing the *Roman Catechism* that became the teaching tool for Catholic pastors throughout the world, standardizing the Roman missal for the celebration of mass, the Roman Breviary, which was the official liturgical prayer for priests and religious, and by a vigorous campaign to reform the mores of the Roman clergy. Pius and his successor, Gregory XIII, pushed for reform in Catholic countries and, more importantly, gave strong support to foreign missions not only in the New World but also, under the aegis of the Jesuits, to lands in the Far East, especially Japan and China. He is perhaps best known today as the reformer of the calendar which was soon adopted by Catholic countries and, with its use of the "leap year" by Protestant ones, although it was not until the seventeenth century that the usage became universal in the West.

Sixtus V (1585–90) encouraged further centralization of Roman customs by adopting a rule which is in existence to this day: the obligation of every bishop to come to Rome and report on the state of his diocese every five years. Known as the *ad limina* (literally, to the threshold) visit, it was a strategy designed to bind the local bishop to the See of Peter in Rome. Sixtus also reorganized the papal curia with distinct offices (known as *dicasteries*) each headed by a cardinal; these offices functioned as the managerial office of the papacy. It was this pope who fixed the number of cardinals at seventy, a number that would not be changed until the middle of the twentieth century.

THE SEVENTEENTH CENTURY

Protestantism was, by the seventeenth century, a fact, and the papal reaction to that fact was a dialectical one: to demonstrate to the world that the Catholic Church was vigorous and dynamic on the one hand and to enforce Catholic orthodoxy through the use of suppression on the other.

The vigor of the Roman Church was amply demonstrated when hundreds of thousands of pilgrims flocked to the city for the jubilee year and culminated when Pope Paul V (1605–21) finally put the architectural façade and porch on the nearly finished Saint Peter's (it would finally be formally dedicated in 1626 under Urban VIII) while, characteristically enough, trumpeting his family name (Borghese) over the new façade. Anyone who has ever entered Saint Peter's realizes quickly enough that the basilica possesses a baroque theatricality designed to magnify the powers of the papacy with the barrel vaulting of the nave pointing down towards the papal altar and beyond to the altar of the Chair of Saint Peter. It was the same pope, however, using the powers of the Roman Inquisition, who censured the opinions of Galileo, putting his works on the Roman index of forbidden books.

Gregory XV (1621–3) demonstrated another aspect of the dynamism of the Catholic Reformation. He established a congregation for missionary work (Propaganda Fide) in 1622, which was to become the headquarters and dynamic center for Catholic missionary efforts both in mission lands and in those places where Protestantism had taken firm root. His successor, Urban VIII (1623–44) enlarged those efforts by founding a polyglot press in the Vatican and a university in 1627 for the training of a missionary clergy. Both institutions still flourish in Rome to this day. Again, following the example of his predecessor, he reiterated the censures against Galileo. Finally, Pope Alexander VII (1655–67) permitted the use of Chinese in the official liturgy of the Church by Jesuit missionaries who had penetrated the Forbidden Kingdom and dispensed Chinese priests from praying the canonical hour in Latin. This far-reaching and early attempt at inculturation had enormous implications for mission strategy, and the withdrawal of that permission in later times was a tragedy of the first magnitude. It would not be until the twentieth century that the need to inculturate the liturgy would get official sanction. The earlier attempts were resisted by those who desired uniformity with Roman customs as an indispensable instrument of Catholic solidarity – mistaking uniformity for unity.

TOWARDS THE FRENCH REVOLUTION

The story of the popes in the eighteenth century continued themes familiar to the previous one. They had to contend with life in the city of Rome and the papal states, monitor the life of the Church in the West (with vexatious problems, especially in France, where an ultraorthodox version of Augustinian Catholicism known as Jansenism created problems), contend with vigorous anti-Jesuit sentiments in parts of Europe (the order was actually suppressed for a time late in the century), oversee the vastly expanding missionary activity of Catholicism in the New World, and, of course, try to implement fully internal reform.

Benedict XIV, who reigned in mid-century from 1740 to 1758 was, in many ways, a model of the early modern papacy. Among the many reforms he undertook was the establishment of a congregation in the

Vatican to select good pastorally minded men for the episcopacy, and he continued the demand (not always observed) that bishops live in their diocese and actually shepherd their faithful instead of living where they wished on the incomes derived from their bishop's office. He also modernized the Index of Books, wrote a definitive set of laws for canonizations which served the Church into modern times, and enhanced the Vatican libraries as well as founding scholarly academies in the city. A recent German study of the papacy named Benedict as the most able pope of his century and, based on his reputation as a studious expert in law and his general cultural level, as one of the most learned popes in the history of the papacy.

The last pope to serve the See of Peter in the eighteenth century, Pius VI (1775–99), lived through the French Revolution. His problems, however, were manifold. Joseph II of the Austro-Hungarian Empire checked papal intervention in his kingdom, granted full recognition of all religions, and attempted to subject the Church to state control. Attempts were made to distance the Church from Roman control in Italy itself (in Tuscany), and, after the French Revolution, priests were made civil servants; all clerics had to make oaths of allegiance to the State. Diplomatic relations between Rome and France were broken off, and the pope deemed all state bishops and those who took the French oath as acting sinfully and illicitly. In 1802, Napoleon Bonaparte invaded the Papal States, annexed portions of them to France, and carried away, as indemnity, many manuscripts and artworks to Paris. The pope himself was carried into exile, where he died, in Valence, pitied by European sentiment, and buried until his remains were later returned to Rome.

THE NINETEENTH CENTURY: THE END OF THE PAPAL STATES

Relative to the papacy, the single most important event that occurred was the loss of the Papal States mid-century during the reign of Pius IX. The popes had been temporal rulers of an area of Italy that ran from the Romagna in the north down towards the kingdom of Naples. Their claim to that territory had been legitimized by the "Donation of Constantine," which, in fact, had been a forged document as was clearly shown in the Renaissance period by the humanist scholar Lorenzo Valla. Nonetheless, the Papal States had been maintained under the rule of Rome. As early as the time of Dante, who wrote scathingly of the matter in the *Divine Comedy*, it forced popes to act simultaneously as temporal rulers with specific political interests and also as the spiritual head of the Catholic Church. More often than not, these two duties could and did come into conflict. It has been recognized in retrospect that the loss of the pope's temporal power was an enormous blessing, but it was not so recognized as events unfolded.

Pius IX was the longest reigning pope in history. He assumed the papacy in 1846 and died in 1878. He began his papacy as a social and political moderate, which was a welcome relief after the arch conservative Gregory XVI, who not only refused to allow a railway in the Papal States but even forbade inoculation against smallpox as an act contrary to nature. The new pope's reign began on a happy note, but unrest developed when it became clear that the pope had no intention of creating a constitutional democracy. The Italian insurgents, driven to create a free Italy, slowly annexed parts of the Papal States, and finally, after some protracted battles, the Italian forces entered Rome in September 1870 and later incorporated Rome into the new Italian state. The pope was guaranteed his own person but now was virtually confined to the Vatican.

Pius responded to these events by declaring himself a prisoner of the Vatican, withheld recognition of the new state, and forbade Catholics from participating in the new political process. The pope had been, for a time before the events of 1870, profoundly suspicious of the new political order coming to life all over Europe. His 1864 encyclical, along with a list of contemporary errors (the so-called "Syllabus of Errors"), stated the matter baldly when it condemned the proposition that the pope ought to reconcile himself to and agree with "progress, liberalism, and modern civilization." In 1869, a year before the capture of Rome, the First Vatican Council also defined the doctrine of papal infallibility (which will be discussed in detail elsewhere in this volume) – a definition at least in part urged on the Council as a way of enhancing the prestige of the papacy at a time when its role as a political leader was being eradicated by the nationalist spirit that brought about the end of the Papal States. The intransigence of the pope, who never wavered in his belief in his claims and the work of the Council (which ended abruptly due to the outbreak of the Franco-Prussian War), did not at that time enhance the prestige of the papacy. Events in other parts of Europe, in fact, were leading away from papal control of church life, most notably in Bismark's *Kulturkampf* in Germany, which sought to subordinate the Catholic Church to the control of the Prussian State. In Rome itself, Pius was deeply unpopular. As the dead pope's cortege went through the city, a Roman crowd attempted to seize the papal remains to throw them into the Tiber. Many thought that the papacy was coming to a sad end.

THE RECREATION OF VATICAN CITY STATE

Leo XIII ushered the papacy into the twentieth century; he reigned from 1878 to 1903. While he followed the policy of his predecessor relative to the new Italian state (he forbade Catholics from voting or taking part in the political life of the Church), he showed himself, in other ways, to be a progressive pope. His most famous encyclical *Rerum novarum* (1891) was the first great papal encyclical on social justice; he asserted the rights of private property but he also asserted the rights of workers to organize and to be paid a decent wage – with the right to private ownership came the obligation of justice. All subsequent Catholic teaching on social justice down to this day looks back to this (then, rather audacious) encyclical. Leo also encouraged a revival of Thomism, thus inspiring the intellectual life of the Church, and wrote on biblical scholarship and letters reiterating the Church's condemnation of slavery. His first forays into ecumenism (he was the first pope to call other Christians "separated brethren") began with the premise (enunciated in his 1996 encyclical *Satis cognitum*) that Christian reunion depended on acceptance of the primacy of the Bishop of Rome. In the same year, perhaps influenced by Anglican movements towards a more Catholic understanding of their faith, he pronounced that Anglican ordinations were invalid. Although he worried about the North American doctrine of the separation of church and State, he at least took cognizance of a vibrant growing church there and, for the first time, in 1893, appointed an apostolic delegate to the USA.

Leo died at the age of ninety-three. Pius X assumed office barely a month later and reigned until 1914. Saintly in his own personal life (he was later canonized), he was in person a fierce reactionary who not only would not find ways to accommodate the Church to secular governments but also broke off relations with some (France in 1906; the Government responded by seizing all church properties a year later) and alienated others. Although he did some laudable things, such as encouraging a reform in church music, insisting on more frequent communion for people when they were at mass, and beginning the revision of canon law as well as liturgical books, he is today best remembered for his fierce reactionary attitudes crystallized in the anti-modernist movement.

Pius X did not like trade unions, which were not expressly under Catholic aegis, because he was profoundly suspicious of most modern ideas. This distrust led him to condemn a rather amorphous intellectual movement within the Church which came to be known as "modernism," and, to be sure that it was rooted out of Catholic circles, he demanded oaths against it and set up boards to root it out when denounced. It is no exaggeration to say that his suppression of modernism, going beyond whatever modernism might have been, in fact, all about, set back the intellectual life of the Catholic Church by decades.

Pius X died in 1914 after a serious illness, which was most likely exacerbated by his reaction to the outbreak of hostilities that led up to World War I. His successor was Benedict XV (1914–22) about whom it was said (legendarily?) that the first thing he found on his desk after his election was a secret denunciation of him as a modernist meant for the eyes of Pius X. He soon called a halt to the witch hunt for modernists but really spent most of his energies to create a peace plan for the then raging war; his efforts came to nought because both sides saw him as a pawn of the other. He did support enthusiastically the League of Nations at the end of the war in the hope that such a forum might forestall armed conflicts, although, as history would show, that turned out to be a dashed hope.

With respect to the relationship of the Vatican and the Italian State, he lifted the ban forbidding Catholics to enter political life and gave encouragement to Don Luigi Sturzo's popular party. More importantly, he had his curia enter into secret negotiations with the Italian State (in the person of Benito Mussolini) to solve the vexatious problem of the annexation of the old Papal States. For the first time since 1870 he also gave his papal blessing "to the city and to the world" from the balcony of Saint Peter's to the crowd in Saint Peter's Square.

It was also in his pontificate that the code of canon law was promulgated – the legal handbook of the Western Church (the Eastern Catholic Church had its own code) – in 1918. The code would govern the Church until the new code was issued in 1983 in the papacy of John Paul II. Conscious of the ancient rights and rites of Eastern Catholicism, he made the Congregation of the Oriental Church autonomous and founded in Rome the Pontifical Oriental Institute under the supervision of the Jesuits.

It was for Pope Pius XI (1922–39) to bring to a final conclusion the issue of the old Papal States. In 1929, the Italian government and the Vatican signed the Lateran Treaty. The Vatican recognized the legitimacy of the Kingdom of Italy with Rome as its capital in exchange for the recognition of the independence of Vatican City State and reimbursement for losses. Certain places connected to the Church outside the physical confines of Vatican City State (for example, the summer residence of the pope at Castel Gandolfo) would have an extra-territorial status which meant that they were under control of the Vatican and not the Italian State. The Italian Government, further, recognized Catholicism as the official religion of the country and mandated religious instruction in secondary schools. Those latter conditions would endure until 1985 when the Lateran Treaty was renegotiated with the mandated religious instruction now abrogated.

Pius XI was not inattentive to the modern world. He established the Vatican Radio in 1931. He reaffirmed the teaching on Leo XIII's *Rerum novarum* on social justice with an encyclical on its fortieth anniversary (*Quadrigesimo anno*) and reaffirmed and extended its doctrine on behalf of working people. Acutely aware of dangerous movements in Europe, the pope also published scathing encyclicals condemning the atheistic character of Soviet Communism (1939), the anti-Christian ideology of German Nazism (1937), and, even earlier, Mussolini's Fascist attempt to control every facet of Italian life in 1931. Pius XI died in the same year that would see the beginnings of hostile movements that would explode into World War II, 1939.

PIUS XII AND JOHN XXIII: A STUDY IN CONTRASTS

Pius XII was an aristocratic Roman with vast diplomatic experience in the service of the Church. He had served the Church in Germany, spoke many languages, and was, as his papacy would show, not immune to new ideas. Pius had a profound loathing of Soviet Communism, and, even though he knew full well the evil character of the Nazi regime, he tried to be as even-handed as possible during the conflict. Subsequent historians have faulted him for his reticence in reacting to the Nazi persecution and extermination of the Jews, but an intense debate rages to this day about the matter. He did keep Rome relatively free from the destructive bombings of the period and did oversee a vast network of shelter for persecuted people. When the war ended, his popularity was at a high point because of his work for peace.

Internal to the life of the Church, he clearly saw the need of a renovation in the pastoral and theological milieux of the times. His justly famous encyclicals on liturgical renewal, biblical studies, a deeper understanding of the nature of the Church, and so on were anticipatory moments which would reach their maturity in the period of the Second Vatican Council after his death. Paradoxically enough, he showed a stern hand in reining in the more adventurous theological minds of his time (thinkers whose moment would come after his death) through the monitoring exercises of the Holy Office. Likewise, he battled vigorously against the Communist Party in Italy and viewed the political power of the countries of the Iron Curtain and their suppression of church life with contempt. In 1950, he declared the dogma of the Assumption of Mary into Heaven to be part of the authentic teaching of the Church. This was the one and only time in the twentieth century that a pope had exercised the function of personal infallibility in the course of promulgating an official doctrine of the Church.

Pius XII was pope for just under twenty years. When he died in 1958, he did so at a time when his personal prestige was at its zenith. His successor, Pope John XXIII, was widely regarded as an interim pope (he was seventy-six when elected) and, as a person, would not have been more of a contrast to Pius XII. Portly, avuncular, and possessed of a peasant sense of humor, John, nonetheless, was a highly intelligent, shrewd, and skilled papal diplomat. In less than a year after his election, he announced, without great fanfare, that he intended to do three things: (1) call a synod of the clergy for the Diocese of Rome; (2) revise canon law; and (3) call an ecumenical council.

There had not been a Roman synod since the eighteenth century. The fact that John wished to have one reminded people that, above all else, he was the bishop of Rome; it was from this position that everything else connected to the papacy emanated. His desire to revise canon law was a reflection of how much the code, adopted in 1918, was out of date. As far as the Ecumenical Council was concerned, the last one had ended abruptly in 1869, so this convocation was, in some sense, the resumption of the unfinished work of Vatican I. Nonetheless, as preparatory work was concerned, it was clear that the Pope did not desire a council that would define doctrines and condemn heresies. He wanted a council that would be pastoral; that would speak to all people of good will (especially other Christians); and that would carry forth what was called, in Italian, *aggiornamento* – renewal or bringing up to date. As he is alleged to have said once, his desire was to open up a window and let in a little fresh air.

The Council would open in 1962, but, by the following year, John was gravely ill, dying in 1963 before the Council was finished. What he had done, however, was to call and convene a council whose deliberations and decisions – to which we will have many occasions in this work to refer – still influence the Church in profound ways. His successor, who would bring the Council to its completion in 1965 was Pope Paul VI (1963–78).

It was the fate of his papacy that the many good things that he had done – bringing the Council to a conclusion, opening lines of communication with the Orthodox Church, reaffirming the papal teaching on social justice, enlarging the visibility of the papacy through travel, etc. – were overshadowed by his decision to reaffirm the Church's traditional prohibition of contraception (in his encyclical *Humanae vitae* in 1968); this triggered a rift in the Church that clearly marked a division among progressive and traditional Catholics, a rift that continues to this day.

The year 1978 was one of "three popes." After the death of Paul VI, the conclave elected Pope John Paul I, who died less than two months after being elected. That gentle man, however, made one important symbolic gesture: He refused to be "crowned" with the traditional beehive tiara with its three levels indicating the pope as "ruler of princes and kings, ruler of the world, and vicar of Christ on earth." By the refusal to use that head covering and his insistence on receiving the miter as bishop of Rome, he was tacitly refusing some claims that had become associated with the medieval papacy, and, in that refusal, he reoriented the papacy back to its origins, namely, that the pope was, before all else, the bishop of Rome.

The Polish cardinal Karol Wojtyla was elected to replace John Paul I in October 1978. He was the first pope in history to come from a Slavic country. He was only fifty-eight when he assumed the papacy and quickly impressed the world with his vigor (he was a dedicated athlete), his academic background (he had been a university professor of philosophy in his native country), and his personal history as one who, along with his interest in poetry and drama, had lived through both the Nazi regime and the oppressive Stalinist government of his country. A true polyglot, he took seriously his role as bishop of Rome and as the universal leader of the Catholic Church. John Paul II understood the power of the media (he had been an actor in his youth) and took full advantage of it, especially through his many travels to all parts of the world.

John Paul II saw the new revision of canon law through to completion in 1983. He wrote many encyclicals (perhaps his most important was his one on ecumenism, *Ut unum sint*, 1995), published books in his own name which were bestsellers, devoted his weekly audiences to catecheses on various doctrinal and moral issues, and oversaw the completion and adoption of the *Catechism of the Catholic Church* – the first universal catechism since the Roman Catechism published at the conclusion of the Council of Trent in the sixteenth century. Many think that his support for the social movement Solidarity and his visit to his native Poland in 1979 were instrumental in the fall of Communism in the Eastern bloc.

John Paul II was, by turns, progressive in matters of social justice and very traditional in matters of faith and morals. He did not condone dissent in theological matters and felt no compunction in using the authority of his office to suppress it. Profoundly, almost mystically, religious, he combined a deep theological faith with a devotionalism that reflected his own roots in baroque Polish Catholicism. His long reign – from 1978 to 2005 – put an indelible mark on the Catholic Church as it moved into the third millennium. At his funeral in early 2005, it is estimated that over 2 million people flocked to Rome to pay the deceased pope homage. How closely his successor, Pope Benedict XVI, the German theologian and close collaborator of John Paul, will continue his policies and to what degree he will put his own mark on the papacy are, at this moment, too early to judge.

CONTINUITY AND CHANGE IN THE PAPACY

The office of the bishop of Rome – the papacy – is the oldest continuous office in Western civilization and one of the oldest in the world. Its foundational claim is that the bishop of Rome is the lineal successor of the Apostle Peter who was martyred in that city during the persecution of Nero *c.* AD 64. When we speak of the "enthronement" of a newly elected pope, we are speaking of his being seated on the Chair of Peter, although, obviously, if he is already a bishop he becomes pope when he is elected.

To that most fundamental position as bishop of Rome there has arisen a whole complex of powers, honors, and legal rights which have accrued to the pope over the nearly two millennia of Catholic history. It is useful to remember that the papacy, like every ancient institution, brings to itself certain customs, expectations, and privileges over time. As we have seen in the rapid history sketched above, certain papal claims to power were introduced over time. The temporal power of the pope over the so-called Papal States was an accident of history, reinforced by legal documents of dubious historical worth, which, as was already recognized in the Middle Ages, was an unnecessary burden and a real distraction. No Catholic today laments the loss of that temporal rule. Similarly, the right of the popes to judge the secular princes, and, at times, to claim power over them was a product of the politics of the Middle Ages. Doctrinal developments such as papal infallibility had their own contentious history of development, and the correct relationship of the local bishop and his powers was not addressed at Vatican I in the nineteenth century and is still a matter of lively discussion in theological circles today.

Over the centuries, the papacy has accrued a number of titles that run
from the honorific to those which actually describe what the Church
believes about the papacy. That he is bishop of Rome and successor of
Peter is a fundamental claim of Catholicism. From the fifth century,
bishops and priests were called "vicars of Christ," but the popes arrogated
that term to themselves in the medieval period. The Second Vatican
Council applied that term to bishops as vicars for the local church and to
the pope as vicar of Christ for the universal Church. The term "supreme
pontiff" (from the Latin *pontifex,* "bridge builder") derives from a fourth-
century title for a bishop even though the term goes back to pagan
Roman usage. Although, as the Second Vatican Council says, the term
should be used for Christ (who is the supreme head of the Church), it is
still used in the Church but, correctly, as the "Roman Pontiff." The titles
"Patriarch of the West" and "Primate of Italy" are purely honorific titles
with no legal authority. The pope is, legally speaking, "Sovereign of the
State of the Vatican City" because the Vatican is a territory legally recognized as independent and sovereign. Today, it is common in papal
documents to use one of the most lovely of the papal titles (first used by
Gregory the Great): "Servant of the servants of God."

In the period after the Second Vatican Council, the eminent theologian (and later, Cardinal) Yves Congar suggested that titles for the pope
should not be exaggerated. The Vatican's International Theological
Commission listed, as the preferred titles, Pope, Holy Father, Roman
Bishop, Successor of Peter, Supreme Shepherd (Pastor) of the Universal
Church. This development, at first seemingly trivial, has some theological
importance in the attempt of the Church to situate the papacy in relationship both to the Church as a whole and to the bishops of the world in
particular.

Modern popes, and especially Popes Paul VI and John Paul II, have
openly said that the papacy is, for other Christians, a point of contention.
Indeed, John Paul II actually called on the Christians who are not united
to Rome to discuss ways in which the office of the papacy (or, more
commonly called today, the "Petrine Office") can be understood in a
fashion that makes Christian unity more attractive. Surely, the Catholic
Church is not going to (and cannot) abolish the papacy since the Catholic
Church defines itself as a body in which all the bishops of the Church are
in union with one other and with the Bishop of Rome, but how that
office is exercised, and how it is to be understood in relationship to the
Orthodox Churches and those of the Reformation is a matter for present
and future discussion.

Box 2   Cardinals in the Catholic Church

The Latin word *cardinalis* comes from the Latin word *cardo* meaning a hinge. It was first used in Christian Rome to designate those deacons who administered the Church's charitable works in the seven designated deaconal stations in Rome. Some time thereafter, the term was extended to include the parish priests within Rome and for the seven bishops of the small dioceses that ringed the city. In the early twelfth century, for the first time, they jointly elected the pope. In 1179, Pope Alexander III decreed that only the cardinal bishops, priests, and deacons could legitimately elect a new pope. At end of the twelfth century, it became customary for the pope to designate certain eminent clerics to hold the title of cardinal even though they lived away from Rome. It is necessary to distinguish (as we do to this day) between residential cardinals (those who live and minister in Rome at the Vatican) and those who live outside the city in their own dioceses.

Pope Sixtus V set the number of cardinals at seventy, and this limit pertained until Pope John XXIII in the early 1960s exceeded that limit. His predecessor, Pope Pius XII, began to internationalize the College of Cardinals in order to reflect more authentically the widespread growth of the Church outside of Europe. That trend has continued down to the present time. Although they enjoy prestige and certain ecclesiastical privileges, the most important task entrusted to the cardinals – apart from those duties performed in the Vatican by residential cardinals – is to come together to elect a new pope. Recent legislation stipulates that only cardinals under the age of eighty can vote in the conclave which meets after the death and time of mourning for the deceased pope. During the period of interregnum (known by the Latin phrase *sede vacante* – "while the chair [of Peter] is vacant"), the ordinary administration of the Church continues but those cardinals who head the various congregations lose their office until reappointed by the new pope. The Dean of the College of Cardinals is given the privilege of ordaining the new pope as a bishop should he not already be a bishop at the time of election. All Eastern patriarchs of the Oriental Churches in union with Rome are now made cardinals at the time of their elevation to the patriarchate. On some occasions, a pope may designate a new cardinal *in petto* – which is to say, name a cardinal in secret but, for reasons of safety (for example, if the person lives in a State where the Church is persecuted) or prudence, he is not formally installed publicly as a cardinal.

In a sense, being named a cardinal is an honorary title but has its own particular power because, for the past millennium, it is to the cardinals alone that the task of naming a new pope is given. That privilege, of course, is the result of a long historical process and does not mean that in some future time the procedure could not be modified or radically changed, although there is little indication that such a change is in the offing. In the present order of things, the cardinals more and more come from various parts of the world; that variety serves the Church well since, informally, the College of Cardinals serves as the senate of the Church and rightfully reflect the needs and aspirations of the Catholic Church world wide.

FURTHER READING

Bellito, C. M., *1001 Questions and Answers about the Popes and the Papacy* (New York, N.Y.: Paulist, 2008). Popular but useful information.

Duffy, Eamon, *Saint and Sinners: A History of the Popes* (New Haven, Conn.: Yale University Press, 2001). Best historical survey in English.

Eno, Robert, *The Rise of the Papacy* (Wilmington, Del.: Glazier, 1990). The evolution of the papacy in the patristic period.

Kelly, J. N. D., ed., *The Oxford Dictionary of the Popes* (London and New York: Oxford, 1986; revised 2006). Very solid historically.

Lampe, Peter, *From Paul to Valentinus: Christians at Rome in the First Two Centuries* (Minneapolis, Minn.: Fortress, 2003). A scholarly investigation about the beginnings of the Christian Church in Rome.

McBrien, Richard, ed., *Lives of the Popes* (San Francisco, Calif.: Harper, 1997). Excellent ancillary information – a chronological survey of the popes.

O'Grady, Desmond, *Rome Reshaped: Jubilees 1300–2000* (London and New York: Continuum, 1999). Popular social history of papal Rome from the Middle Ages to the dawn of the new millennium.

Steimer, Bruno and Parker, Michael G., eds., *Dictionary of Popes and the Papacy* (New York, N.Y.: Crossroad, 2001). Translated from the German *Lexikon fur Theologie und Kirche*, an alphabetical listing of popes with excellent entries on various topics connected to the papacy.

Tillard, Jean Marie, *The Bishop of Rome* (Wilmington, Del.: Glazier, 1983). A solid theological study by the late Catholic ecumenist and theologian.

CHAPTER 3

Being Catholic: Some typologies

INTRODUCTION

In the previous chapter we viewed the Catholic tradition "from on high" by a consideration of the history and development of the papacy. We started at that level because, as we noted, if there is one element that is peculiar to the Catholic Church it is its insistence that the bishop of Rome, the pope, is central to the self-identification of the Church in his role as the center of Catholic unity. Everyone who knows anything about Catholicism understands that. In the official writings of the Church, in everything from its magisterial and papal documents to its official catechism, it is almost a commonplace to say that what makes the Church Catholic is the unity among all Catholic bishops and their common unity with the bishop of Rome, the pope.

However, Catholicism cannot be understood only from the top down or from its center outward. The Catholic faithful are all members of the Catholic Church; they share a common baptism, are held to the same moral order, profess the same rule of faith, recognize a common life of worship, and are challenged to the same imperatives of the Gospel. For that reason alone, it is necessary to take into account the history of the Church not only as a record of what its hierarchy does but how Catholics through history have lived their faith. This chapter, then, hopes to give some account of that history, not from an institutional angle but, as it were, "from below."

That is not an easy undertaking given the fact that the Catholic Church has been present in (largely) Western culture for nearly 2,000 years. We know next to nothing about the many Christians who made up the congregations of believers in most periods of the Church. We rely almost exclusively on texts or readings "behind texts" which might give us some perspective on what ordinary Catholics believed and practiced. Nonetheless, in classic works such as the prologue to Chaucer's *Canterbury Tales* or Dante's *Divine Comedy* we have had set before us idealized types who represented a broad stretch of humanity. In the case of Dante, he peopled his great poem with those who were condemned to eternal damnation or those aspiring to beatitude as they climbed the mount of purgatory as well as those who have already achieved it and enjoyed the vision of God in Heaven as he made his imagined journey through the world which is beyond our own: Hell, Purgatory, and Heaven. In those places, he met a whole parade of saints and sinners from every class and condition. To even attempt to replicate such a panorama as we look at the Church from below is no easily managed task and, we will not attempt to do so. Nonetheless, we will attempt to set out some ideal types who represent eras of the Church.

AN APPROACH TO HISTORY

Almost all traditional histories try to organize their narrative into chronological periods although everyone knows that history does not always fit neatly into such categories. The history of Western civilization is fair proof of that need for caution. The Renaissance period is not an abrupt break with the Middle Ages just as the Middle Ages is in some ways moored to its Roman and Greek past. The same thing is certainly true of the history of Catholicism. Catholicism is rather like a very old house in which generations have lived. The current owners may have put in air-conditioning units, but the old porch where grandparents sat to get a summer breeze is still there, and the attic stores things no longer in use. Similarly, to cite a more precise example, Saint Peter's basilica in Rome stands in its present configuration from seventeenth-century modifications of a Michelangelo plan, which was still incomplete in the sixteenth century but was designed to replace a basilica which was built in the fourth century over the purported grave of Peter first mentioned in the second century and modified all through the Middle Ages; some additions are additions made in the twentieth century. To analyze Saint Peter's is to analyze a building which bears within in it both continuities and novelties. Even discrete elements such as architecture have a compressed history within them.

Thus it is with the larger history of the Catholic Church itself. It is a story which has continuities and abruptions both large and small. It is too complex a history to tell whole in a reasonable space (the late Herbert Jedin's history of the Catholic Church runs to ten fat volumes in English translation and gets us only to the end of the Second Vatican Council), both because the Church has a 2,000-year history and because to write the history of the Church one must write that history with reference to specific places: The history of Catholicism in Ireland is not quite its history, say, in Canada. Nonetheless, those Churches, as well as other national ones, have certain ties with other Churches and with the Roman Church itself. Therefore, no attempt will be made to attempt a brief history of the Catholic Church in this volume.

What will be attempted in this brief chapter is to mark out some conspicuous ideal types which set some eras of Church history but with the added caution that these typologies are not only characteristic of the past but exist today albeit in somewhat different ways: There was a period characterized as a period of persecution, but that is not all past; persecutions were as vicious in the twentieth century as they were before Constantine in the fourth. It can be argued, however, that these idealized types did appear in history and then were built upon subsequently. The typological figures we will call upon are, of course, ideal types, which in the concrete take on the varieties characteristic of different cultures and the peculiarities of different people.

To study the experience of "ordinary" Catholics as crystallized in the story of the various "types" of the faithful throughout history is to get closer to the popular religious expressions which are part of the very texture of Catholic experience. It is to get some sense of what the theologians call the "consensus of the faithful."

Popular piety/popular religion

Popular piety and religion creatively combine the divine and the human, Christ and Mary, spirit and body, communion and institution, person and community, faith and homeland, intelligence and emotion. This wisdom is a Christian humanism that radically affirms the dignity of every person as a child of God, establishes a basic fraternity, teaches people to encounter nature and understand work, provides reasons for joy and humor even in the midst of a very hard life. For the people this wisdom is also a principle of discernments and an evangelical instinct through which they spontaneously sense when the Gospel is served in the Church and when it is emptied of its content and stifled by other interests. (*Catechism of the Catholic Church*, No. 1676)

MARTYRS AND MARTYRDOM

When Christianity began to spread in the Roman Empire after the earthly life of Jesus, it very soon began to attract the suspicion and then the hostility of the Roman authorities. In a way, this was not characteristic of

Roman practice. Typically, the Roman authorities were quite indifferent about the religious practices of their conquered people. They did not like the Druids they found in Gaul since few Romans had a taste for the druidic penchant for human sacrifice. They simultaneously disdained the Jews but, at the same time, had a grudging admiration for their staunch monotheism and the antiquity of their sacred literature. They could tolerate them and did so until the Jews revolted against Roman rule in Palestine some decades before and after the life of Jesus. Nonetheless, we know from Roman sources that in the mid-first century, Christians were the subject of persecution in Rome itself. The historian Tacitus, writing some years after the event, describes Nero as shifting blame on the Christians, whom he describes as haters of the human race, and inflicting on them atrocious tortures and, finally, death. Early in the second century, Pliny the Younger wrote to the Emperor describing the arrest and execution of Christians in a remote area of the Empire near the Black Sea. If one can judge from Pliny's letter, it was the very name of being a Christian that brought down the wrath of the imperial authorities.

Why? It is not clear, but judging from the surviving reports of the trials of Christians in the second century, Christians were seen as recalcitrant in their unwillingness to worship the gods of Rome. Had they venerated them even by the small gesture of a pinch of incense or the pouring out of a libation and, at the same time, practiced their faith, they would have most likely been left in peace. What made the Christians dangerously subversive in Roman eyes was their unwillingness to exhibit that veneration (*pietas*) towards the gods which alone, according to the Roman way of seeing things, insured the civil order. When there was *pietas,* there was harmony among family, State, and the heavens; the result was the *pax deorum,* the peace of the gods. Christians, in short, were considered a fifth column within Roman society for refusing to honor the gods, despite the pleas of a number of highly literate Christians (called the Apologists) who argued that one could be a good citizen and not worship the gods. It is for that reason that the Romans called Christianity a *superstitio* and not a *religio.* A *superstitio* was a name for religion that was irrational, culture-hating, and destructive.

The persecutions by the Romans were at first tending towards the episodic, and they were also location-specific (there were more outbreaks of persecution in North Africa than in Rome itself) until the middle of the third century. In the year 250, the Emperor Decius, who had more than a handful of problems in governing the Empire, ordered every citizen to honor the Roman gods and to get a temple certificate to that effect. Some Christians complied to save their lives; others got bogus certificates to show that they did sacrifice when they, in fact, did not; and a large number refused and were either executed, condemned to the imperial mines (a slow death), or had their properties seized and were sent into exile. The persecution under Decius was the first empire-wide one, but others were to follow culminating in the ferocious decade-long persecution of Diocletian at the beginning of the fourth century. It was only in the period after Diocletian that Emperor Constantine issued the edict of toleration for Christians at the beginning of the fourth century.

From the perspective of the Christians, persecution was something which their very founder had endured. Jesus was the preeminent martyr (the word means "witness") and so it is not strange that the Christian community saw a link between those who died and Jesus himself. The early second-century Christian text *The Martyrdom of Polycarp* indeed drew parallels between the impending execution of Polycarp and the passion narratives of the Gospels. In addition, the community honored the martyrs after their death by recalling their death dates (known as their "birthdays," *dies natalis*), visiting their burial places, and maintaining stories about their bravery and their witness for the truth. The North African writer Tertullian called the blood of the martyrs the seed of the Church. The cult of the saints in Catholic Christianity begins in the veneration of the martyrs.

Even though the period of Roman persecution ended at the beginning of the fourth century, martyrdom remained a constant in the history of Catholicism, perhaps no more than in the twentieth century when more Catholics died for their faith than in all of the Roman persecutions combined. The late Pope John Paul II was instrumental in recalling the powerful witness of those who died in our own times either out of hatred for the faith or for witnessing against social injustice or by uttering a prophetic protest against the suppression of human rights. In fact, the Pope said that dying for the faith was a truly ecumenical bond since many Christians who died in the twentieth century were not Roman Catholics alone. If the old tradition of depicting a martyr with an ancient instrument of death (a sword or arrows), the more recent symbolism would have to show barbed wire, automatic rifles, electric cattle prods, and other forms of violence.

The history of martyrdom is an excellent example of how a certain way of being a Christian enters into the history of the Church in a certain period and then is remembered in the tradition as a model for the Christian life. That "remembering" happens through various vehicles: via worship in the liturgy where the memory of the martyrs is recalled; in literature where their deeds are recounted, and in art where their sufferings are illustrated. The periodic eruption of martyrdom (in the foreign missions in the early modern period; those who died in persecutions in the twentieth century) keeps the martyr from merely being a museum character. Indeed, one of the ironies of the contemporary period is that some of our most notable martyrs (think of Bishop Oscar Romero of El Salvador) have died at the hands of baptized Catholics who pursued them to death not because of a hatred for their faith but because they loved justice and had compassion for the sufferings of the poor of the world. It is also worthwhile that martyrs cut across class, status, and gender. Martyrdom is an equal-opportunity possibility for every Christian.

Of course, every Christian is called upon to be a martyr/witness to the faith by their lives. Most frequently, this kind of witness does not draw violence to itself but it may draw scorn, pity, or indifference. In our times, there are also moments when it was necessary to pay a costlier price for fidelity, but, as Pope Benedict XVI pointed out in the first encyclical of his papacy (*God is Love*), the task of witness is an essential function of those who are in the Church, and that more benign sense of witness must be seen against its more restricted sense of giving up one's life for faith in the preeminent martyr, Jesus.

ASCETICS AND MONKS

The term "asceticism" comes from a Greek word which means athletic training or discipline. In Christian usage, it means either practices in which bodily impulses are sublimated for a greater good, such as fasting as a mark of penance or as an identifiable trait of self-denial as a regime of life undertaken as a form of Christian living. Saint Matthew's Gospel, Chapters 5–7 mentions three traditional pillars of ascetic practice taken over from Judaism: fasting, almsgiving, and prayer. There are, of course, ascetic parallels in all of the world's religions, but our concern here is with the development of asceticism in the history of Christianity.

With the end of the Roman persecution in the fourth century, and the ever-closer identification of Christianity with the Roman State (Christianity was made the official religion of the Roman Empire by Emperor Theodosius in AD 381), some Christians felt that the Church was becoming too worldly and too comfortable. As a reaction against such laxity, it became common for some to flee the Roman cities and to take up a simple life of withdrawal, prayer, self-denial, work, and the exercise of some gospel values such as poverty and freely chosen celibacy. One particular area of the Roman Empire, Egypt and, to a lesser degree, Palestine, was a popular destination for these people. Many of these men and women saw themselves as living a kind of countercultural life regarding their choice as a new kind of martyrdom (witness) for Christ. One of the earliest biographies of those who chose such a life was written by the fourth-century bishop, Athanasius of Alexandria. In his *Life of Antony,* Athanasius claimed that Antony was a "martyr every day of his life"; Antony lived in the desert free from the city and "free from the tax collector."

These desert dwellers were, in many instances, simple country people drawn from the agricultural classes of Roman Egypt. Soon, such folks, both male and female, were to be found in various parts of the Roman Empire but especially in the deserts of Egypt. Their sayings and teachings were collected over time into compilations known as the "Sayings of the Desert Fathers and Mothers." It was from these collections that monastic "doctrine" would later evolve. Many lived alone (the word "monk" comes from the word for "alone") but gathered for common prayer and mutual sharing as well as for the liturgy of the eucharist on Sundays.

Out of this somewhat sprawling and informal movement, monasticism emerged by the simple expedient of organizing those who wished to embrace such a life into a community under a rule of life. A number of such rules have come down to us but, generally speaking, the Rule of Saint Basil in the Christian East became over time normative for Orthodox monasticism while in the West, after a long complicated evolution, a rule written by Saint Benedict of Nursia (?480–?550) became the rule most commonly adopted in the West. Both Orthodox and Catholic monasticism have had a long history in Christianity, but the important point is that the way of monastic living becomes a hallmark of both traditions and exists down to the present day.

The ascetic life was fundamentally embraced and developed first by laypeople, both male and female, not by clerics. Indeed, in the earlier period of its history there was a reluctance to admit clerics to its communities even though, in time, male monastic communities became increasingly clericalized. Despite that fact, it is crucial to recall that a monk is not a synonymous term for a priest even though some monks are priests. Monasticism is a vocation in its own right.

With the waning of the Roman Empire in the West and the decline of city life, monasticism became one of the most conspicuous elements of Christian living in the early Middle Ages. It was well suited to do so. Monasteries were self-contained entities; they had expertise in agriculture, medicine, education, hospitality, and so on. During the early medieval period (the so-called "Dark Ages"), they constituted the major locus of learning and education. Monks also "planted" monasteries in areas which had yet to be evangelized. One could say that the spread of Christianity in the early Middle Ages was largely the result of monasteries from which radiated Christian life. In the absence of towns, many monasteries took on the role of the town. It was to the monastery that people came for medical care, the rudiments of education, food in time of famine, and shelter in periods of distress.

Although monasticism maintained its vigor and presence in the high Middle Ages, it was also challenged by the rise of the mendicant friars such as the Dominicans and Franciscans who were more mobile and more attuned to the new challenges of city life (G. K. Chesterton caught the difference crisply when he wrote that what Benedict had stored, Saint Francis scattered). Monasticism itself had the dynamics for internal reform, and such reforms occurred periodically in Catholic history. When the young convert Thomas Merton (1915–68) entered a Trappist monastery in Kentucky in 1941, he entered a monastery which took its name from the seventeenth-century reform (at La Trappe – hence its name) of the twelfth-century Cistercian reform of the sixth-century Rule of Benedict, which, in turn, was based on still earlier monastic models.

It should be noted that monasticism was never solely a male preserve. Women ascetics and monastics were a feature of Catholicism from its beginnings down to the present day. Monastic life was one attractive model of feminine living because the communities were relatively autonomous, there were opportunities for education, and the possibility of an exemplary life of holiness was highly esteemed enough that women could serve, albeit without the power of priestly ordination, as spiritual guides, reformers, and even, rarely, as preachers and writers. In the contemporary Church, three women have been named "doctors" of the Church: The Church recognizes their lives and bears witness that they have "taught" (the word "doctor" is from the Latin *docere* meaning to teach) the Christian faithful because of their outstanding role as spiritual teachers. All of them were shaped by life in the cloister: The Dominican Saint Catherine of Siena (d.1380) and the two Carmelites Saint Teresa of Avila (d.1582) and Saint Thérèse of Lisieux (d.1897).

The different ways in which people have lived the ascetic life are many in the Roman Catholic Church. In the early modern period, groups of women began to live in community under various religious rules devised for them. This sisterhood needs to be distinguished from the traditional nuns who led a cloistered life. Most congregations of religious sisters as opposed to the traditional more monastically oriented orders of nuns were founded after the French Revolution – they are a modern phenomenon. They undertook a variety of good works ranging from caring for orphans, the elderly, and so on, to hospital and nursing work or education. Similarly, groups of men, without taking on the priesthood, joined congregations of brothers for similar sorts of missionary works, especially in the field of education and care of the sick.

Unlike the Orthodox Church, which has conceived of the monastic life as a single way of life for both men and women to live under the fourth-century Rule of Saint Basil, either as contemplatives or for the service of the needy or a combination of both, the Catholic Church has a history of the proliferation of new religious orders (and continues to see them today) founded and approved by the Church at different times for different needs. Some of these orders bear a similarity to monastic life but many do so only in the sense that, like monks, they accept a vow of chastity, obedience to superiors, and a form of poverty variously understood. The Jesuits, founded in the sixteenth century, were a significant instrument for the Church during the time of the Catholic Reform, while many foreign missionary orders were founded during the expansion of European interests during the colonial period in Latin America, Africa, and Asia.

Obviously, these many different forms of religious life were not open to all Catholics since they all shared the common vows of celibacy, the sharing of goods or poverty, and obedience to a superior, but they were "another way" of being Catholic. Many laypeople affiliated themselves to these orders in order to share in their spirituality and their good works. Such laypeople were often called *tertiaries* because they followed a third rule next to those men and women who followed a regular rule of life. Finally, history demonstrates that over the course of the centuries many orders died out either because their original purpose no longer served or because of laxity of spirit that diminished their attractiveness to people. As certain orders waned or disappeared, others would be (and continue to be) founded.

It should be noted that there is a distinction to be made between monks (who are called to a stable life in community), friars (who are mobile and traditionally lived from alms – hence they are also called *mendicants* [beggars]), and members of religious congregations, both male and female, who lead a common life and take vows but who have a plethora of missionary activities.

Those who follow the ascetic life make up only a small percentage of Catholics but the values which they ideally exemplify – frugality of life, disciplining one's behavior, concern for the other, regular prayer, and so on – are values for all Christians but are magnified in the lives of those who follow the regular path of religious living. Furthermore, no member of the Church is fully exempt from the ascetic ideal of self-denial for a greater good, as every student who works instead of plays, every parent who sacrifices for a child, everyone who fasts for the sake of the poor, etc., understands. The foundations of Catholic asceticism can best be understood as the carrying out of the three things recommended by Jesus in the great section on the sermon of the mount (Matt. 5–7): prayer, fasting, and almsgiving.

PILGRIMS

In the early fourth century, when Christianity was no longer the subject of legal disabilities and, indeed, began to receive the patronage of the State, Christians became more and more inclined to visit the shrines of the martyrs in Rome and to travel to the Holy Land to visit the places associated with the life of Jesus. The idea of pilgrimage was closely entwined with the cult of the martyrs and other saints as well as a desire to make their own, the places sacred to the memory of Jesus. By the end of the fourth century, the holy places in Palestine were filled with ascetics and monks (they also were an object of interest to pilgrims), and visits to those places was made easy by the fact that Palestine was under the control of Roman authorities. Jerusalem itself was a thriving Christian center with a massive church built over the burial tomb of Jesus erected by the generosity of Emperor Constantine and his mother, Helena, who had a keen interest in the places made sacred to Jesus.

One of the most interesting texts about pilgrimage is a narrative of a late-fourth-century ascetic woman named Egeria (from Spain), who traveled from Europe to Egypt, the Holy Land, Edessa, Asia Minor, and on to Constantinople (the manuscript is incomplete; it was only discovered in the late nineteenth century), who provides us with a vivid description of the purported holy places as well as a detailed description of the liturgy, the reception of converts into the Church, and the practices of the ascetic and monks living in Jerusalem around the years 381–4.

The Islamic conquest of Palestine in the eighth century made such pilgrimages increasingly difficult but the memory of the holy places was

Map 1   Pilgrimage routes of the Middle Ages

a leading cause of the medieval crusades beginning in the late eleventh century in order to wrestle them away from the Muslims. The desire for pilgrimage, however, was a hallmark of medieval life. People would go off on pilgrimage either as a penitential journey or as an act of devotion. Some undertook pilgrimage as a way to expiate their sins. Many places in Europe provided destinations for pilgrims who would go to pray at shrines of the Blessed Virgin Mary or the saints or to the tombs of the Apostles Peter and Paul in Rome. Geoffrey Chaucer described the Wife of Bath in his Prologue to the *Canterbury Tales* as an indefatigable pilgrim: "thrice she had been to Jerusalem / She had been and at Boulogne / In Galicia at St. James and at Cologne . . ." Canterbury itself was the destination of Chaucer's pilgrims, but Galicia in Spain was where the pilgrimage site of Campostela was located (still a popular pilgrimage destination), and Cologne's cathedral in Germany held, it was believed, the relics of the Three Magi who were the archetypes of pilgrims.

Of course, such pilgrimages could be the source of abuse, and some simple-minded people felt that just going to a pilgrimage shrine absolved one of sin. The Reformation had scant use for pilgrimages, but such sentiments were known even earlier. William Langland's fourteenth-century poem *The Vision of Piers Plowman* argued strenuously that it was better to seek out "Saint Truth" than to go to Rome or to make the traditional pilgrimage to Campostela. Despite such criticisms (they go back into the early Middle Ages), the idea of pilgrimage so gripped the medieval imagination that one scholar has called it "The Medieval Journey to God." Indeed, it could be said that it was a common metaphor to describe the Christian life itself as a pilgrimage. Saint Thomas Aquinas called Holy Communion the "bread of pilgrims" (*esca viatorum*), and Dante reaches for the metaphor of the pilgrim when he finishes his imaginary journey through Hell, Purgatory and Heaven: "And like a pilgrim who is refreshed in the temple of his vow as he looks around it and hopes some time to tell of it again" (*Paradiso, XXXI: 43–5*).

While Catholics to this day still go on actual pilgrimages to everywhere from Rome to the shrine of Guadalupe outside Mexico City, it is the image of the pilgrim that has remained deep in the Catholic imagination (and, to some extent, the Protestant: Think of John Bunyan's class *Pilgrim's Progress*) as a metaphor for the Christian life. That metaphor has renewed currency thanks to the Second Vatican Council which described the Church as the "Pilgrim People of God" in the seventh chapter of its dogmatic constitution on the Church (*Lumen gentium*). The power of that metaphor rests in the fact that it conceives of the Church not as a hierarchical pyramid with pope at the top and laity at the base but as a vast pilgrimage throughout history in which each individual bound to a community moves through time until the final consummation in Christ when the fullness of the Church, the Body of Christ, is realized. Like an actual pilgrimage, and unlike a mere walk, the pilgrim moves towards a final destination with its promise of grace: "The pilgrim church, in its sacraments and institutions, which belong to this present age, carries the mark of this world which will pass, and it takes its place among the creatures which groan and until now suffer the pains of childbirth and awaits the revelation of the children of God" (see Rom. 8:19–22).

The Catholic tradition has preserved a vast literature from its beginnings down to the present day in which the faith has been defended, explicated, and meditated upon. In the first centuries, a number of Christian writers composed works to defend the faith in the face of pagan hostility in a time of persecution. The so-called Apologists argued that the Christian faith, far from being an enemy of culture, was, in fact, a way of being that both held up virtue and had a plan of life that was revealed by God. In the same Early Church, a number of other writers argued with some vigor against false readings of the Christian message. The so-called "Fathers of the Church" were, for the most part, members of the clergy whose writings were destined either for the Christian faithful in the form of treatises or sermons or directed to those who held heterodox views of Christianity. Such writers produced works in Greek and Latin as well as in Syriac (a Semitic dialect) and Arabic. Some of these authors – Tertullian, Ambrose, Augustine in the West and Greek writers such as John Chrysostom, Gregory of Nyssa and others – left a permanent mark on the development of Catholic theology.

In the period after the fifth century, most scholars wrote from the setting of monasteries. With the decline of city life due to Barbarian invasions in the West, the monasteries became havens of civilization in which texts, both Christian and profane, were preserved and literacy maintained. Monastic authors were especially well known for their commentaries on sacred scripture (which demanded a knowledge of grammar and rhetoric), so that we possess a body of writing that runs from writers such as Pope Gregory the Great, who was a monk, through to the Venerable Bede in England and Anselm of Canterbury down to the golden age of the Cistercian monks of the twelfth century, who, as one author nicely put it, gave up everything for God except the art of writing well.

In addition to biblical commentaries, the same monastic centuries also produced a vast spiritual literature both for internal consumption and as aids for the instruction of those outside monasteries. It was in this area where monastic women as well as men were able to use their talents to produce books, compilations, anthologies, and collections of lives of the saints. It is well to remember that literacy itself was available only to a minority who had the leisure to learn to read and write as well as the circumstances of time and resources to copy books by hand in an age when paper was unavailable and the making of a book was a true form of labor.

It was towards the end of the twelfth century when independent scholars in the cities (and especially in Paris and Bologna) began to gather themselves into a community to have some control over instruction and some way to certify that students had done their course of study to satisfaction in order for them to become teachers. That community became known as the *universitas,* from which we derive the modern word "university." Whereas the monastic authors read the Bible as a contemplative exercise, the teachers in the university began to apply dialectical argument to solve apparent difficulties or contradictions in the biblical text. This form of teaching, traceable to the Parisian master Abelard (1079–1143), became typical in the universities, thus giving rise to what has become known as "scholasticism." The golden age of scholasticism was in the thirteenth century in Paris, represented by teachers such as Saints Bonaventure and Thomas Aquinas, with both dying in 1274. The university masters were charged with three duties: to read (i.e. to comment on scripture); to dispute (over seeming contradictions); and to preach. When a student finished his work and passed his oral examinations, he was known as a "master" who was qualified to teach from set texts; with further training, he could be called a "doctor" and was thus permitted to compose his own commentaries.

Universities flourished in the high Middle Ages. The one in Bologna had a great reputation in the study of law; Salerno was famous for its medical school; and Paris was best known for its theology. Universities developed all over Europe in this period. The Universities of Oxford and Cambridge were founded at this time and, by the fourteenth century, similar schools were found as far east as Budapest and as far west in the Iberian Peninsula (present-day Spain and Portugal). They were centers for the study of the liberal arts, law, medicine, philosophy, and theology.

The universities were not open to women; in fact, Oxford did not admit women to degrees until the twentieth century. We do possess a literature from women from the Middle Ages, but almost all of it was produced by religious women who lived the cloistered life. The most famous of these women scholars was Hildegard of Bingen (1098–1179), who composed music, wrote scientific and medical treatises, wrote plays for her music, and compiled a vast composite work called *Scivias* including illustrations she made for the work. She corresponded with popes and prelates and made at least two preaching tours in her lifetime. Hildegard is representative of a number of women who did serious writing but almost exclusively within the confines of the cloister or aristocratic courts.

One of the characteristic developments in the Renaissance period was a renewed interest in classical studies, and, especially in the north, scholars thought that this study could serve as an instrument of reform in the Church. Creating critical editions of the Bible and the Early Fathers (especially Saint Augustine), learning Hebrew, and finding their way back to sources before the scholastics marked the work of such figures as Erasmus of Rotterdam and his friend Saint Thomas More. The impact of the humanist movement was felt strongly in the universities. When John Fisher, later a martyr under Henry VIII, became Chancellor of Cambridge University in 1504, he not only greatly enlarged the library but also established funds for the teaching of Greek and Hebrew and brought Erasmus over from the Continent to teach. This interest in philology led to the opening of any number of "trilingual" (i.e. Latin, Greek, and Hebrew) schools in Europe.

The turn to the intense study of scripture and the Fathers, as well as the nurturing of the study of biblical languages, coincided with the rise of printing after the invention of movable print in the mid-fifteenth century and the easy availability of paper instead of reliance on parchment or vellum made from animal skins. The easy accessibility of books and the technical study of scripture was surely a factor in the success of the Protestant Reformation. Martin Luther's translation of the New Testament into German was done from a Greek critical edition done by Erasmus, and John Calvin began his career as a humanist scholar in Paris. One force in reaction to the Reformation was the establishment of the Company of Jesus (the Jesuits) in the latter half of the sixteenth century by Ignatius of Loyola (d.1556), which specialized in an educational program that fostered an organized curriculum of study which would lead a student from the classics through philosophy to a culmination in theology. Jesuit education, both at the secondary and at the university level, continues down to this day, and, until recently, the education provided in seminaries was modeled on the Jesuit trajectory of the study of scholastic philosophy and theology after a grounding in the classics.

The Catholic tradition continues to foster scholarship in harmony with the Church's belief that reason and faith are not antithetical but complementary. Rooted in the conviction that the human desire to know is ultimately a desire for God, Catholicism continues to encourage the search for wisdom. It sees the gift of faith as a completion of the human endeavor of knowledge. Writing on the relationship of reason and faith, the late Pope John Paul II, himself a former academic, wrote in his encyclical *Fides et ratio*: "the Catholic intellectual life is inescapably not something finished and settled or even potentially so but a *quest* for 'faith seeking understanding' – a quest which verges towards Wisdom, fully possessed in revelation, but never fully 'understood' though understood ever more deeply [. . .]."

Of course, history also demonstrates that with the rise of modern science there can be instances where the relationship of faith and reason can come into apparent conflict. The contemporary Church tries to use the Galileo affair as a cautionary example to avoid creating such conflicts. The condemnation of Galileo's heliocentric picture of the planetary system came into conflict with the old inherited belief that the Earth was the center of the universe in which, as time would show, the Church was wrong and Galileo was right has made the modern Church more modest as it has had to confront older apparent discrepancies between faith and reason (think of debates over evolution) and more contemporary ones on a range of issues especially in the life sciences regarding everything from cloning to embryonic cell research.

MISSIONARIES

Catholicism has, from its beginnings, been a missionary religion in the sense that it has the deep conviction that its message is intended for everyone. It has tried to be obedient to the great command given by Jesus that closes the Gospel of Saint Matthew: "Go, therefore, and make disciples of all nations, baptizing them in the name of the Father and of the Son and of the Holy Spirit, teaching them to observe all that I have commanded you. And behold, I am with you always, until the end of the age" (Matt. 28:19–20).

In the early centuries of the Church's history, the Church seemingly grew somewhat analogously to cell division. Small communities of believers would gather in house churches, and, when those communities became a certain size, they would split, and new communities would form. People learned about the Christian way of life from traveling evangelists who followed the trade routes within the Roman Empire. These teachers had the advantage of a relatively peaceful period in imperial Rome, a common language used in the Empire (*koine* or common Greek), fairly good roads and a Mediterranean sea which had been pacified by the Roman military. Their message of mutual help and support, forgiveness of sin and the hope for eternal life and their willingness to accept that everyone (Saint Paul said, famously, that in Jesus Christ there was neither Jew nor gentile, male or female, slave or free person) had a certain innate attractiveness despite the fact that they were at odds with the reigning official religion of the time.

In the period after the persecutions, Christianity spread largely through the planting of monasteries in areas which had been at the borders of the old Roman Empire. That is the way in which Catholicism spread in the British Isles, into Ireland (thanks to Saint Patrick who was not, however, a monk) into what is present-day Germany and Eastern Europe. In the high Middle Ages, the new religious orders of mendicant friars began to go further abroad, with Franciscans seeking to evangelize the Middle East (this effort produced more martyrs than converts) with some friars even getting as far as China. With the discovery of the New World in the fifteenth century, Catholicism spread in tandem with the colonization of the Americas so that by the time of the early modern period, French-speaking Canada was Catholic as was most of Central and Latin America. In the modern period, the missionaries were part of the efforts of colonial expansion into the continent of Africa, and the waves of immigration into the present-day USA accounted for the growth of Catholicism there, especially from the second half of the nineteenth century on. Every major city in the USA still has parishes which betray their ethnic roots.

It is one of the curious facts of demographic change that in the contemporary period former "mission lands" now supply priests and religious to the Western world as vocations decline so that many American parishes which were founded by Italian, Polish, or Irish immigrants are now staffed by religious from Nigeria, India, and other parts of the once mission territories.

Missionaries have always had to confront the issue of making the Gospel intelligible to people whose culture and traditions are apparently alien to its message. The delicate task of the missionary is to remain faithful to the essential message of the Gospel while presenting it in a fashion compatible to the potential hearer. This adaptation of the Gospel to different cultures, known as inculturation, can be seen in the example of the Jesuit missionary of the sixteenth century, Matteo Ricci (d.1601). Ricci managed to penetrate China, normally off limits to Westerners, as far as the forbidden city of Beijing. He mastered classical Chinese; he took the rigorous examinations obligatory for those of the Mandarin class. Ricci was convinced that the Catholic liturgy could be modified to add Confucian elements. He asked permission for the right to celebrate the liturgy in Chinese. After some years, such permission was denied, and, eventually, the so-called "Chinese Rites" were forbidden. In some ways, Ricci was ahead of his time in terms of inculturating the Gospel, and one can only speculate how the Catholic faith in China might have turned out differently had he succeeded. The lessons of the Chinese Rites controversy still enter into discussion today for missioners who attempt to preach in areas where the culture is different from the world in which Christianity had been born. Of course, the growth of clergy and religious in former "mission lands" has had the advantage of eroding the impression that Christianity is a Western religion and strengthening the picture of Catholicism as a world Church.

The need to preach the Gospel in areas of the world which had ancient cultures with no links to the West requires not only a familiarity with those cultures but ways of speaking intelligibly to those cultures. Just to cite an extreme example: What were missionaries to do who first began to work with the Arctic peoples? How would the New Testament make sense to a people who had never seen grass, who had no knowledge of foods mentioned in the Bible such as bread, who could not make sense of a person who called himself a "Good Shepherd," who could not supply bread and wine for the mass, etc.? How does one "translate" the Gospel in such a setting? Missionary activities, of necessity, demand a shift in worldviews, which means that the missionary activity demands some sense of everything from cultural anthropology to linguistics.

Missionary efforts are not the sole domain of the ordained clergy or the vowed religious. Nor is it a matter of going out to alien peoples or places since every baptized Christian has an obligation to be a missionary – one who is sent to live and speak the Good News. At a more specialized level, it is increasingly a lay phenomenon. Many traditional religious orders and some independent organizations educate and support missionaries for both domestic and foreign missionary work. At the university where the present author teaches, about 10 percent of every graduating class of undergraduates volunteers for a minimum of a year to serve the needs of the Church in some part of the country, with a small portion going abroad for a two-year commitment.

Christianity is, by its very nature, missionary. It is so much a part of the self-identification of Christianity in general and Catholicism in particular that later in this book we will study its missionary mandate and its various strategies in greater detail.

MYSTICS

The Greek adjective *mustikos* means "hidden" or "concealed." The word was often used in the Early Church to describe the scriptures which had a plain meaning but, through the eyes of faith, also had a hidden, more spiritual meaning. The word was also used to describe the Holy Eucharist because what was seen to the observant eye was bread and wine, but "hidden" under those earthly realities was the true presence of Christ. It was the Syrian monk writer known as Dionysius, who was working around the year 500, who coined the term "mystical [i.e. hidden] theology." Dionysius argued that there were many things we could say about God; scripture calls God "father," "rock," "refuge," "shepherd," etc. However, these are all terms that are used by analogy and do not really come close to describing the mysterious reality of God, who, in essence, is beyond naming because of the divine majesty and the divine otherness. Some of this unknown monk's ideas can be traced back even earlier into the writings of the Greek Christian writer, Gregory of Nyssa.

Even before the time of Dionysius, Christian writers talked about the deep experience of sensing the presence of God in prayer. There is a famous passage in Augustine's *Confessions* where Augustine and his mother are described as having an ecstatic experience of the mysterious reality of God beyond words and sounds as the two of them overlooked the Roman port of Ostia. The Greek writer Gregory of Nyssa, in his *Life of Moses,* saw the experience of God that Moses had as first being in light (at the incident of the burning bush described in Exodus 3), but also the later experience of Moses ascending Sinai and entering into the "dark cloud" where Moses met God in the obscure blackness of the cloud.

It should be noted that this spiritual tradition, recoverable mainly from texts, seeks to articulate not ideas about God but, rather, the experience of God, however elusive or momentary such experiences may be. Indeed, it may be more appropriate, as one contemporary scholar Bernard McGinn has insisted, to speak of the mystical tradition as describing a "consciousness of the presence of God." Such descriptions appear in a wide variety of vocabularies. For some writers, this presence is paradoxically both presence and absence while in others it appears under the guise of lover and beloved. The experience is always described as being deeper than merely objective knowing. The great late-fourteenth-century mystic, Julian of Norwich, tells us in her book *Showings* that she often had deep insights or interior illuminations about the presence of God or the love of Christ which went far beyond simply knowing "about something."

The Catholic tradition testifies to a continuing witness to such deep experience from the literature of early monasticism through the great Cistercian and Carthusian masters of the medieval period continuing in the early modern age down to the present. It was, however, only in the seventeenth century that we begin to see the use of the discrete words "mystic" and "mysticism." Before the introduction of those words, it was most common to speak of "mystical theology," which meant, simply, the experience of God which was "dark" or beyond words. The term was used in that way by the great sixteenth-century Spanish mystic, Saint John of the Cross, who borrows from Dionysius. Commenting on his own poetry, John says that "mystical wisdom comes through love [. . .] need not be understood distinctly in order to cause love and affection in the soul, for it is given according to the mode of faith through which we love God without understanding Him" (Prologue to *The Spiritual Canticle,* No. 2).

Perhaps the word "mystic" has become so compromised in our contemporary vocabulary that it is difficult for moderns to hear it correctly. As understood in the Catholic tradition, however, it means simply that, aided by the grace of God, it is possible to have a deeply profound experience of the presence of God in our lives, and the tradition witnesses to many who have not only had such experiences but have also given us a vast literature about them.

The Catholic tradition further argues that this deep experience of God is available to every person who attempts to live out the Gospel life. The twentieth-century spiritual writer Thomas Merton (1915–68) argued that at the center of every human person was a profound point where God dwells within us, sustaining us with his providential love. If we are truly human, we can have some recognition of that deep reality if we are open to God's grace.

One of the pressing issues facing the contemporary Church, particularly in the West, is to recover the ancient tradition of mystical or contemplative living because, with the collapse of so many traditional forms of religious life in the West, there has been a concomitant rise in which is broadly called "New Age" spirituality. New Age, in many of its manifestations, is simply a rebirth of an old antagonist to Christianity: Gnosticism. Gnosticism, which traditionally has held out a promise to a "secret" knowledge (*gnosis* means knowledge in Greek; hence the term "Gnosticism") known only to the few, in its New Age manifestation offers strategies or mechanisms by which people can have (not always well-defined) "experiences" which can be broadly called spiritual. Such experiences are frequently oriented to the therapeutic promising better self-esteem or a sense of wholeness and satisfaction. The Christian response to these therapeutic promises emphasizes both the ordinary practice of religion through the sacramental life of the Church but also the assurance that we can experience the presence of God within us as graced persons and a wholeness of life that can take into account and turn into grace our pain and weaknesses. It also promises that to the degree that we genuinely love God and experience God in our lives we will also grow in love of others and pour out that love in service.

Those who have experienced these deep encounters with God have left to the Church a vast literature that still nourishes Christians today. Some of these books have taken on the status of classics, which is to say that their meaning overflows from the time when they were written in such a way as to illumine our own spiritual development. It would not even be possible to give a beginning list of such books, but it is interesting to note that well into our own age, the most read book after the Bible was the fourteenth-century Thomas à Kempis's *The Imitation of Christ.* Other works – Augustine's *Confessions* comes immediately to mind – are recognized as world classics by believers and non-believers alike.

SAINTS

Saint Paul often addresses his letters to the "saints." In Paul's understanding everyone who is a follower of Christ is a saint or, to translate more precisely from the Greek *hagios,* "a holy one." Paul understood that God is holiness and the source of all holiness while everyone else (and everything else – the Earth is holy) is holy to the degree that people participate in the holiness of God. It is for that reason that the Second Vatican Council, in its dogmatic constitution on the Church (*Lumen gentium*), devoted a whole chapter (No. 5) on this issue under the title "The Universal Call to Holiness." That chapter puts the matter simply: "all in the Church, whether they belong to the hierarchy or are cared for by it, are called to holiness, according to the apostle's saying 'For this is the will of God, your sanctification' [1 Thess. 4:3; cf. Eph. 1:4]." Further, in that same chapter, the Conciliar Fathers go on to say: "It is therefore quite clear that all Christians, in whatever state or walk in life are called to the fullness of Christian life and to the perfection of charity and this holiness is conducive to a more human way of living even in society here on earth."

The kind of holiness described above – fully living the Christian life which is the perfection of love – means, fundamentally, that everyone is called to be a saint. The consequence of that fact means that it is too restrictive to think of saints exclusively in terms of those who already live with God beyond this earthly life. In other words, we need to resist the idea that saints are only those who are canonized and publicly venerated as saints in Heaven.

Nonetheless, it is a constant tradition within Roman Catholicism to venerate the saints, to name our children after them, to dedicate churches under their patronage, to invoke their names as we pray, to honor their memory in the liturgy, and to seek out their example for our own way of life. The one point which we do need to underscore is this: Holiness is not only open to everyone but is each Christian's destiny. Thus, we should not restrict the word "saint" or "saintliness" to a select coterie of persons within the Church.

How did the veneration of certain persons, called restrictively "saints," develop in Catholicism? The answer to that question brings us back to the very beginning of this present chapter. During the period of the Roman persecution of the Church, the Christian communities kept in their memory the example of those who professed their faith publicly to the point of death. They saw in their example of suffering and death a kind of imitation of the Lord himself who was persecuted and condemned to death. Already in the second century, their bodies were buried with care, their stories were told in texts that were written for the community, the date of their death entered into a calendar of memory, and, before long, chapels or shrines marked the spot of their burial. Christians, especially after the end of the persecutions, would visit their burial places and pay honor to them with the same ceremony that citizens show to the tomb of the nation's Unknown Solider, but with this difference: Christians believed that the memorials of the saints exhibited power to heal or to answer prayers. Thus, the rise of devotion to the saints had a number of desired ends: The saints could intercede for us from their place with God; their lives were a source of inspiration and emulation; they were part of the universal body of all believers – they became what was later called the "communion of saints" – a term used in the creeds to this day.

Saints, in a basic sense, were paradigmatic persons. After the era of persecution ended, there was a tendency to offer the same reverence and to express the same confidence in figures who, even though they were not technically martyrs, did serve as a model for a certain way of Christian living. Thus, again to look back on this chapter, certain exemplary ascetics, monks, pilgrims, scholars, and so on, who performed their state in life in such a fashion later became part of the common Catholic memory to be held up as models of how to live. When one looks back over the vast catalog of saints who are venerated either in the whole Church or in a particular locale, it is clear that as human beings they run the gamut from the poorest peasant to royalty, from male to female, from brilliant intellectuals and scholars to illiterate workers. Somehow, the Church has remembered them to show how diverse and complex the ways of Christian living are.

The late Jesuit theologian Karl Rahner once wrote that the saint is a person who teaches us that it is possible to be a Christian in this or that particular way. How such a life is to be lived out differs greatly. The late Mother of Teresa of Calcutta was universally recognized as a saint in her own lifetime and will, in due time, be so recognized by the institutional Church. When one looks at her life, however, it is clear that how she lived and what she did for the poor of India (and, by extension, the world) had a certain traditional timelessness about it. Had she been, by some magic, transported to the Middle Ages, she still would have been serving the dying poor and living a life of personal asceticism and prayer. What Mother Teresa demonstrated in her life was that the perennial demand of the Gospel has a timeless presence to it which can be lived out at any age.

By contrast, some saints in the tradition demonstrated, and often either with the resistance of the official Church or its indifference, that it was possible to lead a new kind of life in service to the Gospel. Thus, the seventeenth-century French priest Vincent de Paul and his close collaborator Louise de Marillac had the innovating (and daring) idea that women could be vowed religious without living a totally cloistered life. Vincent thought that the Daughters of Charity could make the streets of Paris their cloister and the local parish their chapel while they worked with the poor in everything from hospitals to direct feeding. It was largely through the initiative of this pair that in the modern period we saw the flourishing of hundreds of congregations of active religious women doing a wide variety of pastoral work. What they began would be a new age for women in the Church, which, when they began, seemed radical.

A scan of the list of canonized saints venerated in the Church does reveal a preponderance of persons in religious life or the priesthood with men outnumbering women. With the reiteration of Vatican II's reminder that all are called to saintliness (and not just religious "professionals") the Catholic Church must search for new models of sanctity. Of course, it is a commonplace to say that at every age and in every place there are "hidden saints" whose reputation never goes beyond their immediate surroundings. When the creed describes the Church as "holy," what it means is that there is always within the Church the means of holiness – the liturgy, the sacraments, the schools of prayer – and, equally, that there are those who live out fully the life of Jesus. It is that conviction that allows the Church to assert, as it did at the Second Vatican Council:

> Accordingly, all Christians, in the conditions, duties, and circumstances of their lives and through all these, will grow constantly in holiness if they receive all things with faith from the hand of the heavenly Father and cooperate with the divine will, making manifest in their ordinary work the love with which God has loved the world. (*Lumen gentium*, V.41)

By holding up the image of the "saint" – freed from the stereotypes of the popular imagination – the Catholic Church invites us to look around our own contemporary world to seek out models who live exemplary self-giving lives who best show forth the deepest meaning of the gospel life. Such persons are an apologetic indication of the power of the Christian faith since, as we have observed throughout this work, the Gospel is not a book to be read but an action plan to be performed.

The various "ideal types" that we have outlined above help us to understand one way of thinking about the very nature of catholicity. Catholicity, in this sense, does not mean the aggregate whole of Catholicism but, rather, the inner dynamism of the Catholic tradition that allows a person to live the gospel life in a rich variety of ways. Certain times call forth certain models, and those models reappear at other times while other models remain a constant in the tradition. If there is a further lesson to be drawn by thinking of models of being Catholic it is that exigencies may draw forth new models. It is quite possible, as Catholicism spreads vigorously in the non-Western world, that new ways of being Catholic will emerge as a natural adaptive response to those new conditions. If such responses do not flourish, then the Church always runs the risk of losing the dynamic character of its tradition and thus reducing itself to a museum, showing off old ways of being that lack pertinence in the world today.

Box 3   The cult of the saints

Veneration of the saints began with the respect that the Church paid to those who died in public witness for the faith during the era of the Roman persecutions. Their sufferings were recorded in writings which were circulated to the various Church communities. As early as the second century, the *Martyrdom of Polycarp* informs us, relics of their persons were gathered up and their bodies were buried with respect. It was the custom on the anniversary of

Box 3 (cont.)

their deaths to pray at their tombs, and, with the end of the persecutions, it was common for people to visit their shrines as pilgrims. That custom continues to this day.

For nearly 1,000 years, the veneration of the saints was legitimized by the application of two criteria: did the local bishop or another church authority permit veneration to take place at the various shrines, and was there some evidence that through the miraculous intervention of the saint that healings or other miraculous events took place? It was only in the tenth century that a pope actually canonized a person by his personal authority, and it was only in the thirteenth century that the process of canonization was restricted to the papal office.

In the seventeenth century, Pope Gregory XIV, a noted canonist and theologian, issued a set of instructions for the process of canonization which lasted, with some modifications, until the late twentieth century when the late Pope John Paul II modified the procedures. Canonization technically means that a person may be added to the list (canon) of those who may be venerated publicly in the Church. In the present day, the procedure for canonization begins at the local level when persons, under the authority of a bishop, begin to gather evidence of the holiness of the person's life and an attestation of the person's faith and fidelity to the Church's teaching and practice. If such evidence seems plausible, the dossier is forwarded to Rome where the person is known as "a servant of God."

The investigation in Rome continues (there is a separate congregation "For the Causes of the Saints" which handles these matters), and, in due time, the person is then beatified, which means that in a given place one may pray for the intercession of the beatified person. If an authenticated miracle is attested to, the person can then proceed to canonization when the pope so stipulates. Historically, the process of canonization was a lengthy one (some "causes" are centuries old), but, during the papacy of John Paul II (1978–2005), it was speeded up because of the pope's conviction that such canonizations are evidences of holiness in the Church and, as such, are important gestures for evangelization. Some, even in the Vatican, thought that the process was too speedy and should be more considered. Under Pope Benedict XVI, John Paul II's successor, there are subtle signs that he may, in fact, slow down the procedure. For instance, Pope Benedict does not preside over beatifications as his predecessor did but only canonizations.

Many argue that the spectrum of canonizations is too narrow. Such critics argue that too many priests, religious, and members of the hierarchy are canonized and too few ordinary men and women. The result of that imbalance, unwittingly, is to indicate that the religious are "professionals" at piety who do not model holiness for the vast majority of those in the Church. The need to hold forth new kinds of models is the only way to make the critique of the present system irrelevant.

FURTHER READING

Cunningham, Lawrence, *The Catholic Heritage* (New York, N.Y.: Crossroad, 1983). A study of some "Catholic" types.

Cunningham, Lawrence, *A Brief History of Saints* (Oxford: Blackwell, 2005). A summary of the history of the cult of the saints and of canonizations.

Ellsberg, Robert, *All Saints* (New York, N.Y.: Crossroad, 1997). A story of outstanding Christians not only those canonized.

Haight, Roger, *Christian Community in History*, 3 vols. (London and New York, N.Y.: Continuum, 2005–8). The Church "from below."

Harmless, William, *Desert Christians: An Introduction to the Early Literature of Early Monasticism* (London and New York: Oxford University Press, 2004). A user-friendly but authoritative introduction to the literature.

Harmless, William, *Mystics* (London and New York, N.Y.: Oxford, 2007). An accessible book on the topic of mysticism and some representative examples.

Sumption, Jonathan, *The Age of Pilgrimage* (New York, N.Y.: Hidden Spring/ Paulist, 2003). Updated version of a standard work on medieval pilgrimage.

CHAPTER 4

Catholicism in place and time

INTRODUCTION

The Catholic Church as an empirical reality is, at one level, a place that can be identified: For example, "That is a Catholic church on the other side of the street." Before we enter into a further discussion of what Catholics believe and how they worship, it might be instructive to think about the "where" of Catholicism not in a universal sense but as the Church makes itself manifest locally. In a sense, we will attempt to answer the empirical questions: Where is the Catholic Church? Can you point me to that church? The thesis of this chapter is that if someone actually looks at the place where Catholic believers gather, both historically and actually, one can learn a good deal about Catholic practice and belief. That thesis will first lead us, for a short space, into the area of architecture. The history of Christian church architecture is, obviously, a highly complex one, but we at least sketch out a broad outline that will be of service to discussions that will take place in later chapters. We shall discuss a few historical examples of the evolution of floor plans of Catholic churches to see how the changing shape of churches reflect a widening of Catholic belief and practice.

In this chapter, then, we will focus not on the assembly of Catholic Christians (which is the *ekklesia*) but where they gather, which is in what generally we call the church. The English word "church" has its roots in the Greek *kuriake*, "the place of the Lord." As a further etymological note, one is reminded that in the Orthodox world the church is often called the *katholikon*, "where all gather."

This approach to matters architectural and spatial may seem a bit odd at first glance, but it derives from a long-held conviction, namely, that were an interested person attempting to understand Catholicism, a good place to visit might be the nearest Catholic church building to have a "look around."[1] There is a way in which, if a person looks at a typical church with a tutored eye, it would raise a lot of interesting questions behind which one would find a lot of history: What is the focal point of the interior? Why is there a chapel or a space with an image of the Virgin Mary? Why is there a burning lamp before a highly decorated box container called the tabernacle? What is the significance of those stained-glass windows? Why are there padded kneelers before each chair or pew? What is the significance of the fourteen plaques illustrating the Passion, known as the Stations of the Cross, of Jesus which one finds fixed to the side aisles? Why is there a large font at the front of the church? If one is in the church at the time of Sunday worship, one might simply ask, What is going on? Does the placement of congregation and priest tell us something?

To address each of those questions (and others that could be thought of) would take one far back into the Catholic Tradition (note the capital T) as well as its added traditions (small t).

The visit to the church, in addition, would be rather like an archeological investigation in that certain parts of the church are ancient and others are of more recent vintage. Some elements are accidental and could easily be removed, while others reflect unassailable elements of the Catholic Tradition. Again, certain aspects of the church are open to theological debate within the larger Christian family and, for example, their absence, say, in a Reformed church says something about deep theological matters.

THE EVOLUTION OF THE CATHOLIC CHURCH BUILDING

As we noted in the first chapter, the early Christians met in private homes: "Aquila and Prisca, together with the church in their house, greet you" (1 Cor. 16:19). We are not sure what those early homes exactly looked like but archeologists have found remains of them under church buildings which were later built over them. Visitors to Rome today can see such architectural remnants under churches such as Saint Clement (San Clemente) and Saints John and Paul (Ss. Giovanni e Paolo). Those house churches are instructive because they put us in touch with some of the most ancient evidences of early Christian belief.

An extraordinary find in the town of Dura Europos on the Euphrates river below Baghdad in Iraq give us a much better sense of what a house church might have looked like. The town had been destroyed and

---

[1] Of course, the experiment would even be more interesting if one compared a typical parish church to, for example, the cathedral of Chartres or Saint Peter's in the Vatican.

subsequently covered by sandstorms before the Constantinian Peace of the early fourth century. When excavated, mainly in the twentieth century, scholars found pagan sites, the earliest known synagogue with frescos depicting biblical scenes, and a Christian house church which dates, probably, from the first half of the third century since the town itself had been destroyed *c*.256 during Persian incursions from the East. The town remains were rather well preserved because sands from the desert had pretty much enveloped the area. What this community did to renovate a private dwelling was to remove a wall partition to change two small rooms into a single larger one with a raised platform at one end (possibly for an altar). A third room seems to have been used for baptisms. This third-century building modified a private dwelling to make a space where the assembly could gather for worship. The building tells us, at a minimum, that space was needed to gather (the large room) and a place for the separate rite of baptism was evidently also desired. That latter fact in itself is interesting because it tells us that in some instances Christians were baptized not in "living waters" of a stream or a lake but in a building designated for the purpose.

What is even more surprising for a house church of such an early period is that the building has a number of interior frescos depicting, among other things, the Good Shepherd, the healing of the paralytic, the woman at the well, and women bringing spices to anoint the dead Jesus, as well as more symbolic decorations of wheat, grapes, and pomegranates. Many of these biblical scenes are also commonly found a bit later in paintings in the Roman catacombs and as sculptural decorations on early Christian sarcophagi.

When Christianity was granted toleration in the early fourth century by Emperor Constantine, it became possible to build churches without fear of suppression since the era of official persecution had ended. The earliest public churches, often funded from the public coffers by the imperial rulers, patterned themselves after the large public Roman building known as the *basilica*. Typically, a basilica had an outer courtyard known as an atrium with a narrow porch (*narthex*) leading into the building itself. A glance at a typical floor plan tells us rather quickly how the building was to function (see Figure 4.1).

There would be a large central space (the nave) with two side aisles separated from the nave by supporting pillars. In the semicircular apse there would be a place for the assembled clergy with a seat for the presiding bishop in the center. Between the space in the apse for the clergy there would be an altar for the celebration of the public liturgy. Typically, the

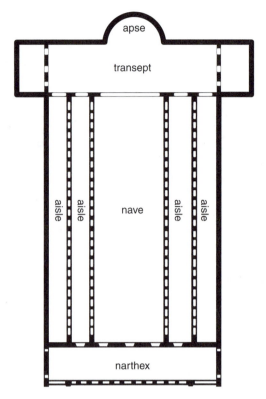

Figure 4.1   Basilica floor plan of Old Saint Peter's, Rome

people would stand during the entire worship service, and the bishop, when he preached, would sit at his place. The bishop's chair was called a *cathedra* from which word we get the modern term "cathedral."

What that kind of basilica space tells us is that the building was designed for the gathering of a large assembly with the focal point on the chair (*cathedra*) of the presiding bishop who would preach and then celebrate the eucharistic liturgy. A basilica was designed for public worship with relatively little to indicate a space for private devotion.

By the early Middle Ages, roughly around the year 1,000, a new style of architecture began to emerge in Europe known as the *Romanesque* (because the principles of design were derived from Roman models of building; see Figure 4.2). The Romanesque church was characterized by heavy thick walls which supported an arched roof, but, most importantly, there began to appear smaller chapels radiating from the apse, each with its own altar.

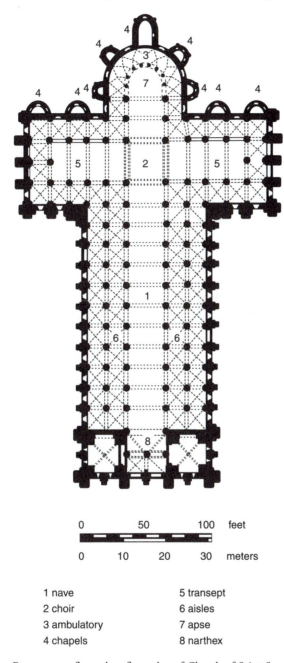

0   50   100   feet

0   10   20   30   meters

1 nave	5 transept
2 choir	6 aisles
3 ambulatory	7 apse
4 chapels	8 narthex

Figure 4.2   Romanesque floor plan: floor plan of Church of Saint Sernin, Toulouse

This new design accommodated the rising practice of individual priests saying mass (the eucharistic liturgy) individually. Thus, a new development in architecture signaled a newer practice where the shift to private masses (and their multiplication) began to be the norm. From the basilica to the Romanesque there was a shift from one central mass to accommodations for many masses. As we shall see, this new practice also meant that a different understanding of worship was emerging in the Western Church. In addition, an *ambulatory,* which permitted visitors to walk all the way around the main altar area reflected the increasing interest in the veneration of relics buried under the altar or in the space before the altar.

The high Middle Ages saw a new and soon popular style of architecture: the *Gothic.* Driven by a desire to heighten the walls of churches, medieval architects learned that the roof would not collapse under its own weight if it were buttressed from the outside, where the buttresses would give added support to the walls. This innovation allowed the walls to increase in verticality and, more to the point, allowed the wall to be pierced with windows of stained glass. In many of the major Gothic cathedrals built in the twelfth through to the fourteenth century, the walls became skeletal frames for glass windows. Anyone who has ever walked into such a cathedral as Chartres in France or Winchester in England instinctively looks up because every line pushes up vertically from the thin pillars to the Gothic points of the frames of the windows.

There was a theory behind such buildings. When the worshiper entered such a church, the architecture itself raised eyes to the world beyond while the light pouring in from the windows illumined the stories of the Bible depicted in the stained glass. The sensual experience of the Gothic church was designed to make visitors think that they were in the forecourt of Heaven bathed in light, eyes moved up towards God, listening to the music of the choir, and breathing the sweet scent of incense from the liturgy. The Gothic experience was meant to be a transcendent otherworldly one.[2]

By contrast, the Renaissance church was centrally planned, most frequently utilizing a Greek floor plan with the nave and the transepts crossing under a centralized dome. That is what Michelangelo had in mind when he designed Saint Peter's in Rome. His great dome was to act

---

[2] The term "Gothic" was a pejorative one developed in the modern period to designate the sense that such medieval buildings were barbaric.

as a canopy over the papal altar, which, in turn, covered the purported grave of the Apostle Peter. The long nave of Saint Peter's was not part of Michelangelo's plan but was added later. The Renaissance central plan became a baroque church, which signaled the splendors of the papacy as a kind of rebuke to the Protestant denial of the papal claims. If the intention of the Gothic was to lift the eye to the heavens, the realm of light, the focus in Saint Peter's was to have the eye look down the nave to the papal altar and beyond to the altar of the Chair (see Figure 4.3).

Subsequent church architecture, well into the modern period, drew eclectically on the inherited architectural ideas from the past so that one can see traces of basilican, Romanesque, Gothic or Renaissance architectural styles in churches built in the nineteenth and twentieth centuries in addition to whatever advances were made in more modern or contemporary architectural styles.

THE THEOLOGICAL MEANING OF ARCHITECTURE

When one looks closely at the very space of a Catholic church, either historically or actually, one learns a great deal about what the builders intended to teach by the very way in which space was organized. The early Roman basilicas were organized to emphasize the role of the presiding bishop who not only celebrated the liturgy but also preached with authority. The Romanesque church, with its radiating chapels, made allowance for the multiplication of private masses, including masses for the deceased, as the role of priests as celebrants of mass began to take on greater significance. Hence, these churches marked a development not only in the understanding of the eucharist but also in the fate of people after death – the two states of Heaven or Hell were interspersed with the idea of a purgatorial period of purification whose duration could be modified by the prayers of the Church and the celebration of masses for that end.

The great Gothic cathedrals were so designed to confront the senses of the worshiper who entered the sacred space of the Church while leaving the profane (the word "profane" etymologically means "outside the temple"). Often these churches would have inscribed over the entrance the phrase "This is the gate of Heaven," signifying that the cascade of the colored windows, the music of the liturgy, the odor of incense and candle, and the solemn rite of the services were a kind of foretaste of Paradise. The sheer emphasis on the vertical naturally caused the congregants to raise their eyes.

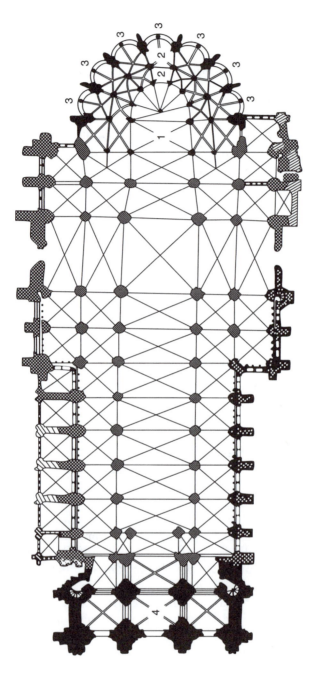

1. choir; 2. ambulatory; 3. radiating chapels; 4. narthex

Figure 4.3   Gothic floor plan: plan of Abbey Church of San Denis

Abbot Suger of Saint Denis (1081–1151) is considered the founder of the Gothic style. Over the west door of his royal Abbey of Saint Denis near Paris, he had the following words inscribed to emphasize the theological significance he gave to the light streaming through the stained-glass windows and the doors within which the faithful would enter: "Bright is the noble work, but, being nobly bright the work / should brighten the minds, so that they may travel through the true lights / to the True Light where Christ is the true door / In what manner it be inherent in this world the golden door defines: The dull mind rises to truth through that which is material / And, in seeing the light, is raised from its former subservience [. . .]"

By contrast, the centrally planned churches of the Renaissance period tended to focus the eye on the altar and its surrounding sanctuary as it sat under the cupola at the center of the axis of the nave and transept. When one considers, to cite a conspicuous example, the interior of Saint Peter's basilica in Rome, it is clear that the intention of the architects was to create a space almost theatrical in its environment: The long nave leading toward the baroque canopy designed by Bernini was perfectly oriented to highlight the splendor of papal liturgies with their vast assemblage of prelates and the implied authority of the pope (as a counterstatement to the Reformation claims against the papacy) who celebrated over the tomb of Saint Peter, which is located under the papal altar. Behind that altar is the baroque shrine of the "chair of Peter," held up by Fathers of the both the Western and Eastern Church. The window with the figure of the dove representing the Holy Spirit was so positioned that light would stream through the window and cast a line right down the expanse of the main aisle.

Churches designed after the Second Vatican Council were most frequently designed to create the sense of the Church as a community at worship. The floor plan is almost always semicircular so as to embrace the altar and the pulpit and to highlight the sense that both the Word and the eucharist make up the sum of the eucharistic celebration at the liturgy. It is quite instructive to contrast churches built before the Second Vatican Council with their renovation afterward to see how the focus shifted away from the tabernacle on the altar as a primary focus to the newer arrangement where the altar and pulpit become central and the tabernacle is no longer centrally located. In our discussion of the sacraments and the liturgy we will understand more fully how that change comes about.

THE CHURCH BUILDING AS PEDAGOGY

The architectural layout of a church in a given era was not the only symbolic marker of what a church wanted to "say" to the faithful. After the peace of Constantine (early fourth century), church building began in earnest. Constantine himself was responsible for building two monumental places of worship which exist to this day: old Saint Peter's, which marked the burial place of the Apostle Peter on the Vatican Hill, and the Church of the Holy Sepulchre in Jerusalem, which honored the burial place of Jesus and the spot where he was raised from the dead. Hence, from the earliest days, churches marked off sacred spots which served as magnets for believers who wished to pray at places identified with the life of Jesus or at buildings that covered the graves of saints. In that sense, there was a connection between church architecture and the ever-so-increasingly popular devotional practice of pilgrimage.

Church buildings were also meant to instruct. Again in the period immediately after Constantine, Christians made use of the already established art form, inherited from pagan Rome, of decorating churches with mosaics that depicted the mysteries of the faith, mainly biblical stories, in "living color." Whole cycles of mosaics such as those in the basilica of Saint Mary Major in Rome, created in the fifth century, gave pictorial evidence of the stories from the Bible read out at the weekly liturgy. By the early Middle Ages, it became popular to tell similar stories by the use of stained glass in the windows. As walls became thinner, under Gothic influence, windows became more elaborate. That fact that they were viewed from inside the church, illumined by the light coming from the sun, had the added symbolic advantage of indicating the warming love of God lighting up the stories of the inspired words of scripture for the worshipers. Indeed, it was not uncommon to call such window picture cycles the "bible of the poor" since books, before the age of paper and moveable type, were the possessions of only those who had the will or the means to buy them. Along with mosaics and windows, there was also the artistic technique of painting on fresh plaster so that when the plaster hardened there remained permanent pictures on the walls. This technique of fresco (the Italian word *fresco* means "fresh") was widely used (and is used today) as a former of artistic expression of the faith.

To these artistic endeavors we should also add, in the West at least, the near-universal custom of three-dimensional art in the form of sculpture. Since stone was so durable, it was common to develop in larger churches a whole sculptural program (one of the most famous was at the cathedral church in Chartres) on the exterior of buildings while inside there were affixed to the walls or in niches other sculptural forms that ranged from crucifixes over the main altar to single statues of the Virgin Mary and some of the patronal saints in side chapels along the nave of the church.

It has not always been appreciated how much one can learn about devotional and theological ideas by an examination of these artistic productions, but simple reflection shows that every age has contributed its own response to the art which is found within the churches of various eras. The great figure of Christ found in Byzantine-influenced churches is not the same thing as the Christ of the large painted crosses of medieval Italy, which is not the same as the Christ of the Renaissance or the baroque, which provides its own angle of vision.

To study the different ways in which Christ is depicted is to get some insight into the ways in which a particular period or a particular culture understands the person of Jesus. Art is instructive because the human imagination can "construct" an image of Christ. The construction is possible because nowhere in the New Testament do we get any hint at all about what Jesus might have looked like. We can only intuit that he must have looked like a first-century Palestinian Semite, but the particulars are completely hidden from us.

This is not the place to treat artistic development in any detail, but one example might suffice to show how profitable it is to know something about artistic evolution. Let us think of the developing iconography of the cross and the crucifix (the latter includes crosses with the figure of Christ on them). We can see, roughly, various stages of this evolution. Very simply that evolution runs something like this:

- In the period before the end of the Roman persecutions, we find no clear examples of crosses in Christian art except in an occult fashion (for example, an upside-down anchor or the famous Chi/Rho which derives from the first two letters of the word "Christ" in Greek). This absence might well be explained by reason of the fact that crucifixion was seen as a shameful form of death in pagan eyes. Most of the art of this period tends to depict symbols or stories that hold the promise of bodily resurrection. Christian iconography of this era emphasizes the promise of life more than a fixation on death even though we know that as early as the late second century Christians made the "sign of the cross" on themselves as a devotional act and as a sign of faith.
- Early in the post-Constantine period, we find a growth in the depiction of the cross (for example, in the fifth- and sixth-century mosaics in

Ravenna), but they appeared without a corpus attached and frequently were shown jeweled – a sign of the cross triumphant – linking the cross with the resurrected Christ. The use of a cross in art becomes more and more common.

- The transition from cross to crucifix becomes more frequent in the early Middle Ages, most likely as a way to signify that Jesus was a real human being and not merely, as some heretical movements insisted, only someone who "seemed" human. The more frequent depiction of a corpus on a cross was also an implied argument against those who tended to understate the true humanity of Jesus or who downplayed his suffering.
- In the Middle Ages, more attention was paid to the sufferings of Jesus on the cross. The corpus on the crucifix increasingly showed signs of the nails, the crown of thorns, the pierced side, etc. This emphasis on the suffering humanity of Jesus reflected both the intense meditation of monastic authors from Anselm of Canterbury in the eleventh century and the Cistercians of the twelfth but especially due to the influence of Saint Francis of Assisi, who, it was claimed, actually bore the wounds of Christ (the so-called *stigmata*) on his own body. The impact of Franciscan piety cannot be overestimated. The bloody crucifixes that have been a hallmark of medieval piety (transported to Latin America by missionary clergy) derive mainly from the energies unleashed by the Franciscan movement and its constant preaching about the significance of the Passion of Christ.
- The Renaissance, with its intense study of the human form, added to the iconography of the crucifix by increasing attention to the human anatomy of the one who was crucified. The accumulated tradition of the iconography of the Passion was further developed by a loving attention to the sheer physicality of Christ as is clear from any number of examples from both Renaissance artists (for example, Michelangelo) and those who became the leaders of the baroque such as Peter Paul Rubens.
- In the modern period – witness the crucifixes available in any religious-goods shop – the crucifixes are the inheritance of this long tradition. What has happened most recently, of course, is that the traditional iconography has been "read" in the light of contemporary experience so that a Chagall crucifix alludes directly to the Jewishness of Jesus while others have replaced the crown of thorns with the barbed wire of the contemporary concentration camp.

Typical crucifixes found in many Catholic homes or schools today are, as it were, compressed figures that reflect nearly two millennia of meditation on the crucifixion of Jesus. This excursion into the crucifix is only one example of how the Catholic tradition remembers, meditates upon, and rereads the gospel story in order to present it to the age in which it lives (one could do a similar analysis, for example, of the figure of Mary or any other well-known religious token). Such art, common in churches, is both an instrument of teaching as well as a fruit of the meditations, prayers, and theological reflections of the centuries.

THE CHURCH BUILDING EXPANDED

Up to this point we have concentrated mainly on those churches which were designed for communities of the faithful as their primary gathering place of worship. We have not spoken of the many church buildings which have been erected for more particular uses. Those would include churches built as destinations for pilgrimages or those adjacent to monasteries, chapels located at cemeteries or hospitals or other places of Christian service.

When churches were considered at the level of the parish (or the cathedral church of the local bishop), it was inevitable that other buildings would be annexed to the primary church to carry out other functions. Such expansions are so numerous that they can, at best, only be mentioned in passing even though their naming gives fair indication of the ways in which the evolving history of the Church's practice becomes more complex as time passes. Among the more conspicuous of these additions would include the following:

A. **Separate Baptisteries**. In the period after Constantine it was common to build a separate building to house the baptismal pool. Such baptisteries – many going back to the pre-medieval period, such as the baptistry at the cathedral of Saint John Lateran in Rome – not only emphasize the fact that baptism is the central rite by which people are received into the Church but also indicate how solemnly the Church understood that rite. Many of these early baptismal buildings were octagonal in shape; the octagonal shape was meant to remind the congregation of the "eighth day" (after the seven-day week described in Genesis 1) when God "recreates" a person. New converts, immersed in the baptismal pool, would then process to the main church to experience the eucharistic liturgy fully as members of the Church. Many contemporary churches, unable to duplicate a separate building, give a nod to that practice by installing the baptismal font at the very entrance of the church's nave as a symbolic "first step" towards the altar. Typically, these baptismal fonts are also octagonal in shape so as to echo the ancient shape of baptisteries.

B. **Presbyteries.** With the emergence of the clergy as having a kind of separate status, it become increasingly common to have a separate quarter for the housing of the clergy or, in the case of cathedrals, a canonry (i.e. a house for those priests attached to the cathedral) and an episcopal residence. In more contemporary times, the presbytery or rectory was part of the general plan for the church complex.

C. **Schools.** The education of the young grew in time to be part of the general mission of the Church's outreach. Some schools, such as the catechetical school of Justin Martyr or the one in Alexandria under the direction of Origen, date back to the second century. Cathedral schools were a common addition to the medieval cathedral, and, in the modern period, the parish school was a regular part of the local parish in many countries. In fact, the so-called "parish plant" in countries such as the USA would typically include a parish church, a rectory for the clergy, a school for children, and a convent for the religious sisters or brothers who would administer and teach in schools. Each of those elements reflect an historical evolution over time.

TRAJECTORIES FOR THE FUTURE

At a certain level, one can think of the Church as a vast skein of inter-woven places which go to make up the visible church as an empirical reality. At the local level there are parishes of varying sizes which may or may not have the luxury of a resident priest and a school, but the parishes, large or small, are in communion with the local bishop and his cathedral (from *cathedra* – chair). That bishop, in turn, is in communion with all other bishops, who, in turn, are in communion with the bishop of Rome, the pope. Woven into that web of mutual unity are the manifold number of shrines, religious houses, pilgrimage sites, schools, hospitals, chaplaincies, and other institutions which are part of this large picture. If anyone wishes to make a measure of the Catholic Church, to recognize that web of interwoven concrete realities, simply mapping out the visible institutions is one way to do it. It certainly does not "explain" the entire reality, but it does give one a kind of template for seeing the Church as a recognizable whole. To get a fuller picture, of course, one needs to grasp what goes on in those places as well as getting some sense about what radiates from them and, finally, towards what end(s) does the visible reality look and yearn.

AMBO AND ALTAR

If one were to strip back all of the interior furniture, decoration, app-urtenances, and so on from a typical church, there are two foci which would remain that tell us much about the essential rites that take place within a church. These are the ambo (also called the lectern or the pulpit) and the altar. They are essential because they involve the two parts of the Church's public worship: the proclamation of the Word and the celebration of the eucharist.

Originally, in the early Christian basilicas, the ambo was a raised platform for the reading out loud of the scriptures and for the reflections on those readings by the priest who presided over the Sunday celebration. We can take that "reading" to stand for the "telling the story" of salvation as it was recorded in the biblical narrative of the Old and New Testa-ments. It was also from that same place that the priest reflected on that story in what was called the homily (or sermon). In time, the raised platform gave way to a more or less elaborate reader's stand, but, however, much as the ambo turned into an elaborate pulpit, the basic function was to proclaim the Word.

The altar, by contrast, was simply a table on which the offerings of bread, wine, and water were placed as an offering. Almost universally, Catholics prefer the language of "altar" to that of "table" to make the doctrinal point that the eucharist is a re-presentation of Christ's sacrifice. These offerings were prayed over in a thanksgiving (the word "eucharist" comes from the Greek "to give thanks"), after which the congregation would partake in them as a form of communion. Again, in time, the table which served as an altar would become more elaborate, and its setting would become more complex. The crucial point, however, is that the ambo and the altar are the two crucial foci for the Catholic liturgy. The Second Vatican Council put it succinctly: "The Church has always venerated the divine scriptures as it has venerated the Body of the Lord [. . .]" (*Dei verbum*, VI.21). In other places in this work, we will talk about the evolution of the liturgy, but, for now, it suffices to keep in mind these two elements. We have a description of this act of worship that goes back to the mid-second century.

TIME

Just as we can ask, "Where is the Church?" and mean a specific place – this parish or that basilica – we can also ask, "When is the Church?"

meaning at what time(s) does the *ekklesia* gather? In other words, we can speak of the church in terms of concrete place and also as a reality that exists in time. Catholicism has a strong sense of its own existence in time. We envision the College of Bishops as being somehow linked to the Apostles; we enumerate our popes as having a genealogy back to Peter; we search our tradition to learn about our present by understanding what has been handed down from the past. The vibrancy of the Church, Catholicism asserts, comes from living in the present, oriented to the future, while being in communion with the past; that sense of continuum is encapsulated in the affirmation that Jesus Christ is the same yesterday, today and forever. The Catholic Church symbolizes that truth when, on Holy Saturday, the Easter (Paschal) Candle is inscribed by the priest. He does so while intoning, "Christ, Yesterday, Today and Tomorrow."

Christianity in the first place is a historical religion, and history is a record of a revelation in history. It did not begin "Once upon a time" in the swirls of myth, but at a historical moment. As the beautiful opening lines of the *Epistle to the Hebrews* puts it, "In times past, God spoke in partial and various ways to our ancestors through the prophets; in these last days, he spoke to us through a son whom he has made heir to all things and through whom he created the universe" (Heb. 1:1–2). Christianity began with the birth of Jesus at a particular place (ancient Palestine) and at a particular time (in the reign of Caesar Augustus) even though it had long antecedents in Jewish tradition that makes it understandable in terms of both its place and its time.

The early Christians met on the first day of the week (our Sunday) most likely as a way of distinguishing themselves as different from the Jews who celebrated their sabbath on the seventh day – the day, according to the creation account in *Genesis,* when God rested. Justin Martyr, writing in the mid-second century, explains that the choice of the first day was not accidental: "Sunday is the day on which we hold our common assembly because it is the first day on which God, having wrought a change in darkness and matter, made the world; and Jesus Christ our savior on the same day rose from the dead" (*Apology,* Chapter 67). From that initial decision to worship on a given day there developed a complex calendar of liturgical observance which we know today as the liturgical year. The historical evolution of the liturgical calendar is far too complex to describe here, but its main outline, as it is observed today in the Catholic Church, can be briefly summarized.

- The liturgical year begins with the so-called Christmas cycle. There are four weeks known as the Advent season, which leads up to the feasts of Christmas and ends with Epiphany.
- The Easter cycle begins with the first Sunday following Ash Wednesday (the dates are variable depending on the dating of Easter) and reaches its high point in Passion Week, beginning with Palm Sunday, culminating in Easter, and ending on the feast of Pentecost, fifty days after Easter.

Interspersed between those great cycles are the weeks known as the "ordinary weeks." When seen as a whole, the liturgical year unfolds the whole story of the mystery of Christ: In the Advent season the great prophets are heard foretelling the coming of the Messiah; Christmas and Epiphany celebrates Christ's birth and his "showing forth" (Epiphany). The Easter cycle unfolds the penitential preparation of Lent for the great paschal mystery of Christ's Passion, suffering, death, and resurrection at Easter and concludes with the outpouring of the Spirit at the feast of Pentecost.

The Church year is a telling of the Christian story from the anticipated coming of Christ through his birth, life, passion, resurrection, and the coming of the Holy Spirit upon the Church at Pentecost. One of the fundamental tasks of the Church is to tell that story. The great narrative of Christianity triangulates the story of Jesus, the story of Jesus remembered in the Church, and our story as we encounter it as believing Christians who gather together.

Today, it is somewhat difficult to follow that unfolding of the story of salvation in the liturgical calendar because the Church's year overlaps with the secular calendar. In most modern cultures, Christmas is hardly recognized as a religious feast. Most people do not see New Year's Day as the great feast of Mary, the Mother of God. Easter has been commercialized as a time for finery and chocolate eggs, unconscious of the fact that the egg is an ancient symbol of Christ's resurrection since new life (a chick) breaks open the shell of the egg to be born. Many competing civil holidays such as memorial days or thanksgiving days have further attenuated the sacred round of time.

To complicate matters even more, interwoven into that liturgical calendar is a second subsidiary calendar known as the *sanctoral cycle* – feasts that honor the Blessed Virgin Mary, the Apostles, martyrs, confessors, and other saints who are listed in the universal canon or the list of those persons whose intercession is sought in liturgical fashion. This cycle never supersedes the temporal cycle of the liturgical year and varies, depending on place, according to the degree of solemnity. The sanctoral cycle is a characteristic of the Catholic (and Orthodox) liturgy because of the strong conviction that the Church is a "communion of saints" (as the creed affirms) which includes not only those on Earth but those who now enjoy the vision of God in eternity. Only on a few occasions does the calendar of the saints coincide with the larger story of Jesus. One example is conspicuous: On March 25 we celebrate the feast of the Annunciation to Mary that she is to become the mother of the Savior. That feast day occurs exactly nine months before Christmas day, which celebrates the birth of Jesus.

The celebration of specific times – most commonly by Sunday worship – is part of the larger understanding of time which is part of Catholic theology. Indeed, the moment when time and place most perfectly coincide is when the Catholic people gather together for worship on Sunday. Although it would be too simplistic to say that Catholic faith can be reduced to the liturgy, it is nonetheless true, as Vatican II's *Constitution on the Sacred Liturgy* asserts: "the liturgy is the summit towards which the activity of the Church is directed; it is the source from which all its power flows" (No. 10). In the liturgy, the Catholic community gathers in place and time to celebrate the saving mysteries of the life, death, and resurrection of Jesus Christ.

As we will have seen elsewhere in this book, we also mark as sacred the various stages of an individual's life. This is most strikingly done through the sacramental life of the Church. We celebrate birth by the rebirth of the child in baptism; we mark that person's "coming of age" in confirmation; we consecrate a change of individual life to the common life of people by celebrating the sacrament of matrimony. We have end-of-life rituals annexed to the sacrament of the sick, to aid in the passage of one life to another. It is worthwhile noting that when we celebrate a sainted martyr we do so on the date of the person's death, which has been called his or her birthday (*dies natalis*) into the realm of God in Paradise.

In addition to those formal sacramental rites, the Church, in various places and cultures, blesses and sanctifies fields at planting and harvesting times; recommends evening and morning prayers; and, in some cultures, has ceremonies to mark the passing over from adolescence to adulthood. It has long been a custom to sound the hours by the church bell. We pray for the dead on All Souls' Day. Homes and residences were traditionally blessed during the Easter season. Visits are made to the burial grounds to keep the area hallowed. All of these informal rites and ceremonies are reminders of our passage through that slice of time which we call "our life."

There are also other ways in which Catholicism understands time. Drawing on a biblical distinction, the Church understands the marking of ordinary time – the time of the calendar – as *chronos,* which is the Greek term for time. The scriptures also speak of another kind of time: those moments which are decisive, which open up the opportunity for conversion or commitment. The New Testament calls this kind of time *kairos.* The *kairos* moment happens each time God's invitation in Christ is presented to us. It may well happen that at a religious event which we are observing in chronological time we might experience some grace of conversion which becomes a *kairos* moment for us.

Catholic doctrine further teaches that time has a direction, that the world has come out from God and will return to God in the final age. Time, in the Catholic tradition, is not ultimately understood as being either without direction or as an unending cycle of eras. The Catholic understanding of creation is not that God creates and then retires from the world. The biblical doctrine of creation insists that God creates and sustains the world at every moment. As humans we are cooperators in God's creation, which God watches over (as God watches over us) by providence. In that sense, at least, we not only live in our time but also in God's "time" which creates, orders, watches over all creation, and will bring it into a final consummation when, as the creed says, he "will come again in glory."

In the creed, it is said that we expect the "resurrection of the dead." In the brief phrase is the deep conviction that our earthly life is not the sum total of our existence. It is for that reason that our funeral rites, while allowing a large space for mourning and grief, affirm that just as Christ rose from the dead so we also, at the end of human history, will rise up to live again as whole persons glorified as Christ is already glorified. To be quite precise about this: Catholics do not believe in some vague form of the immortality of souls but in the resurrection of the person. That is why we cover the casket of the deceased with a white pall and place the Easter candle near it so that we recall that while we mourn our dead we also have the conviction of faith that the person will rise on the Last Day.

A consequence of this belief in the direction of time towards a final end means that Catholicism accepts both the limitation of the present and the hope for a final resurrection. It is that looking towards the future that explains why we pray for the dead, why we honor the saints whom we believe to be with the Lord, and why we pray in hope for ourselves. Those sentiments are all expressed in part of one of the eucharistic prayers in the liturgy: "Remember those who have died in the peace of Christ and all the dead whose faith is known to you alone. Father, in your mercy grant also to us, your children, to enter into our heavenly inheritance in the company of the Virgin Mary, the Mother of God and all your apostles and saints" (*Eucharistic Prayer,* No. 4).

The fact that Catholicism sees time as leading to a future does not mean that it encourages anyone to disparage the present or to be indifferent to it. Karl Marx, famously, called religion the opium of the people because he believed that religion, like a powerful painkiller, relieved human injustice and suffering by holding out a future happiness beyond history. Catholic theology does not accept that judgment. A more precise way to think about present and future time, as Catholicism understands it, is to consider the metaphor of pilgrimage.

A pilgrimage is a journey with an end in mind; one starts off with the intention of reaching a destination. The Second Vatican Council, famously, described the Church as the pilgrim people of God. Like any pilgrimage – think of the ideal types described in the prologue of Chaucer's *Canterbury Tales* – the members come from various backgrounds, of different genders, of diverse skills, and with diverse gifts, but they are all joined democratically towards the common purpose of making the journey and reaching the destination.

The people of God, which is the Church, has a dual destination: to use the gifts and graces they have to fulfill their temporal duties, whatever they may be, and also to reach their final end, which is God. What distinguishes a pilgrimage from a mob is common purpose and common support.

A final note: It is within the confines of the Church that, in one real sense, time and space coincide. Catholic infants are brought to the baptistery after birth; they will mark their first communion and confirmation in the church precincts. As adults, they will make public witness of their love before a priest at the time of their marriage. At the end of life, their bodies will be received at the church for a final commendation. In many places, they will be buried in the churchyard adjacent to the church. Thus, for most Catholics, the lifecycle of their individual growth will intertwine with and be celebrated in the church.

There was a time in the not-distant past in which the local church was the custodian of the vital records of a person's life from birth to death, as they were inscribed in parish archives. This is no longer generally the case. Under the pressures of contemporary mobility, the tenacious hold that the local parish had on the Catholic population is eroding for those who live in a highly mobile urban society. No longer is it generally the case that people mark the day by the sound of the church bell, nor is it common to have local festivals connected to the round of the liturgical season or the feast days of the saints. One should resist looking back on those times in nostalgia, but, rather, ask, how we can articulate the old Catholic sense of space and time given the very different world in which most of us live today.

SOME PROBLEMS CONSIDERED

While we have insisted in this chapter that Catholicism is located in a definite place by pointing out that where the Catholic assembly meets has a definite theological significance, it is also true that Catholicism is a missionary Church, which means that it is both anchored in place but also on the move. The Second Vatican Council devoted an entire document to the missionary character of the Church (*Ad gentes*). When one reads that decree, it is striking how frequently it uses the language of movement rather than the vocabulary of place. After asserting in its opening page that the Church is missionary by its very nature, it goes on to note that the Church must "walk the road Christ himself walked" and the Church must, like the Apostles, "walk in hope and by much trouble and suffering fill up what was lacking in the sufferings of Christ for his body which is the Church" (No. 5).

The Catholic Church is both located in place and constantly on the move. That is another reason why the image of the pilgrim Church is such a fruitful one. To fail to recognize the tension or paradox between a church located in place and its necessarily pilgrim character has been a constant challenge in Catholicism. Missionaries to lands which did not have a long tradition of knowing Christianity presented a challenge: What was the "place" for these new Christians to look like? One obvious mistake would have been to import to these areas "places" that resembled those from where the missionaries came. It took some time to recognize that it was not appropriate to build Gothic structures in Kenya but, rather, places that reflected the cultural values peculiar to the new lands where missionaries went to preach. The failure to adapt to local cultures led, not always unjustly, to the charge that Christianity was a colonial import.

Another problematic area in the consideration of church space is this: What happens when an historical church building, representative of its own age, now becomes an unfamiliar place or even one detrimental to the purposes of worship. Do the elaborate baroque or rococo churches of the eighteenth century even speak to people of today? Churches with elaborated reredos (backdrops) to altars which once were a feature of such churches now seem oddly out of place for congregations that are encouraged to participate in the liturgy rather than to be simple spectators at distant celebrations of the old Latin mass.

The *Constitution on the Sacred Liturgy* issued at the Second Vatican Council devotes an entire chapter (VII) to the issue of sacred art and architecture. The Church is justly proud of its artistic heritage but is also acutely aware that bad architecture and inappropriate art can not only be detrimental but also of dubious theological correctness when not considered prudently. The Council was clear about these issues: "When churches are to be built, let great care be taken that they are suitable for the celebration of liturgical services and for the active participation of the faithful" (VII.124). Furthermore, as it did in the sixteenth century, the Council reiterated the legitimacy of images in church to foster devotion (see Box 4 below) but also warned that such images "should be restricted in number and their relative position should reflect right order lest they cause confusion among the Christian people or foster devotion of doubtful orthodoxy" (VII.125).

That last point about the correct use of images demands a further reflection. The church building fundamentally is a place for the eucharistic liturgy and for the celebration of the other sacraments of the Church. Over the course of the centuries, the churches also became places where certain popular devotions developed. Already in the fourth century, many churches had a *confessio* where people would come to pray at the tomb of the martyr buried there. In addition, the church may have housed a particular image of the Madonna or a saint which attracted the devotion of people. It was quite common from the Middle Ages on that groups such as lay confraternities would donate chapels or images in honor of a patron saint. Increased devotion to the real presence of Christ in the eucharist triggered a movement from the fifteenth century on to place the tabernacle containing the consecrated eucharist on the main altar. The tabernacle, as a result, became the main focus of the church rather than the altar itself. The net result of these evolutionary developments was that the church building housed a whole series of foci for people who visited the church outside the time of the liturgy or even during the liturgy. It was not uncommon in the past to see people at side altars or burning candles before an image even during mass.

It is precisely because churches lost a certain sense of focus that the Second Vatican Council foresaw a return to an emphasis on the fundamental needs of the Church. Most churches place their baptismal font at the entrance to remind people symbolically that it is through baptism that one enters the Church. The sanctuary typically has its focus on the altar and the ambo to state strongly that it is there that the liturgy of the word and the liturgy of the eucharist are celebrated. The tabernacle containing the eucharist is set either to the side or behind the main altar. There are still places for the images of the Blessed Mother and, perhaps, a patronal saint since this is a long-standing custom in the Catholic Church as are the stations of the cross, which have been part of the devotional life of the Church since the early modern period. The design should also find an appropriate place for the choir. The central concern, though, is to give the altar and the ambo or pulpit center stage for when the people gather to hear the Word proclaimed and for the celebration of eucharist that we the *ekklesia* have gathered.

Box 4   Christian art

Some of the earliest evidence we have for Christian beginnings comes from the art found decorating the walls of catacombs and the tombs (sarcophagi) dating from the period of late antiquity. In addition, certain ephemeral archeological finds indicate that the early Christians used art as part of their self-expression.

We have already seen that in the period after the Roman persecutions it was common to use art in the church. It became quite common to decorate churches with biblical scenes in order to illustrate the truths of the faith and to further the piety of the Christian faithful. Early churches built in the Byzantine style had quite elaborate programs of art in mosaic covering large parts of the church interior. There was a problem with the use of such art in that the Old Testament, accepted as canonical in the Church, forbade the making of images. The Ten Commandments have an express prohibition against artistic depictions: "You shall not carve idols for yourselves in the shape of anything in the sky above or on the earth below or in the waters beneath the earth; you shall not bow down before them or worship them" (Exod. 20:4–5). Judaism, as a consequence, has always had a vigorous aniconic tradition in its practice although this prohibition was not evidently universally observed, as the synagogue at Dura Europos clearly shows.

Although Christians certainly did not worship idols or adore the artistic representations used in their churches and homes, there was nevertheless a long tradition of the use and veneration of art especially in the form of icons

Box 4 (cont.)

(images). This practice came under strong challenge, mainly in the Christian East, in the early eighth century, in a movement which became known as the iconoclastic (literally: "image-breaking") controversy. Possibly influenced by the rise of Islam, which fervently forbade religious imagery, a number of Christian emperors in the East not only forbade the use of icons but also ruthlessly suppressed them and their supporters. Despite such supporters as Saint John of Damascus in the East and Pope Gregory III in the West, it was not until the convocation of the Ecumenical Council of Nicaea in 787 that the legitimacy of the use of icons was affirmed by the universal Church. That council distinguished the *veneration* permitted for the use of icons from the *adoration* that was due to God alone. The Council's decision was based on the broad principle of sacramentality, namely, that the material things (icons) can serve as a mediatorial way of bringing divine mysteries into the consciousness of people just as the Word was made flesh in the incarnation of Jesus. The affirmation of the legitimacy of images (icons) was so important to the Eastern Church that each year the anniversary of Nicaea II is celebrated as the "Feast of the Triumph of Orthodoxy."

Both the Orthodox and the Catholic Church have maintained the legitimacy of the use of art both for instruction and as an aid in devotion down to the present. At the time of the Protestant Reformation, a new wave of iconoclasm broke out, and, as a consequence, one way to distinguish the Catholic and the Protestant sensibility is to be aware of the use of images or the lack thereof in the two traditions. One shorthand way to understand that tradition is to be found in the fact that in Protestantism one frequently finds the use of a cross in churches but the Catholic tradition favors crucifixes – crosses with images of the body of Christ affixed to them.

The Catholic Church is justly proud of its long patronage of the arts by insisting that authentic Christian art is not only an aid to devotion but also an instrument for instruction and another way of "doing" theology, that is, reflecting on the truths of faith.

FURTHER READING

Chupunco, A., ed., *Handbook for Liturgical Studies: Time and Space* (Collegeville, Minn.: Liturgical Press, 1997). The fifth volume of an authoritative resource. An excellent resource for the topic relative to Catholic worship.

Connell, Martin, *Eternity Today: On the Liturgical Year*, 2 vols. (Collegeville, Minn.: Liturgical Press, 2006). A useful survey of the liturgical calendar of the Catholic Church with much ancillary information.

Finney, Paul C., *The Invisible God: The Earliest Christians on Art* (Oxford: Oxford University Press, 1994). A highly competent study of the emergence of Christian iconography in the era before Constantine.

Kieckehefer, R., *Theology in Stone: Sacred Architecture from Byzantium to Berkeley* (Oxford: Oxford University Press, 2004). Excellent analytical study with good bibliography.

Ouspensky, L., *The Theology of the Icon*, 2 vols. (New York: St. Vladimir Seminary Press, 1992). Classic study by an Orthodox thinker.

Seasoltz, K., *Sense of the Sacred: Theological Foundations of Christian Architecture and Art* (London and New York: Continuum, 2005). Both culturally and theologically sophisticated.

Vosko, Richard, *God's House is Our House* (Collegeville, Minn.: Liturgical Press, 2006). A study of contemporary worship space with an extended theological meditation on sacred architecture.

White, James, ed., *Documents of Christian Worship* (Louisville, Ky.: Westminster/ John Knox, 1992). A handy resource for primary documents.

Wilde, J., ed., *At that Time: Cycles and Seasons in the Life of a Christian* (Chicago, Ill.: Liturgy Training Publications, 1989). A popular but instructive survey written by a variety of authors.

CHAPTER 5

Catholic worship

INTRODUCTION

Catholicism is not merely a belief system. While it is true, as we will develop at length in the next chapter, that there are criteria for the basic beliefs of the Church set out in the rule of faith, it is equally true that Catholicism is also a worshiping community and not simply a movement with a collection of ideas or concepts. The relationship between worship and belief is, in the Catholic understanding of things, symbiotic: What we believe is expressed in how we worship as a Church.

As we have already noted, the New Testament word for church – *ekklesia* – means a gathered congregation. The New Testament succinctly sets out the reasons for that coming together as an *ekklesia*: "They [i.e. the early Christian community] devoted themselves to the teachings of the Apostles and to the communal life, to the breaking of bread, and to the prayers" (Acts 2:42). In that terse description we see that the gathered community first received the apostolic preaching and teaching and, in the second place "broke the bread" and prayed, which is to say, they engaged in a form of ritual activity ("broke the bread" is a shorthand description in the New Testament for the eucharist), and they offered prayers to God.

This chapter will focus particularly on the formal worship of the Church, which frequently is referred to as the liturgy. The word "liturgy" comes from a Greek word *leitourgia*, which originally meant, roughly, a public work. In the Catholic sense of the term, liturgy means the public worship of the Church. The Second Vatican Council, in its *Sacrosanctum concilium* (*Constitution on the Sacred Liturgy*), stated,

Liturgical services are not private functions but are celebrations of the Church which is the "sacrament of unity," namely, the holy people united and organized under their bishops. Therefore, liturgical services have to do with the whole body, the Church. They make it visible and have effects on it. But they also touch individual members of the Church in different ways, depending on ranks, roles and levels of participation. (No. 26)

In general, the Catholic Church understands the liturgy to consist of two broad categories: the sacraments of the Church and the official public prayer of the Church. Each of these broad categories and their particularities will be discussed in that order.

THE CONCEPT OF SACRAMENT

The word "sacrament" has been understood in the Catholic tradition to mean a visible sign of divine power manifested to humanity. Understood in that non-technical, broad sense of the term, the first sacrament or sign of God's presence and power is the created world itself, which is a sign of the creator who brought forth the world. Thus, the psalmist says: "The heavens declare the glory of God / and the firmament proclaims his handiwork" (Ps. 19:1); the Book of Wisdom chides the foolish "who from the good things seen did not succeed in knowing him who is, and from studying his works did not discern the artisan" (13:1); and Saint Paul confessed "Ever since the creation of the world, his invisible attributes of eternal power and divinity have been able to be understood and perceived in what he has made" (Rom. 1:20). It has always been a fundamental datum of Catholic belief that the world itself gives us, if we see with the eyes of our humanity, some glimpse into the power and majesty of God.

If the world itself is the first sacrament, then Catholics believe that the coming of Jesus Christ, who was the Word made flesh (John 1:14), was the next great sacrament because Christ was a visible sign of God's presence on the Earth and God's love for it. Christ, Paul writes, "is the image of the invisible God, the firstborn of all creation . . . for in him all the fullness was pleased to dwell" (Col. 1:15, 19). It is thus common for the Catholic tradition to say that Christ is the Great Sacrament in the sense that he is the efficacious sign of God's presence among us. It is often said that if one wants to know what God is like, one should look at Jesus Christ who is God made man.

Jesus Christ, in turn, left a visible sign of his continuing presence in the world in the Church so that it was common enough for the early Christian writers to use the word "sacrament" to describe the Church. They often called the Church the "great sacrament" (which sacrament/ Church, in turn, also worked through visible signs in the liturgy). Catholic theology has always insisted that the Church, as a visible sign, is the sign of the presence of God in Christ in the world.

In the Early Church, the word "sacrament" was further used very fluidly to refer to a wide range of things. Saint Augustine of Hippo, for example, considered the Bible itself a sacrament, and he used the term broadly to refer also to objects, events, and practices found in the Bible (the temple, circumcision, exorcisms, the Lord's Prayer, etc.), although the same Augustine also began to use the word in a somewhat narrower sense to describe the formal liturgical functions of the Church as vehicles for God's grace to people. Augustine was the first theologian to describe the sacraments as composed of a recognizable word and a material element (for example, the utterance of the baptismal formula and the pouring of water) – a distinction which would lead the medieval theologians to clarify the sacraments as the main instrumental means by which the Church is built up by making holy its people and thus leading them to salvation.

Eventually, the Church designated seven principal sacraments in the Church, namely: baptism, confirmation, Holy Eucharist, penance or reconciliation, anointing of the sick, matrimony, and holy orders. That order of sacraments has been hallowed in official Church teachings. However, the enumeration of the sacraments as being seven, as we shall see, is more symbolically potent than mathematically strict. The concept of "seven sacraments" is an enumeration that goes back into the medieval theologian's desire for tidy categories. For example, we now number baptism and confirmation as separate sacraments, but, historically speaking, they were part of a complex of initiatory rites that, for many complex historical reasons, became separated. What was clear from the very beginning is that the gateway to all the sacraments is baptism, and, in the order of significance, it is the Holy Eucharist that is at the core of the whole sacramental system. Since, however, it is traditional, at least since the medieval period, to speak of seven sacraments, we will honor that custom and treat each of them in turn.

BAPTISM

If there is one thing that is clear in the New Testament, it is that the rite of baptism (from the Greek verb *baptizein*, "to dip" or "to immerse") is a central feature of the Christian faith. The first Apostles were ordered to preach the Gospel to every person on Earth and to baptize them in the name of the Father, the Son, and the Holy Spirit (Matt. 28:19–20), while John's Gospel demands that all be cleansed in "the water and the Spirit" (3:1–21). The Acts of the Apostles says that the first Apostles baptized everyone who believed in what they preached (see, for example, Acts

2:37–41). Saint Paul not only preached the necessity of baptism but also provided a meaning for the symbolic rite. Just as Christ died, was buried, and rose again, so the person who is baptized goes down into the waters and comes up again as a new person through the Spirit of God (see Rom. 6:3–11). Paul sees in baptism a new form of living in the Christian *ekklesia* which frees one from sin, joins one to Christ, and provides a new status for the one who is baptized: "For all of you who were baptized into Christ have clothed themselves with Christ. There is neither Jew nor Greek, there is neither slave nor free person, there is no male and female; for you are all one in Christ Jesus" (Gal. 3:28). What is clear about this primordial rite is that it used the symbol of cleansing in water as a sign of entrance into the body of believers and as a way of symbolizing a cleansing from sin. Paul used the further analogy of understanding baptism as a kind of reenactment of Christ's saving death. Just as Christ died, went into the tomb, and then rose again, so does a believer "go down" into the waters to rise up a new person: "All of us who have been baptized into Christ Jesus have been baptized into his death" (Rom. 6:3).

We are not certain how the baptismal rite was performed in the earliest period of the Church, but indications are that it was by a process of immersion in some kind of body of water. We do know that until the sixth century there was a long process of initiation for potential Christians (called *catechumens*) which involved a period of instruction, a series of exorcisms accompanied by anointings, a gradual set of instructions, and, usually on the evening before Easter, a triple immersion into the baptismal waters after the threefold profession of faith in the Holy Trinity. By the Middle Ages, this elaborate catechumenate had all but disappeared, but the main lines of the ceremonies were maintained for the baptism of infants even though the ritual renunciation of Satan and the profession of faith were done by the godparents, who spoke in the name of the infant.

We also know that from the fourth century, the place where baptism was performed was separate from the church building itself and that separation was maintained for a very profound reason: The act of baptism was the entrance rite into the Church. One entered the baptism for the sacramental washing which then permitted one to enter the church building proper to participate in the full liturgy of the Church. Many of these ancient baptisteries, as we have seen earlier, were octagonal in shape to symbolize that the eighth day was the day of recreation.

One of the reforms of the liturgy at the Second Vatican Council resulted in the restoration of the old process of the Roman catechumenate, which is now widely used in parishes. The RCIA (Rite of Christian Initiation of Adults) is a process for those adults who wish to enter the Catholic Church. This rite envisions four stages:

1. The rite of becoming a catechumen – a welcoming ceremony.
2. An intense forty-day period during Lent in which the catechumens are "elected" for baptism.
3. The sacramental rites of baptism, confirmation, and the reception of Holy Eucharist are celebrated.
4. A post-baptismal period of further instruction is provided.

For those who are already baptized, these rites are not fully observed. A validly baptized person in some other Christian community who enters into full communion with the Catholic Church simply makes a profession of faith after due spiritual formation. That person is then ready to make a sacramental confession (i.e. the sacrament of reconciliation), to be confirmed, and to begin the reception of holy communion. This reception may occur at the same time as the RCIA, but it should be so done as to distinguish clearly the two rites.

The necessity of baptism for salvation is a constant teaching of the Catholic Church. What happens to those who are not baptized? This has been a vexed question in Catholic circles. Two things must be kept simultaneously in mind: the necessity of baptism and the full salvific will of God. Some have posited a "baptism of desire" for those who, in good faith, yearn for God as well as a "baptism of blood" for those who die without baptism but who are martyrs for the truth. The *Catechism of the Catholic Church* wisely insists that for both unbaptized adults and children we should have confidence in the mercy of God who wants all to be saved and says this explicitly in its funeral liturgy for children which entrusts such children to the tender mercy of God (No. 1260–61).

A medieval tradition, but never part of the authentic doctrine of the Church, assigned righteous unbelievers and unbaptized infants to an intermediate state of natural happiness called *limbo*, but that theory, and it never moved beyond the status of theory (mainly developed as a solution to the problem of what happens to unbaptized children), has not received much endorsement in the present age and is probably better left to the history of theology as a flawed theory that deserves little credence. A recent proposal made in Rome by a body of theological advisers to the Vatican has suggested dropping the theory altogether, and that proposal received the endorsement of Pope Benedict XVI in 2007.

Summary: It is Catholic belief that all stain of sin is removed in baptism; that the person is "born again" as a child of God; such a person is illuminated by the grace of baptism and is incorporated in the mystical body of Christ which is the Church. When a person is baptized, the rite not only signified death and purification but also regeneration and renewal: "now you have had yourselves washed, you were sanctified, you were justified in the name of the Lord Jesus Christ and in the Spirit of our God" (1 Cor. 6:11).

CONFIRMATION

The sacrament of confirmation is inextricably linked to baptism. It was only in the Middle Ages that discussions arose as to whether it was even a separate sacrament from baptism or not. In the Early Church, the bishop would lay hands on and anoint with oil the head of every catechumen who was presented for baptism. In the early medieval period, this rite was separated from baptism while theologians began to insist more that the rite was connected with the reception of the gift of the Holy Spirit. It then became common to speak of baptism as the sacrament of Christian (re)birth and confirmation as the sacrament of Christian maturity. Ideally speaking, the order of sacraments ought to be baptism, confirmation, and reception of holy communion.

In practice, apart from the full observance of the RCIA for those entering the Catholic Church as adults, it is most commonly the practice that Catholics baptized as infants receive the sacrament of reconciliation and holy communion before they are confirmed. Confirmation today is most commonly seen as a "rite of passage" which signifies the time when a young person "confirms" (strengthens) what was done in baptism, i.e. accepts the full Christian life. Most commonly, confirmation is done by a bishop (a simple priest may confirm when necessary or convenient) and involves the dual rite of laying on of hands and anointing with sacred oil (the oil is called *chrism*). As the bishop lays on hands and anoints, he says "Be sealed with the Holy Spirit." It is a common practice as well as a pious custom for candidates to choose a confirmation name – typically of a saint to whom they have a special devotion and whose virtues they hope to emulate. The person also chooses a sponsor at confirmation. Ideally, that person or persons would be the same ones who stood as godparents at baptism because that would symbolically link the two sacraments. The full meaning of this sacrament is economically expressed by the prayer of the bishop (with a direct echo of Isaiah 11) who extends his hands over those to be confirmed and prays aloud:

All-powerful God, Father of our Lord Jesus Christ,
By water and the Holy Spirit you freed your sons and daughters from sin
And gave them a new life.
Send your Holy Spirit upon them to be their helper and guide.
Give them the spirit of wisdom and understanding,
the spirit of right judgment and courage,
the spirit of knowledge and reverence.
Fill them with the spirit of wonder and awe in your presence.
We ask this through Christ Our Lord.

Like baptism, the rite of confirmation occurs only once, for, through this sacrament, the person is indelibly marked with the seal of the Holy Spirit which incorporates them fully as children of God and as full members of the congregation of the bishop in union with all other Catholics. The person thus sealed must have attained the age of reason, willingly profess the Catholic faith, and be ready, through God's grace, to accept the role of a true disciple of Christ and as a witness to Christ both in the Church and in the world. It is usual in almost all parishes for candidates who are to be confirmed to go through some catechetical instruction, and it is not uncommon for the bishop, when he comes to the parish, to quiz the candidates about their knowledge of the faith.

HOLY EUCHARIST

The sacraments of baptism and confirmation lead up to and find their fulfillment in the Holy Eucharist. That is why these three sacraments are called collectively the "sacraments of initiation." The eucharist is at the center of the life of the Church so its meaning and significance can be discussed under a number of headings.[1] Thus, words such as "eucharist," "holy communion," etc. are all different ways of speaking about a similar reality.

Eucharist as a symbolic meal

We can begin with the earliest text in the New Testament which deals with the eucharist. Writing in the early 50s to the Christian community in Corinth, Saint Paul said:

[1] As did the late Pope John Paul II in his 2003 encyclical letter *Ecclesia de Eucharistia* (*The Eucharistic Church*).

For I received from the Lord what I also handed on to you, that the Lord Jesus on the night before he was handed over, took bread, and after he had given thanks, broke it and said: "This is my body that is for you. Do this in remembrance of me." In the same way also the cup, after supper, saying: "This cup is the new covenant in my blood. Do this as often as you drink it in remembrance of me." For as often as you eat this bread and drink the cup, you proclaim the death of the Lord until he comes. (1 Cor. 11:23–6)

That text, in somewhat different words, is found also in the synoptic gospels of Mark, Matthew, and Luke. Allusions to Christ as bread, and to the breaking of the bread in conjunction with the act of thanksgiving (the word "eucharist" comes from the Greek work for giving thanks), are frequent in the New Testament. What seems to be going on here is quite simply this: On the night before his death, Jesus, at the close of a Passover meal, celebrated a rite involving bread and a cup of wine which he saw as being his body and his blood. He left this rite as a memorial of his own death and enjoined those who were with him to repeat this action in memory of him. Paul adds that this was something that he had received and handed on to the Church at Corinth and further explained that this was to be done until the Lord comes again (i.e. at the end of time at the Last Judgment).

Now what is striking about this and similar passages in the New Testament is the vivid realism with which Jesus identified this rite with his own body and blood. What the Catholic tradition has always maintained is that when the eucharist is celebrated, Christ is *truly* present although, clearly, under the appearances of bread and wine. Writing only a century or so after Paul, Justin Martyr, in his *Apology*, makes clear not only the nexus between baptism and eucharist but also states most clearly what was believed about the eucharist:

The food we call eucharist, of which no one is allowed to partake except one who believes that the things we teach are true, and has received the washing for forgiveness of sins and for rebirth, and who lives as Christ has handed down to us. For we do not receive these things as common food or common drink; but as Jesus Christ our savior being incarnate by God's word took flesh and blood for our salvation, so also we have been taught that the food consecrated by the word of prayer which comes from him, from which our flesh and blood are nourished by transformation, is the flesh and blood of that incarnate Jesus. (*Apology* 66)

The eucharist as sacrifice

Like all orthodox Christians, Catholics believe that Christ's sacrifice on the cross was a single, unrepeatable, and full sacrifice for the sins of humanity.

What, then, is the connection between the eucharist and the sacrifice of Christ on the cross? Why do Catholics call their central liturgical act the "Holy Sacrifice of the Mass"?

That Jesus had sacrificial emphases with respect to the Last Supper's institution of the eucharist seems clear. After all, the eucharist was instituted during a Passover meal whose central focus was the lamb slain for the feast. Paul would later make the link explicit: "Our paschal lamb, Christ, has been sacrificed" (1 Cor. 5:7). Mark tells us that when Jesus took the cup at the Last Supper he said over it, "This is my blood of the covenant which will be shed for many" (Mark 14:24). John says that the bread which Jesus gives "is my flesh for the life of the world" (John 6:51).

The Church, from its earliest centuries, began to understand the eucharistic liturgy as a sacrificial rite which made present the one sacrifice of Christ. Hence, the liturgy remembered, reenacted, re-presented, recalled, and made present in the eucharist is the sacrifice of Christ in time. So the Church offers again, through sacramental gesture, what Christ did in his passion and death. When Catholics attend the eucharistic liturgy, that make them contemporaneous with the death of Christ on the cross acted out by the consecration of the bread and wine, which is – not merely symbolized but *is* – the body and blood of Christ.

This sacrificial offering, done through the agency of the priest celebrant, is aptly summed up in words which are said in the eucharistic prayer known as the Roman Canon: "Father, we celebrate the memory of Christ, your Son. We your people and your ministers, recall his passion, his resurrection from the dead, and his ascension into glory; and from the many gifts you have given us we offer to you, God of glory and majesty, this holy and perfect sacrifice: the bread of life and the cup of eternal salvation." This "recalling" or, as it is called, *anamnesis* makes present sacramentally today what Christ did historically.

To underscore that the eucharist is a sacrifice, it is appropriate for the celebrant or president at the liturgy to be called a priest since a priest is, by definition, one who offers sacrifice. Similarly, it is preferable, in Catholic circles, to speak of an "altar" and not simply a "table" because an altar is the place where a sacrifice is made. To make this point is not to make a simple point about vocabulary. The classical reformers of the sixteenth century quite explicitly called their leaders pastors or ministers or preachers for the precise reason that they did not accept the notion of the mass as a sacrifice but as a memorial – a distinction of grave theological importance. Obviously, a Catholic priest ministers in a variety of ways, but, fundamentally, he is a priest who offers sacrifice.

The eucharist as liturgy

Holy communion refers to the eucharistic elements of the consecrated bread and wine which are distributed at the liturgy to the congregation or taken to those absent due, for example, to sickness or infirmity. In that sense, holy communion is part of the larger reality, which is the mass or the eucharistic liturgy. It is in the mass where the sacrament of the eucharist and the proclamation of the Gospel meet. Even though the mass has undergone a long historical evolution over the centuries, the two main parts go back to apostolic beginnings. The liturgy is divided into two major divisions:

1. The liturgy of the Word: The people gather for an opening prayer. There then follow readings from sacred scripture, a prayerful response to these readings typically taken from the Book of Psalms, a homily from the presider explicating or enlarging the readings, ending with a common profession of faith with the recitation of the Nicene Creed.[2]
2. The liturgy of the eucharist: The gifts of bread and wine are brought forward; the priest recites the eucharistic prayer (called the eucharistic *canon*), which concludes with the great Amen (the word means "so be it" – it is an affirmation of faith which means, in essence, "we affirm this"). The Lord's Prayer is recited in common, the kiss of peace is exchanged, holy communion is distributed, and the congregation is dismissed.

Over the centuries, elements accrued to this basic framework, but the basic distinction of liturgy of the Word and liturgy of the eucharist remains as the basic scaffold of the Sunday liturgy.

> The Roman Catholic Church celebrates the eucharistic liturgy in the vernacular language according to the reforms established at the Second Vatican Council. It is permissible also to celebrate the same liturgy in Latin according to the liturgical form established in the sixteenth century as part of the reforms of the Council of Trent. The sixteenth-century Council of Trent made its liturgical reforms mandatory for the entire Roman Catholic Church except for those religious orders (the Dominicans, Carmelites, and Carthusians) that were allowed to maintain their ancient liturgical practices. Some places in Europe also had an ancient liturgical tradition, and those traditions were maintained. They are the Ambrosian Rite in Milan, the Mozarabic Rite (Toledo, Spain), the Braga Rite (Portugal), and the rite(s) observed at the cathedral of Chartres. The Eastern Church, of course, has its own liturgical tradition.

[2] In many parishes the homily is preached by a deacon among whose duties is the office of preaching.

Real presence

The Catholic Church has always taught that Jesus Christ is truly present
in the Holy Eucharist. The elements of bread and wine are not mere
reminders or symbols but somehow are – to use Justin Martyr's phrase –
transformed into the body and blood of Christ. After all, Saint Paul
warned the Church at Corinth that "whoever eats the bread or drinks the
cup of the Lord unworthily will have to answer for the body and blood of
the Lord" (1 Cor. 11:27). The Catholic tradition affirms the presence of
the resurrected and glorified Christ in the gathered community at prayer,
when the Gospel is preached, and when he is called upon by the faithful
in time of need. Nonetheless, it has always been part of Catholic belief
that Christ is present in an intimate and real way in the eucharist.

The theological issue for Catholics is not that Christ is truly present in
the eucharist but how to explain that presence. It was not really until the
early Middle Ages that the question was discussed in any seriously systematic fashion. At the fourth Lateran Council in 1215, the Church used,
for the first time in a universal official magisterial document, the term
transubstantiation. The term, utilizing terminology derived from the
philosophy of Aristotle, argues that every reality has something that
makes it what it is and not something else (i.e. the breadness of bread
which distinguishes it from the treeness of a tree). That something is its
substance. Every substance has accidental qualities that specify the substance: weight, color, extension, etc. Transubstantiation is the theory that
says, in effect, that in the eucharist the substance of bread and wine are
changed into the substance of the person of Jesus Christ while the acci-
dents (taste, color, etc.) remain. In other words, the substance of one
thing – "breadness" – is changed into the substance of something else:
Jesus Christ. That understanding of the "how" of the eucharistic presence
was reaffirmed at the sixteenth-century Council of Trent against alternative theories proposed by Protestant reformers. That council insisted on
two things: (1) Christ is substantially present in the eucharist; and (2) that
the best way (*pace* Luther and others), the preferred way, of speaking
about that change is via the language of transubstantiation.

Although some twentieth-century Catholic theologians, uneasy with
the language of Aristotle and the physics undergirding it, have proposed
other understandings, to this date the Magisterium of the Church has
stood by the older understanding, resisting newer attempts at explain-
ing the "how" of Christ's sacramental presence in the eucharist. This

resistance to tampering with the language is best explained by the fear that were one to attempt new understandings of the "how," this could result in weakening the firm conviction of the Church that Christ is "truly" present in the eucharist.

The Catholic Church has traditionally "reserved" the eucharist in the church building to bring it to those who are sick and dying; this reserved eucharist is commonly known as *viaticum,* which means, beautifully enough, "bread for the journey." It is the custom to keep a lamp burning in the church to indicate that the eucharist is reserved, typically, in an ornate chest or box known as a tabernacle.

One development that evolved as a result of the Catholic emphasis on the real presence of Christ in the eucharist was a series of devotional practices that underscored this belief in the real presence of Christ: the custom of praying before a tabernacle where the eucharistic elements are preserved to carry them, when necessary, to the sick; the development of practices that "exposed" the eucharist for adoration; the blessing of people with the consecrated host in a vessel known as a monstrance, etc. Even the design of churches in the second millennium tended to place the tabernacle on the main altar for such extraliturgical practices, even though this had never been the custom earlier. Today, through the liturgical reforms of the Second Vatican Council, such tabernacles are more fittingly placed to the side of the main altar where the liturgy is celebrated or even, when feasible, in a side chapel as we have noted in an earlier chapter.

PENANCE/RECONCILIATION

The sacrament of penance, or, as it is more commonly called today, reconciliation, is the ritual act by which a person is reconciled to God and to the Christian community after the commission of personal sin. The history of the development of this sacrament is a very complex one because practices in the Early Church varied. Basically, the penitential rite in the early period, both in the East and West, was this: If a person committed a grave public sin (for example, apostasy in time of persecution, murder, adultery, etc.), that person could be readmitted to the worshiping congregation as a communicant only after a suitable period of penance. The act of reconciliation was a public one, done within the confines of the liturgy. Apparently, the rule was that a person could go through this rite only once in a lifetime although this one-time-only act was not uniformly observed. The high point of the ritual was the silent imposition of hands by the bishop on the penitent, which then meant that the person could again receive holy communion at the liturgy. Hence, before this public reconciliation was celebrated, it is correct to say that a person was "excommunicated" – literally "outside of communion."

Among the Celtic monks of Ireland, the common practice was for an individual to make a private confession to an abbot or to another monk, to receive a suitable penance, to perform it, and to rejoin the community as one forgiven. There was no stipulated public ceremony done within the liturgy itself, although it could occur. Through the missionary expansion of monks from Ireland south into Europe, this form of penance became more common, was extended beyond the monastic community to lay persons, and inevitably clashed with Roman reconciliation rites, which were public, once in a lifetime, and liturgical in their celebration.

The Celtic custom won out among the Christian people to the extent that the Fourth Lateran Council stipulated that every Christian should confess his or her sins each year to a duly authorized priest and receive holy communion. Medieval theologians regularized the form of private confession by outlining its main stages. The penitent should feel real sorrow for sins (contrition), confess them to a priest, receive absolution from the priest, and perform whatever penance the priest enjoined upon the penitent. That set of particulars has remained in the practice of Catholics down to this day.

The old "Act of Contrition," traditionally taught to every schoolchild and recited at the end of every confession, contains within it the Catholic understanding of both imperfect contrition (loss of salvation) and perfect contrition (love of God). It also ends with the essential conditions for the sacrament: confession, sorrow for sin, and willingness to do penance and to amend one's life:

O My God, I am truly sorry for having offended Thee
I detest all my sins because I dread the loss of Heaven and the pains of Hell
But most of all they offend Thee, My God, who are all good and deserving
   of all my love.
I firmly resolve, with the help of Thy grace, to confess my sins
to do penance, and to amend my life.
Amen.

The form of private confession described above made the priest the equivalent of a judge whose task it was to adjudicate the weight of a person's sin and to mete out an appropriate penance. It should be noted in passing that right down to the modern period it was thought possible to make a confession of one's sins to a fellow Christian as an act of piety. Saint Thomas Aquinas, in the supplement to the *Summa,* makes allowance for a non-priest to hear a person's confession, and, as late as the sixteenth century, there were instructions as to how this was to be done in the manuals of piety of the time.

About this sacrament known familiarly by Catholics as "going to confession" there arose a very complex set of laws to insure the integrity of the sacrament since it touched the personal lives of people so intimately. The Church very carefully regulated who could hear confessions (only duly trained priests authorized by a bishop); under what conditions they might hear confessions; where confessions were to be heard (confessionals and reconciliation rooms are of relatively modern vintage); the rights of people going to confession, etc. A paramount obligation of a confessor is confidentiality: Any confessor who hears confessions has a strict obligation never to reveal what he has heard in confession. Any confessor who breaches what is known as the "seal of confession" loses the right to hear confessions.

Although the norm today in the Catholic Church (at least in the Roman rite) is private confession of an individual to a priest (so-called *auricular* confession), there are allowances for communal penitential or reconciliation rites under carefully delineated conditions. The liturgical reforms of the Second Vatican Council did insist that the sacrament of reconciliation be so administered and celebrated to underscore that it is a liturgical action; that the place of scripture be made more apparent in its administration; and that while the form of confession may be private, the sacrament itself is a public rite in the Church. Hence, the increasing popularity of a communal rite of reconciliation followed, when possible, by the individual confession of sins. In fact, there is a brief penitential rite celebrated at the very beginning of the eucharistic liturgy which is part of every mass.

The intricate history of the development of the sacrament of penance was paralleled by a development in the field of moral theology and ethics which trained priests in their capacity as confessors; we will take up that issue in the chapter on Christian morality later in this volume since the rise of a separate branch of theology known as "moral theology" was closely connected to the increasing practice of private individual confession of sins in the sacrament of penance.

ANOINTING OF THE SICK

Already in the New Testament there were ritual moments for the care of the sick by the laying on of hands (see Mark 6:13) and the anointing with oil (James 5:13–16). For about eight centuries, it was customary for bishops to bless oil that the faithful, apparently, would keep in their homes to use when sickness befell someone in the household. A later development, linked to the custom of avoiding reconciliation until one was gravely ill, since it could be received only once, where a person would be anointed as part of the final rites for a dying person, led the anointing of the very sick to be reserved to a priest. It was out of this practice that there derived what was once commonly called "extreme unction," that is, the "last anointing." This sacrament was seen as one of the final rites performed before death. It was a sacrament that presumed a community (the family) that would gather for such a solemn moment.

Today, this sacrament emphasizes the efficacy of prayer for spiritual and physical healing as well as a support in the case of serious illness. Frequently, in parishes, the sacrament is offered at Sunday liturgies on certain occasions to all who feel the need of it either because of physical or spiritual ailment. When it involves a person who is gravely ill, it is part of a complex of rites that would include the sacrament of reconciliation, then the anointing of the sick, and the administration of holy communion. If the person is, in fact, dying, the ritual of the Church also provides a complex of beautiful prayers to be said to accompany a person who is undergoing his or her last agony. When it is feasible, the priest who comes to the home may perform these rites within the celebration of mass, which can be said at the home or in a care-giving facility.

Pastorally sensitive parishes have used this sacrament as a form of ritual for those who suffer from addiction or mental illness or some form of terrible inner trauma that afflicts people after loss or separation. All pastoral instructions insist that this sacrament be part of a larger care for those who are ill. The anointing of the sick is not meant to be an emergency one-time rite that substitutes for either other sacramental ministrations such as reconciliation and eucharist or as a substitute for prayerful care and visitation and support for those who are in need because of any of many forms of serious illness.

The *Catechism of the Catholic Church* rightly points out that the final anointing, as it were, completes the anointing done at baptism and confirmation, which "fortifies the end of the earthly life like a solid rampart for the final struggles before entering the Father's house" (No. 1523).

HOLY ORDERS

The precise relationship between the various forms of ministry mentioned in Paul's pastoral letters (1 and 2 Tim.; Titus) has been a subject of much scholarly discussion. What is clear is that by very early in the second century the three distinct orders of bishop, priest, and deacon had been fairly well sorted out. Writing around the year 115, Ignatius of Antioch wrote, "Let the bishop preside in God's place and the presbyters take the place of the apostolic council and let the deacons – my special beloved – to be entrusted with the ministry of Jesus Christ who was with the Father from eternity and appeared at the end time" (*Letter to the Magnesians,* VI).

The relationship of these three offices runs roughly in this order: The bishop presided over a given area as its chief minister, its authentic teacher and in his role as successor of the first Apostles. The presbyters (priests) ministered as an extension of the bishop's office in particular places within the jurisdiction of the bishop (later known as a diocese and a parish respectively), while the deacons oversaw the material goods of the Church and ministered works of charity for the Christian community. By the end of the second century, there was a clear distinction made, for example by the North African writer Tertullian (d.220), between an ecclesiastical order (i.e. the clergy) and the laity.

All three of these offices were made present through the laying on of hands already mentioned in the New Testament (which to this day is the essential gesture for all ordinations), and, by the Middle Ages, ordination to these offices was considered, in our modern understanding of the term, a sacrament. Though it was not universally held in the Middle Ages, it is now not only accepted but also taught by the Second Vatican Council authoritatively that the fullness of the sacrament of orders resides in the ordination of the bishop who is called upon to minister a threefold office of preaching and teaching, sanctifying (through the liturgical life of the Church), and governing the local church. Priests share in the sacrament of orders by being ordained ministers of God's word and ministers of the sacraments and as the spiritual fathers of the local community in which they serve under the jurisdiction of the bishop. The deacon is also ordained and serves as a liturgical minister (for example, baptizing and witnessing marriages), as a preacher of the Word, and exercising the ministry of service to those in need. For a very long period, deacons usually went on for priestly ordination, but Vatican II mandated the office of the permanent deacon who, unlike a priest, may be a married person. The office of deacon, permanent or transitional, is restricted to men, although there is clear evidence of deaconesses in the ancient Church. Whether or not the Church will restore the office of the deaconess, an office common in the Early Church, is a subject of much debate.

Over the course of the centuries, the offices of bishop, priest, and deacon went through many changes. In the first millennium, for example, priests could marry (as they still can in the Eastern Church before their ordination), but under the impetus of monasticism they were enjoined to celibacy for all priests of the Roman Rite. Celibacy became a general norm for all priests in the West only in the second millennium. Formal education for priests is a relatively new phenomenon as seminaries were founded as part of the Catholic reformation of the sixteenth century. As we saw, permanent deacons again became a reality in the past few generations and are trained in educational programs suited for their pastoral needs. Deacons today preside over funerals, can witness marriages, can baptize when a priest is absent – even though in an emergency any person may validly baptize – and are deputized to preach.

It should be noted that the Second Vatican Council did not see the laity as passive recipients of the ministry of those in holy orders. It reaffirmed the New Testament teaching that all baptized persons share in a common priesthood but insisted that from the body of the faithful certain people are called forth to serve the Church through a special ministry which serves all in the Church and is available to those who are ordained by the Church to serve as bishops, priests, and deacons. Bishops alone can confer the sacrament of orders.

The life of the Catholic bishop and priest is one that bears a long and complex history. Some of that history is precisely that: Bishops and priests of the Roman Rite are celibate, but that is a disciplinary practice and not essential to the sacrament. Bishops and priests take on many roles in the community simply as an offshoot of their status in society: They serve as spokesmen of the Church; they organize many activities in the church they serve; they are administrators, counselors, and so on. In the last analysis, however, their main task if they are bishops is to teach the faith authentically, to celebrate the liturgy and to assure its integrity, and to preside over the local church. The priests, by their ordination, share in that work of the bishop.

MATRIMONY

In a very fundamental sense, marriage is a primordial sacrament because the Bible teaches us that God himself created humans male and female and provided Adam with a companion, a helpmate with whom he would live until death. The story of Adam and Eve is not merely a little folk tale about beginnings. It is, rather, a profound theological statement about us as human beings: namely, that it is God's plan for a man and a woman to form that most primordial of relationships from which come the future generations of humanity. That conviction explains why the Catholic Church insists that marriage can only take place between a man and a woman. If a person denies himself or herself the privilege of marriage through a celibate life, it is not because marriage is bad but because it is good – a good one relinquishes for the Kingdom of God.

In the Catholic Church, the union of a man and woman who solemnly consent in a liturgical service to live together as man and wife out of mutual love and for the procreation and education of their children is a grace-filled state which the Church numbers among its sacraments.

For nearly 1,000 years of its existence, the Church allowed civil society and/or family customs to bear the prime responsibility for the rite of marriage even though from its earliest days the Church was ready to bless marriages. In the *Canterbury Tales,* the Wife of Bath mentions her marriages as having been blessed on the "threshold" of the church, which may mean that it was there that the blessing took place in lieu of any elaborate formal ceremony. The Church became more involved in marriage in the early Middle Ages. By the eleventh century, a church ceremony was obligatory for a valid marriage, and, by the twelfth century, there was a recognized rite for the celebration of marriage even though the rite was not always uniform everywhere in the Church. By the thirteenth century, marriage was included on the list of the seven sacraments. In his supplement to the *Summa,* Saint Thomas Aquinas notes that the mutual exchange of the spouses to enter into marriage, and not the blessing of the priest, constitutes the form of marriage. Another way of saying this is that the spouses confer the sacrament of marriage on each other. That is the common teaching of the Catholic Church to this day.

Because of grave abuses with secret marriages or clandestine ones (which could easily be repudiated, with the repudiation almost always to the detriment of the woman), the Church, in the sixteenth century, laid down the rule that it would not recognize as valid or sacramental any marriage that was not celebrated before a priest and two witnesses. It is important to note that the priest is not the minister of the sacrament but its official witness: The couples are the ministers of the sacrament. That general rule has been observed in the Catholic Church until this day.

Theologically speaking, the Catholic Church sees marriage and the family that is the normal consequence of marriage as a domestic church. That is to say, the Church sees one of the foundational elements of the Catholic community to be the family, spouses married by mutual consent and graced by Christ in the Church, as the first place where the faith is taught, nurtured, and sustained. The family is sometimes called, in Catholic writing, the "domestic church."

The Catholic Church today is vehement about the rights of parents to be the primary educators of their children. It regards marital infidelity or family discord or neglect as detrimental not only to those involved but also to the Church and to society as a whole. Consequently, it affirms the Gospel teaching about the permanence of the marriage bond and the caution it enjoins on Catholics who wish to marry outside the faith. Because of these convictions, and in the face of failing marriages in Western society, Church law typically requires some premarital counseling before a sacramental marriage is celebrated.

The Church recognizes as permanent any sacramental marriage between two baptized persons. Hence, the Catholic Church does not permit divorce and remarriage while a legitimate spouse is still alive. There are provisions made in the Code of Canon Law for the annulment of marriages for certain reasons; those annulments are declared through the tribunals of the Church, with each diocese having its own tribunal. The increase of broken marriages in contemporary society has brought to the fore vexatious issues of what to do about irretrievably broken marriages: Can a person, for instance, receive holy communion if that person has remarried after a divorce, especially if that person has lived in complete fidelity to the spouse in a second marriage and was, to make the case harder, the innocent party in the divorce? Under the current discipline, the person should not receive communion, but the issue is so difficult and compelling that many think that the issue should be revisited. While there may be compelling civil reasons for people to go through a civil divorce in those places where it is permissible under law, the Church does not accept that such a civil procedure gives one the right, in the eyes of the Church, to enter a second marriage.

SACRAMENTALITY

In the opening chapter of this work, we noted that sacramentality is one of the signal characteristics of Catholicism. Older catechisms defined sacraments as "outward signs of an inward grace," which meant that there is something visible that mediates God's presence and favor to us. We have already noted that in a broad sense creation itself is a sacrament in that creation lets the goodness of the creator shine forth. The final warrant for Catholicism's confidence in the sacramental is to be found in its faith that what the first chapter of the book of Genesis says is true, namely, that when God called forth creation it was pronounced to be good. The goodness of that creation in general and the creation of humans in particular is triply underscored by the fact that God became man in Jesus Christ; he is the Word made flesh. Of course, the consequence of that central fact of Christianity is, again to repeat, that Christ is the great sacrament. By his incarnation, Christ reveals God's love for us. God shines forth through the flesh in the person of Jesus.

When we look at the seven traditional sacraments of the Church, it becomes clear that they are closely aligned to the journey of a life. The three sacraments of initiation – baptism, confirmation, eucharist – give us new life as we enter and mature in our natural life. Reconciliation and anointing of the sick are remedies for our weak human condition, while matrimony is crucial for the social well-being of human society and holy orders keep intact the apostolic work of the Church throughout history. In that restricted sense, sacraments in the Church can be seen as rites of passage, beginning with birth, extending through one's lifetime, and ending with death.

It should also be noted that the sacramental system is the work of the Church at prayer; sacraments are closely tied to the liturgical life of the Church. All the sacraments flow from the first one, which is baptism. Only baptized persons can receive the other sacraments. While the Catholic Church permits a Catholic to marry a non-baptized person when certain stipulations are observed, it does not consider such marriages, though legally valid, to be sacramental. Much emphasis is placed on not letting the administration of the sacraments be perceived as private affairs. The Church prefers that when people are baptized, confirmed or reconciled to the Church that it be done as a public act and, when possible, in the context of a public liturgical ceremony.

The confidence that Catholicism has in the sacramental – in the mediating power of physical reality – also explains why historically and actually the Church is so sympathetic to anything that touches our senses in a way to remind us of the presence of God. Hence, from the beginning, Catholicism has had a sympathy for the visual, by making use of art and artifact, and the auditory, in encouraging music and chant and the tactile in the generous use of gesture in liturgical celebrations.

SACRAMENTALS

Catholicism clearly distinguishes *sacrament* and *sacramental*. The former are the seven traditional signs which effect what they signify; they are efficacious. Sacramentals, by contrast, are those signs which may be the occasion for greater piety or religious observance. They point to something of faith or observance. There is a huge repository of such sacramentals in the Catholic Church, with many of them being extremely familiar to the degree that they have almost become badges of being a Catholic: making the sign of the cross; the wearing of a religious medal; using holy water; being marked by ashes at the beginning of the Lenten season; displaying a crucifix in a home or a classroom in a Catholic school; the use of "holy cards" etc. Other sacramentals are common across traditions but have a specific context that reflects their status as a Catholic sacramental: the blessing of wedding rings in a marriage ceremony; a Catholic formula for prayers before meals; the reverence shown to the book of scriptures; gestures of reverence in prayer, etc. In a recent manual issued by the Catholic bishops of the USA, *Catholic Household Blessings and Prayers,* there is a whole range of blessings and rituals for various moments in life which may be utilized by people to sanctify further their individual and familial lives.

Some of these sacramentals are very ancient in the Church. Making the sign of the cross is alluded to as early as the second century. Others developed in the course of time. Sacramentals allow for a great deal of flexibility; they are constantly invented as the Church makes use of the familiar symbols, gestures, practices, etc., of a given culture. Catholic people have frequently adapted such sacramentals according to the prevailing custom of a given area. Others have died out in the course of time. In many homes, even in the recent past, pious Catholics lit candles in times of storms, kept a stoop of holy water at the entrance of the house, etc., with those customs now not commonly found.

One could also add that the ceremonial aspects of the liturgy – processions, lighted candles, and so on – can be understood as sacramentals in that they are all signs and symbols to enhance the solemnity of the liturgical worship we direct to God. Sacramentals can be understood as reflective of the popular piety of Christians throughout the ages. In addition to the formal liturgical worship of the Church discussed in this chapter, there is also a vast web of devotional practices which have been part of the worship of Catholics either individually or in the Church as communal activities. Catholics historically have made pilgrimages; they gather for reciting the rosary; they pray at home; they teach their children to pray before going to bed and when getting up. The Church encourages people to pray before meals. They adorn their homes with sacred images.

Some of these customs are very ancient. Tertullian, at the end of the second century, refers to the making of the sign of the cross. Other customs, such as making the stations of the cross as an individual or as a group are of more recent vintage. Various devotions in honor of the Blessed Virgin Mary or the saints and angels have a more distant past. Since Catholicism puts a high premium on visible signs of devotion of many kinds, there is, of course, the danger that these pious practices can quickly turn into superstition or quasi-magical formulae. The Catholic tradition is not insensitive to these dangers. Writers on the eve of the Protestant Reformation mercilessly criticized such superstitious practices as a quick perusal of Erasmus of Rotterdam's *Praise of Folly* attests. The Catholic Church, sensitive to the even more critical rejection of popular practices, made it a point, in the twenty-fifth session of the Council of Trent, to condemn such superstitions: "all superstition must be removed from the invocation of the saints, veneration of relics, and use of sacred images," lamenting the tendency to turn feast days into "drunken feasting" or celebrations of "sensual luxury" (Pelikan II: 871), while still affirming the legitimacy of such devotions, images, relics, and so on.

Anyone who inspects a parish bulletin today will find a wide variety of pious practices suited to the tastes of members of the Church. They might run from bible study or Twelve Step Programs to charismatic prayer groups, communal recitation of the rosary or other pious practices. On the matter of pious devotion, the Church invokes the old principle that in matters of faith there should be unity; in matters of non-essentials there should be liberty; but in all things there should be charity.

Box 5   The liturgy of the hours

One other part of the official liturgy – the public worship of the Church – is the so-called liturgy of the hours which is also commonly known as the *divine office*. In the Early Church, we have evidence that Christians would gather for common prayer in the morning and evening perhaps in imitation of the Jewish custom of reciting the twice-daily prayer formula "Hear, O Israel" from Deuteronomy (6:4–9) known from its first Hebrew word *Shema*. After the edict of toleration issued by Constantine in the early fourth century, this became a common feature in churches, especially in cathedral churches presided over by a bishop. There are some indications that there were also

Box 5 (cont.)
night vigil prayers to mark the coming of the Lord's Day. These communal prayers in churches can be distinguished by the common prayers of monks – the monastic office – which would punctuate the hours of the day. Both the cathedral offices and the monastic ones had a complex evolution which is well beyond our scope to detail.

While the various hours are different in both length and structure, the one thing that they do have in common is that at their heart they make use of the psalms as the basic unit of prayer with readings from scripture and canticles from the same source. Vespers (evening prayer) in a typical parish might have the following order:

• opening prayer followed by a hymn;
• the singing of two or three psalms;
• the singing of the *Magnificat* (Mary's hymn in Luke's Gospel: 1:46–55);
• a final closing prayer.

Morning prayer (called *lauds*) has the same basic structure, but the canticle of Zechariah called the *Benedictus* (Luke 1:68–179) is sung in place of the Magnificat.

The actual situation in the Catholic Church today is that members of religious orders of both men and women recite the hours in common on a daily basis. Diocesan priests are obligated to recite the hours but do so on a private basis using a book known as a *breviary*. Cathedral offices are still recited in some places when the cathedral has canons (clergy who are attached to and minister at a cathedral or a major basilica), and, frequently, laypersons, who have no obligation to do so, use the canonical hours for their own prayer. The Second Vatican Council has encouraged churches to provide for liturgical prayer on some kind of basis, for example, by having vespers (evening prayer) on Sundays. It is also becoming more common for ordinary Catholics to make use of the liturgy of the hours in some modified form, such as the recitation of morning and evening prayers, as part of their own devotional life.

In monasteries where the hours are observed in the full, a typical daily routine might look something like this:

• Vigils (sometimes called matins): early morning before dawn.
• Lauds (sometimes called morning prayer): at dawn or shortly thereafter.
• Prime: the first hour of the day (now largely suppressed).
• Tierce (the third hour): around 9 A.M.
• Sext (the sixth hour): around noontime.
• None (ninth hour): around 3 P.M.
• Vespers (dusk): in the early evening.
• Compline (night prayer): before retiring for the night.

FURTHER READING

Chauvet, Louis-Marie, *The Sacraments: The Word of God at the Mercy of the Body* (Collegeville, Minn.: Liturgical Press, 2001). Excellent work by renowned scholar.

Conference of Catholic Bishops, *Catholic Household Blessings and Prayers*, rev. edn (Washington, DC: United States Conference of Catholic Bishops, 2007).

Jones, C., ed., *The Study of Liturgy* (Oxford: Oxford University Press, 1992). Excellent survey in encyclopedia form.

Fink, Peter, *The New Dictionary of Sacramental Worship* (Collegeville, Minn.: Glazier/Liturgical Press, 1990). Reliable one-volume encyclopedia.

Ganoczy, Alex, *An Introduction to Catholic Sacramental Theology* (New York, N.Y.: Paulist, 1988). Standard introduction by a European theologian.

Jungmann, Josef, *The Mass of the Roman Rite* (Westminster, Md.: Christian Classics, 1986). The classic historical study of the Catholic mass.

Kaska, John C., *Understanding Sacramental Healing* (Chicago, Ill.: Hillenbrand, 2006). A pastoral work on the sacramental care of the sick.

Osborne, Kenan, *The Christian Sacraments of Initiation* (New York, N.Y.: Paulist, 1987). The three sacraments of baptism, confirmation, and eucharist considered as a whole.

Osborne, Kenan, *The Permanent Diaconate* (New York, N.Y.: Paulist, 2007). Important study of this restored office.

Power, David, *The Eucharistic Mystery* (New York, N.Y.: Crossroad, 1992). Excellent theological study.

Power, David, *Sacrament: The Language of God's Giving* (New York, N.Y.: Crossroad, 1999). An insightful survey volume.

Seasoltz, Kevin, *God's Gift Giving: In Christ and Through the Spirit* (London and New York, N.Y.: Continuum, 2007). The sacraments studied under the rubric of gift.

Vorgrimler, Herbert, *Sacramental Theology* (Collegeville, Minn.: Liturgical Press, 1992). A standard handbook on the subject.

Vosko, Richard, *God's House Is Our House* (Collegeville, Minn.: Liturgical, 2007). On liturgical architecture today and historically considered; informative.

Wainwright, Geoffrey and Westerfield Tucker, Karen B., eds, *The Oxford History of Christian Worship* (Oxford: Oxford University Press, 2005). An encyclopedic history of Christian worship in an ecumenical context.

CHAPTER 6

The rule of faith

INTRODUCTION

Every religious body has some kind of standard of belief that is frequently reducible to a core statement that attempts to capture the essence of what that body stands for. For Buddhism, it consists of the "Four Noble Truths" about suffering and its remedy, while for Jews it is the daily repeated prayer or act of faith, drawn from the Torah, known as the *Shema*: "Hear, O Israel, the Lord is our God, the Lord alone. You shall love the Lord your God with all your heart, and with all your soul, and with all your might" (Deut. 6:4). In Islam, the basic creed is simplicity itself: "There is but one God (Allah), and Mohammad is his prophet." Behind those simple formulas, of course, is a fuller body of doctrine that answers questions of inquiring minds: What does this or that phrase mean? Why should it be believed? How does it apply to our daily lives, etc? In other words, simple statements of belief cannot be seen in the abstract. They are uttered by real people in real circumstances and have behind them a complex of rites, convictions, ideas, and moral imperatives.

The earliest writings of the Christian community, the various letters that Saint Paul wrote to Church communities, already reflect disputes about what it meant to be a follower of Jesus. Did these followers have to follow the prescriptions of the Jewish law? Did they have to be circumcised if they were male? Did they have to follow the Jewish dietary laws? In addition, it is clear that there were different nuances about what formed the basic beliefs of those who were followers of Jesus who was called the Christ. Writing only a little more than a generation after the earthly life of Jesus, Paul urged unity and not dissension for the community at Corinth: "I urge you, brothers, in the name of our Lord Jesus Christ, that all of you agree in what you say and that there be no divisions among you, but that you be united in the same mind and in the same purpose" (1 Cor. 1:10).

Later in that same epistle, Paul mounted a lengthy argument to persuade doubters in that same community that Jesus really rose from the dead: "For I handed on to you as of first importance what I also received: That Christ died for our sins in accordance with the scriptures; that he was buried; that he was raised on the third day in accordance with the scriptures" (1 Cor. 15:3–4). In fact, in that very brief passage, one can sense a faint echo of a statement of faith which Paul received and which he handed on to the Corinthians: Christ died, Christ was buried, Christ was raised – and all of this fulfilled what had been written in the scriptures.

There are no set formulas of faith in the New Testament, but one can glean from passing statements and from rhetorical rebuttals of those who held erroneous ideas that there was a kind of core or series of fundamental statements which the New Testament refers to as the "Good News," the Gospel. In the Acts of the Apostles, for example, there are six discourses (2:22–4; 3:12–26; 4:8–12; 5:29–32; 10:34–43; 13:16–41) which, while somewhat differently phrased in words, do reiterate same major points. Modern scholars call these the *kerygma,* from the Greek word for "proclamation" and think them to be a short summary of early Christian faith. The main points of these discourses, when compared one to the other, are the following:

1. Jesus was a man who did mighty deeds and signs by the power of God.
2. This man was delivered up to death by crucifixion.
3. God raised him up on the third day after his death.
4. We (the Apostles) are witnesses to this reality.
5. Belief in this risen Lord will save you from your sins.
6. All these things were witnessed to, and anticipated by, the ancient prophets of Israel.

It is possible to see in that brief summary above a kind of outline for the written Gospels which, undoubtedly, were narrative expansions of these core beliefs. Nonetheless, there is nothing systematic about either the written Gospels or the corpus of writings of Paul and the others which make up what we call the New Testament. In fact, that same New Testament gives ample proof, as we have seen above, that within the communities of early believers there were many who were at odds with each other about the precise character of Jesus Christ, his message, his demands, and his ultimate significance. Not to put too fine a point on it: The Jesus of John's Gospel reflects a different "portrait" to that of the Synoptics.[1]

---

[1] This is not to say that one cannot find some unifying threads in this diversity; see Frank J. Matera, *New Testament Theology: Exploring Diversity and Unity* (Louisville, Ky. and London: Westminster/ John Knox, 2007).

In general, the main lines of the *kerygma* outlined above form the core of Christian belief, but how that faith was to be formulated more precisely was the fruit of struggle for both clarifying the meaning of Jesus as Christ and deepening the meaning of the teaching and acts of Jesus himself. The only thing that the New Testament was in total agreement on was that Jesus in his life, suffering, death, and resurrection was at the core of the faith of those who were the followers of his way.

A CREED EMERGES

We know both from the New Testament and from the practice of the Early Church that the crucial symbolic rite by which a person entered into the Christian community was through a ritual washing called baptism (from the Greek *baptizein,* "to plunge [into water]"). This rite was accompanied by the invocation of Father, Son, and Holy Spirit (see Matt. 28:19) and was freighted with high symbolic meaning which linked the rite of going down into the waters and coming up as a kind of death and rebirth analogous to the death, burial, and resurrection of Jesus. That rite was explored in more detail in the previous chapter.

The issue for the Early Church was this: Who was worthy to receive this rite, which incorporated one into the Christian community? Writing in the second century, Justin Martyr says that those who are "convinced and believe what we say and teach is the truth and pledge themselves to be able to live accordingly" are led to the waters, after fasting and prayer, and are regenerated "In the name of God the Father and Lord of all, and of our savior, Jesus Christ, and of the Holy Ghost" (*Apology,* Chapter 61). Justin goes on to say that this washing is called *photismos,* "illumination," because they now can see a new way and are freed from their sins. This person, he concludes, is baptized in Jesus Christ "who was crucified under Pontius Pilate and in the name of the Holy Spirit" who "predicted through the prophets everything concerning Jesus" (*Apology,* Chapter 61). In other words, only those who subscribed to what the community believed were worthy of undergoing the rite of washing and illumination. It was necessary, in Justin's words, to be "convinced and believe what we say and teach" (*Apology,* Chapter 61). Justin's point about what is required before baptism should not be overlooked: One must agree with the community's teaching before being baptized.

On good evidence from the early third century on, the affirmation of faith as a prelude to baptism was done in the form of an interrogation. *The Apostolic Tradition* (*c.* AD 215), ascribed to Hippolytus of Rome, describes a triple immersion, with each immersion accompanied by a question and a response:

1. Do you believe in God the Father Almighty? (I do believe.)
2. Do you believe in Christ Jesus, the Son of God who was born of the Holy Spirit and the Virgin Mary who was crucified under Pontius Pilate and was dead and buried and ascended into heaven and sat down at the right hand of the Father and who will come again to judge the living and the dead? (I do believe.)
3. Do you believe in the Holy Spirit, the holy church, and the resurrection of the body? (I do believe.)

(Pelikan I: 12–13)

Variations of that triple formula, rooted in a tripartite affirmation of Father, Son, and Holy Spirit, provide the matrix from which all other attestations of faith emerge. These affirmations are often called the rule (Latin: *regula;* Greek: *kanon*) of faith, which is to say, the measurement by which the community attests that someone is "of the faith." Interestingly enough, that triple interrogation is still used today in the Roman Catholic rite of baptism directed either to the person who presents him or herself for baptism or through a proxy (the godparents) in the case of the baptism of an infant.

Perhaps the most common of these creeds, which is still used in the Christian West in a formulaic articulation, is the so-called *Apostles' Creed.* Most likely based on an old Roman baptismal creed in use as early as the second century, it was well known in various forms in the Early Church. An early legend claims that it was written by the Apostles themselves (each contributing a line), but this is surely not the case. It is the creed upon which earlier catechetical instruction was given, and its universal popularity has made it one of the most-recited creeds among Catholics (for example, it is the beginning prayer of the recitation of the rosary). Its authority is such that it is almost universally accepted by all creedal Christian Churches as an ecumenical statement and a prayer for use in common. Here is that creed in a traditional twelve-line version:

I believe in God the Father Almighty, Creator of heaven and earth.
And in Jesus Christ his only Son, our Lord,
Who was conceived of the Holy Spirit, born of the Virgin Mary,
Suffered under Pontius Pilate, was crucified, died and was buried; he
   descended into hell.
On the third day he rose from the dead;
He ascended into heaven, sits at the right hand of God the Father Almighty.

Thence he shall come to judge the living and the dead.
I believe in the Holy Spirit,
The holy, catholic church, the communion of saints.
The forgiveness of sins,
The resurrection of the body,
and the life everlasting. Amen. (Pelikan I: 669)

COUNCILS AND CREEDS

The simple assertion that Christians confess "Father, Son, and Holy
Spirit" brought with it a number of vexatious problems in the Early
Church. The mention of the three persons was used in baptism on the
warrant of the New Testament itself (see Matt. 28:19); prayers were
directed to them ("to the Father," "through the Son," "in the Holy
Spirit"), and so on. For pagans, it could be taken to mean that Christians
were polytheists because they invoked three different words: "father,"
"son," "spirit." For Jews, such an affirmation of belief meant that the
oneness of God was compromised. It was left to Christian thinkers both
to refute the charge of polytheism and to articulate how one could speak
of three and still affirm the one God of the biblical tradition. Various
attempts were made to solve these problems. Maybe the one God
appeared in three different guises (modalism); perhaps the Father took on
the "form" of Jesus and simply appeared to be a human person (patri-
passionism; various forms of gnosticism); perhaps Jesus was not really
equal to the Father but was only the first born of creation (arianism).
None of these models seem to fit the witness either of the Church's
preaching or the testimony of scripture. It seemed clear that the scriptures
clearly distinguished the three while insisting on the oneness of God.

It also seemed obvious that Jesus made claims of divinity but, equally
obviously, he was a real person who was born, lived, suffered, and died.
How was a person to put into one formula the seemingly paradoxical
claims of scripture that the man Jesus, who was hungry, thirsty, weary at
times, given to emotions, capable of suffering and death, was the same
person who could take to himself the sacred phrase "I am," which was
God's self-revelation in the Book of Exodus; who was described, in the
prologue to John's Gospel as the Word who was "with God" and "was
God." The opening verse of John's Gospel seemed to make three high
claims: "In the beginning was the Word" (existence); "The Word was
with God" (relationship); "The Word was God" (predication). Even
more stunningly is an assertion later in that opening chapter: "And the
Word became flesh and made his dwelling among us" (John 1:14).

These matters were debated ferociously in the first centuries of Christianity's life, but it was only in the early fourth century, shortly after Emperor Constantine granted toleration to the Christian Church, that clear fractures broke out that threatened the unity of the Church. Fomented under the leadership of a priest in Alexandria named Arius, who taught that the Word (*logos*) was subordinate to God the Father (his famous catchphrase was "There was a time when the Son was not"), his ideas soon spread all over the Christian East (and later to the West) to a degree that there were large competing factions within the Church that were either for or against Arius's take on the matter. Vexed by this disorder, the Emperor demanded that the bishops convoke a general council to settle the issue and to bring order to the divided Church. The issue before this council was simple enough even though the issues seemed complicated: What is the faith of the Christian Church?

Hundreds of bishops, mainly from the East, with the bishop of Rome represented by two delegates as well as the Spanish theologian Hosius of Cordoba, met in Nicaea (modern Iznik in Turkey) in 325. After much debate, the bishops declared that the Son was of the same substance (*homoousios*) as the Father and inserted that word (daringly, since it is not a biblical word) into a creed which was in use in Palestine. Nearly sixty years later, in AD 381, a second general council was held in Constantinople to further clarify the Church's understanding of the Son and to clarify the status of the Holy Spirit. At the conclusion of that council, an expanded creed, rooted in the faith expressed at Nicaea, was issued. That creed, often but misleadingly, called the Nicene Creed, is the one that is used by the Roman Catholic, Orthodox, and all creedal Protestants to this day. It is the creed which is commonly recited at the Sunday liturgy in all Catholic churches, although some countries also use the Apostles' Creed. That creed, in the version used in the Catholic liturgy, reads:

> We believe in one God, the Father, the Almighty,
> Maker of heaven and earth
> Of all that is seen and unseen.
> We believe in one Lord, Jesus Christ,
>
> The only Son of God,
> Eternally begotten of the Father
> God from God, Light from Light
> True God from true God,
> Begotten not made, one in Being[2] with the Father,

[2] In Greek: *homoousios*.

Through whom all things were made.
For us men and for our salvation
He came down from heaven:
By the power of the Holy Spirit,
He was born of the Virgin Mary, and became man.
For our sake he was crucified under Pontius Pilate;
He suffered, died, and was buried.
On the third day he rose again
In fulfillment of the scriptures;
He ascended into heaven
And is seated at the right hand of the Father.
He will come again in glory to judge the living and the dead,
And his kingdom will have no end.

We believe in the Holy Spirit, the Lord, the giver of Life,
Who proceeds from the Father [and the Son][3]
With the Father and Son he is worshiped and glorified.
He has spoken through the prophets.
We believe in only, holy, catholic, and apostolic church.
We acknowledge one baptism for the forgiveness of sins.
We look for the resurrection of the dead,
And the life of the world to come. Amen.

That creed attained such authority that at the Council of Ephesus in 431 the bishops issued a canon (law) that forbade the writing of any other creed to replace it; in fact, that made it the criterion for conversion to Christianity in quite solemn terms: "Any who dare to compose or bring forth or produce another creed for the benefit of those who wish to turn from Hellenism or Judaism or some other heresy to the knowledge of the truth, if they are bishops or clerics they should be deprived of their respective charges and if they are laymen they are to be anathematized" (Pelikan: I, 167).

When one looks carefully at the Nicene Creed, it is clear that within it are a number of fundamental doctrinal points. First, it is a trinitarian creed in that it invokes Father, Son, and Holy Spirit. That trinitarian affirmation mirrors the three questions asked of those who were to be baptized, since the Nicene Creed is based on an old baptismal creed. Second, in its declarations about Jesus Christ, it is at pains to affirm both his transcendental character and his historical reality. Finally, it ends with expectations about the future wherein we will live in the life of the world

---

[3] "And the Son" was added to the creed by the Latin Church; it is not found in the Orthodox creed; its addition is a matter of grave theological contention between East and West.

to come and, in that fashion, circles back to God who is invoked in the opening sentence of the creed.

Even though that creed (commonly known as the Nicene Creed) became and remains the gold standard, this did not mean, of course, that general councils of bishops could not amplify or deepen doctrinal points that arose because of misinterpretation or outright heresy. Indeed, at the same council of Ephesus, the bishops repudiated the teaching of Nestorius (d.451), the patriarch of Constantinople, who taught that there were two persons in Christ. He further taught that Mary was the mother of the human Christ but not the mother of the incarnate Word. He insisted that Mary be called "Christ Bearer" and not "God Bearer" (in Greek: *theotokos;* in Latin: *deipara*). The bishops rejected that notion and reaffirmed that Mary was *Theotokos*.[4] In their final formula, they insisted that they would not add to the creed but would provide a

full statement, even as we (i.e. the fathers of the council) have received and possess it from of old from the Holy scriptures and from the tradition of the holy fathers, adding nothing at all to the creed put forward by the holy fathers at Nicaea . . . which is sufficient both for the knowledge of godliness and for the repudiation of all heretical false teaching. (Pelikan: I, 169)

Twenty years later, at the next general (ecumenical) council held in a suburb of Constantinople called Chalcedon, the gathered fathers clarified the person of Jesus Christ by stipulating that he possessed two natures – human and divine – in one person and that the two natures in that one person undergo no "confusion, no change, no division, no separation" but "come together in a single person and a single subsistent being; he is not parted or divided into two persons" (Pelikan: I, 181). This classic definition of what is called the *hypostatic union* would stand as the single most important definition of the Catholic doctrine of the person of Jesus Christ. However, the fathers at Chalcedon did not add to the creed but simply reiterated what had been said at Ephesus, namely, that the Nicene Creed is the sufficient articulation of the Catholic faith and required no additions or emendations.

It may be well to stop at this point to make a few observations about the emergence of the rule of faith from the first ecumenical councils in the first five centuries of Christianity since they form one of the bedrock points of Catholicism's self-understanding.

[4] The term *theotokos* had been used before that time; see the interesting article by my colleague Max Johnson: "*Sub tuum praesidium:* The *Theotokos* in Christian Life and Worship Before Ephesus," *Pro Ecclesia*, 17, 1 (2008): 52–75.

1. While the items in the creed are propositional statements they are meant only as the minimum requirements for orthodoxy. As Saint Augustine famously said, the creed "is for the benefit of beginners and those still on milk food; reborn in Christ, they have yet to be strengthened by a detailed spiritual study and knowledge of the divine scriptures and so are presented with the essentials of faith in a few sentences" (*Faith and the Creed* 1.1).[5] The creeds neither stop further clarification (in fact, the deliberations at Ephesus and Chalcedon were exercises in clarification) nor did they block the work of writers and thinkers within the community to enlarge upon or clarify or further amplify what the creeds said in bare propositions.

2. The creeds adopted at the early councils reflect the consensus of bishops who must be understood not as atomized individuals with each speaking on their own but as representing the common faith of the Churches over which they had jurisdiction. In other words, their authority was linked to both their perceived relationship to the first Apostles who handed on the faith (which is why the creed affirms its belief in the apostolic Church) and their role as defender and teacher of that apostolic faith.

3. Creeds had their origin in worship – they were part of the rite of baptism and subsequently became part of the eucharistic liturgy as a sign of the common faith of those who gathered in worship. The nexus between worship and faith was discussed in Chapter 5, but it is worth noting a dictum which was developed a bit after these first councils, namely, that the "rule of worship undergirds the rule of belief" (in Latin: *lex orandi statuit lex credendi* [and vice versa]).

It is worthwhile noting that the Catholic Church is notoriously conservative with respect to the public worship of the Church (known as the liturgy) for the precise reason that public worship reflects the faith of the Church. In the contemporary Catholic Church, all variations of the order of worship, all translations of liturgical texts, etc., must ultimately be submitted to the authority of Rome for the precise reason that liturgy is a vehicle for the expression of faith. The traditional character of Catholic worship and the zeal with which that character is maintained reflect a deep conviction that there must be symmetry between right worship and right belief as the very meaning of the word "orthodox" implies.

---

[5] Augustine's words most likely reflect the custom of teaching the creed during the baptismal rites for new Christians.

The term "magisterium"

Catholics often refer to the magisterium. As the word is used today, it refers to the authoritative teaching office of the bishops who are the legitimate successors of the Apostles. The "ordinary" magisterium of the Church refers to the common teaching of the bishops dispersed in the world. Each bishop is the legitimate teacher in his own place but also exercises his teaching function as part of the College of Bishops. The "extraordinary" magisterium refers to the College of Bishops in union with the bishop of Rome (the pope) when they gather in an ecumenical council. The object of their teaching concerns only matters related to faith or morals.

The magisterial task is to listen to the Word of God, to guard it, to explain it faithfully and to hand it down faithfully. The magisterium does this, as the Dogmatic Constitution on Divine Revelation at the Second Vatican Council says, both by divine commission and with the aid of the Holy Spirit. When the magisterium speaks definitively on a matter of faith and morals, it does so, aided by the Holy Spirit, in an infallible (i.e not leading the Church into error) fashion.

THE POPE AND THE RULE OF FAITH

If there is one thing that every person knows it is that the pope in Rome plays a conspicuous role in the Catholic Church. Most people also know that the pope claims to be "infallible," but most people, including many Catholics, only have a hazy idea of what that might mean. What is the connection between the papal office and the College of Bishops with respect to the rule of faith?

First, we need to stipulate that the pope becomes pope by being elected to the office of bishop of Rome. Catholics believe that Peter, the first of the Apostles, died as a martyr in Rome and that his successors are the bishops of that city. In the early centuries of Christianity, the preeminent authority of the bishop of Rome derived from the fact that he represented the apostolic succession of Peter. When Pope Leo wrote his famous *Tome* in the fifth century to the gathered bishops at the Council of Chalcedon (the treatise which formed the basis for the doctrine of Christ stipulated there), it was said that "Peter has spoken through Leo." Thus, the bishop of Rome is not someone beyond the College of Bishops but a part of it. It is Catholic belief that one of the marks of catholicity is the unity of all bishops within the College of Bishops and with the bishop of Rome as the linchpin and center of that unity. In other words, each Catholic bishop must be in union with all other Catholic bishops, and they, in turn, must be in union with the bishop of Rome. The crucial role of the pope as the source and expression of episcopal unity is called the *primacy of the pope*. The papal duty, among others, is to maintain the unity of the Church, and so the pope has been self-described since the time of Pope Gregory the Great as the "servant of the servants of God."

Second, for historical and social reasons which we noted early in the second chapter of this text but which are far too complex to describe here, papal authority and prestige grew over the centuries so that certain activities once done at a more local or regional level (for example, the naming of bishops, the canonization of saints, the supervision of liturgical books, etc.) became centralized in Rome. Much of that centralizing authority is historical at root and could conceivably be modified as even papal documents have suggested but the core belief that the bishop of Rome is the center of episcopal unity and the role of the pope in keeping that unity intact (for example, an ecumenical council could not be called without the consent and participation of the papal office) are essential aspects of what Catholicism is all about. It goes to the very heart of Catholicism's understanding of the apostolic nature of the Church.

It should be noted, however, that within Catholicism itself there are ongoing discussions among theologians and others about the right balance between episcopal and papal authority. It has been argued, for example, that the papacy, through its offices in the Vatican, centralizes power too much in a manner that is only historical in nature and not central to the understanding of the Church in its essence. Achieving the correct balance between the local bishop (who, after all, is not merely an agent of the pope but one who guides the Church locally with authority) and the bishop of Rome is a profoundly important discussion that vexes the Church to this day. That issue orbits around the larger theoretical issue of how to make the Church, simultaneously, universal and local.

What about papal infallibility? It is absolutely crucial to understand what the term means in its particularity before we specify it in its generality. Infallibility is not to be equated with revelation; it does not mean that something in an essential matter of belief or morality could be revealed or disclosed by the pope which is not in the original faith handed down by the apostolic teaching. Popes do not claim to receive new revelation. The pope, like every Christian, must test himself against the rule of faith. Nor is infallibility the same as inspiration. While Catholics firmly believe that sacred scripture was written under the inspiration of the Holy Spirit, it does not claim that the Holy Spirit guides the magisterium of the Church in each of its utterances. Infallibility is a negative gift, or *charism*. As such, one can call the tradition of the faith taught in council or by the full College of Bishops (which would include, of course, the bishop of Rome) infallible in the sense that those teachings would not err or lead the Church into substantive error about a matter essential to the Gospel. Finally, infallibility does not mean impeccability – it does not guarantee that the actions of the Church or the pope in particular are free from moral error or in their personal opinions particularly intelligent. In fact, not to put too fine a point on it, the long history of the papacy would indicate empirically that popes are not always impeccable and, further, in their private opinions, not infrequently quite fallible.

Since the pope under circumstances we will outline below enjoys the personal charism of infallibility, it may well be better, as a recent theologian has written, to see that the pope exercises infallibility rather than saying "the pope is infallible" since that latter turn of phrase could lead the unwary into thinking that everything the pope says is infallible.

The precise character of papal infallibility was defined at the First Vatican Council in the nineteenth century even though the notion of the infallibility of the pope went back into the past of the Church at least into the medieval period. Let us look at the text of the conciliar document itself and then parse its meaning:

we teach and define as a divinely revealed dogma that when the Roman pontiff speaks *ex cathedra*,[6] that is, when, in the exercise of his office as shepherd and teacher of all Christians, in virtue of his supreme apostolic authority, he defines a doctrine concerning faith or morals to be held by the whole church, he possesses by the divine assistance promised to him in blessed Peter, that infallibility which the divine Redeemer willed his church to enjoy in defining doctrine concerning faith and morals. Therefore, such definitions of the Roman pontiff are of themselves, and not, by the consent of the Church, irreformable. (Tanner: II, 816)

What, in effect, is contained in this statement?

First, there are conditions needed for a teaching to be infallible: The pope must be speaking explicitly in his role as head of the entire Church, stipulating that he is using his supreme authority as teacher and supreme pastor. Clearly, his weekly homilies, his encyclicals, his apostolic letters, and other venues that he uses do not fall under the charism of personal infallibility unless he makes that abundantly clear and in the most

---

[6] *Ex cathedra,* "from the Chair" (of Peter) – i.e. in his role as a successor of the apostle Peter.

explicitly solemn fashion. Recently (2007), Pope Benedict XVI published a book (*Jesus of Nazareth*) under his family name. He made it clear that he was not speaking as part of the magisterium in that book but writing his own take on Jesus. He went on to say in his introduction that "Everyone is free, then, to contradict me" (xxiv). Benedict made it clear in that book that he was not speaking solemnly as the Head of the Church but as a private theologian. He further invited other scholars to criticize his work on the basis of their own scholarship.

Second, the subject must be concerned with a matter of faith or morals. So, expressions of a political, social, or historical nature, even if they touch on matters of faith and morals, do not qualify for falling under the charism of infallibility. A pope, for example, cannot declare infallibly that the free-market economy represents the will of God.

Third, he must be directing his teaching voice to the entire Church, and he must so stipulate explicitly.

Fourth, he will not err in his teaching thanks to the promise of Christ to be with his Church. This guarantee does not mean that he must say something new or that he has had a private revelation or that he is revealing something not already found in the Tradition.

Fifth, what he says does not require prior approval from within the Church. In a restrictive sense, it means that the pope does not have to consult the Church either through a general council or by sounding out the College of Bishops. In practice, the two times in modern history when papal infallibility was clearly exercised (the definition of the Immaculate Conception of the Blessed Virgin [1854] and the Assumption of the Virgin [1950]), the pope in question did consult, in fact, the bishops of the world; it is unthinkable that he would do otherwise.

Vatican I ended before the Council was able to stipulate how this exercise of papal infallibility related to the body of bishops; that task was taken up by the Second Vatican Council. Also, the parameters within which the pope exercises this gift are quite narrowly drawn. Indeed, since the close of the First Vatican Council, only one pope in one instance has exercised that privilege, namely, on the occasion of the definition of the Assumption of Mary into Heaven by Pope Pius XII in 1950. In point of fact, the pope, on that occasion, did not make the definition before sounding out the world's bishops to see if they felt that the doctrine was definable. While the pope enjoys papal infallibility according to the Church, it would be unthinkable for a pope to exercise that authority without taking into account the ordinary magisterium of the Church.

THE SCRIPTURES AND THE RULE OF FAITH

It might come as a surprise to many that we have not up to this point touched on the Bible as a source for Catholic teaching. It is one of the foundational theses of the Reformation that the Bible is the source for all belief and practice – *sola scriptura* were the watchwords of the Reformation: scripture alone. Now, in fact, Catholicism does see the Bible as the infallible and inspired Word of God, and all teaching within the Church must be tested against the witness of the scriptures. It was precisely because the word *homoousios* (of one substance or being) was not attested to in the scriptures that caused the bishops at Nicaea some concern about adding it to the creed. The rule of faith is intimately tied to and a reflection of the witness of holy scripture.

The Catholic Church teaches that there was already a Christian community before there was a settled reality known as the New Testament. In fact, we can say that the New Testament comes from the believing community – the Church – and not vice versa. The issue of what would constitute the authentic list of writings of what would become the New Testament was precipitated by a strange figure in second-century Rome named Marcion.

Marcion (d. *c.*160) arrived in Rome from the East around the year 140. Enormously wealthy, he preached in the city an odd version of Christianity which argued that the Christian Gospel was one of love that was totally antithetical to the God of the Old Testament. He rejected all of the Old Testament and accepted only his own version of the Gospel of Luke and ten letters of Saint Paul. Everything else, according to him, was infected with the spirit of Judaism, which, according to Marcion, understood only a God of Law. Marcion's notions were vigorously rejected by all of the major Christian writers of the time not only because of his ideas on the Bible but also because of his very odd views about Jesus Christ whom, he thought, was not a real human being but only appeared or seemed to be one. Marcion was a *docetist* – one of those who found the idea of the word truly becoming flesh as repugnant. According to Marcion, Jesus only *seemed* to be human and only *seemed* to have died. He also rejected all the writings of the Old Testament as having a deficient notion of God.

His theories, of course, did precipitate a long argument in the Christian community about what, in fact, did constitute the authentic scriptures. Most Christians accepted, taught, and preached from the Old Testament books found in the Greek version known as the Septuagint, a Greek translation of the Old Testament done in the centuries before the time of Jesus. The Christian Church almost exclusively used this version right down to the fourth century.

What made up the New Testament? In the early second century, the four Gospels and thirteen of Paul's letters were mostly acknowledged. There was ambivalence about some other works such as Jude, Revelation, 3 John, etc. By the fourth century, the canon was pretty much as we have it today. Saint Augustine, in his time, gave a good rule of thumb for what was to be accepted as canonical. In his work, *On Christian Doctrine*, written *c*.396, Augustine says: "He will accept this rule concerning the canonical scriptures, that he will prefer those accepted by all catholic churches to those which some do not accept; among those which are not accepted by all, he should prefer those which are accepted by the largest number of important churches to those held by a few minor churches of less authority" (*On Christian Doctrine*, Book 2, Chapter 8). In other words: Read and preach in church (i.e. in the worship of the Church) those works which are read in the churches founded by the Apostles: Rome, Antioch, Alexandria, etc. It was the authority found within the Church that determined the canon of the New Testament. The canon of the New Testament was thus intimately tied to the worship of the Church.

What then is the relationship between the Bible and the rule of faith? It is a dialectical one. In essence, the Catholic Church teaches that Jesus revealed himself and his message to his Apostles, who, in turn, preached and, through their successors, continue to preach the Gospel. Out of the community came written works which the community accepted over time as being inspired by the Holy Spirit. Those books, twenty-seven in number, make up the canon of the books we call the New Testament. That canon is accepted by all Christians. The constant witness of the apostolic Church, contained in sacred scripture, and by the witness of the handing on of the Gospel through that apostolic witness, constitutes the authentic teaching of the Church. This understanding of how the faith is preserved and transmitted has been succinctly summarized by a statement taken from the Second Vatican Council which has been repeated verbatim in the *Catechism of the Catholic Church:* "Sacred Tradition and Sacred Scripture, then, are bound closely together and communicate one with the other. For both of them, flowing from the same divine well-spring, come together in some fashion, to form one thing and move towards the same goal" (No. 80). The catechism then goes on to say: "Each of them makes present and fruitful in the Church the mystery of

Christ, who promised to remain with his own 'always, to the close of the ages'" (No. 80).

It is crucial to understand that the Catholic Church never made the scriptures subordinate to the teaching magisterium; as the Catechism of the Catholic Church says, the magisterium is the servant of the Word of God (No. 86). Hence, the decisions of the bishops or the creeds used in either the liturgy or uttered by councils or the teachings of the papal magisterium must be tested by their fidelity to the scriptures. That is a touchstone for the orthodoxy of belief and practice: Nothing can be accepted as teaching or practice in the Catholic Church if it is not in harmony with the witness of scripture. It is quite possible to object that certain things taught as part of its doctrine in the Catholic Church are not explicitly found in the scriptures (for example, the Assumption of Mary into Heaven or, for that matter, the doctrine of papal infallibility). The Church would not ask whether a doctrine is taught in scripture, but it would ask if a doctrine, or a belief or a practice, is conformable to the witness of scripture. Often a Church doctrine derives from questions asked or from arising controversies to which the Church then says that the rule of faith allows for this but excludes that – this long process is often called the "development of doctrine," which is part of the ongoing attempt of the Church to reach up to the mind of Christ in a faithful fashion.

The sensus fidelium

To this point, we have spoken of the teaching authority of the Church in terms of both episcopal and papal authority. It should not be understood that the laypeople of the Church are mere passive recipients of the Church's teaching. They all witness to the truth of the Gospel by their reception of the Gospel and by their living out of the Christian faith. This common witness of everyone in the Church is often described by the Latin phrase *sensus fidelium,* which means, roughly, the consensus of the faithful. It has been beautifully described at the Second Vatican Council in the document on the Church in these words: The holy people of God share also in Christ's prophetic office: it spreads abroad a living witness to Christ, especially by a life of faith and love and by offering to God a sacrifice of praise, the fruit of lips confessing his name. The whole body of the faithful who have received an anointing which comes from the Holy One cannot be mistaken in belief. It shows this characteristic through the entire people's supernatural sense of the faith which, from the bishops to the last of the faithful, it manifests a universal consensus in matters of faith and morals. (*Lumen gentium,* 12)

It is the unbroken witness of the faith of the people of God which can be reliably used to witness to the fidelity of the Gospel. It has been often

pointed out that when many bishops and other members of the clergy
felt the allure of Arianism, even after the Council of Nicaea, it was the
Catholic faithful who held staunchly to the orthodox faith.

THE DEVELOPMENT OF DOCTRINE

The Catholic Church believes that we will never know the full truth of
God as revealed by Jesus Christ fully in this life. The Church takes very
seriously the observation of Saint Paul that "at present we see indistinctly
as in a mirror, but then face to face. At present I know partially; then
I shall know fully, as I am fully known" (1 Cor. 13:12). The Church strives,
with the aid of the Spirit, to remain faithful to what has been given to
us and, at the same time, to receive a deeper understanding – not proof,
but understanding – of the mysteries of faith. That understanding comes
in various ways.

First, we attempt to understand the faith we profess more fully. When
we say, for example, that we believe in "God the Father Almighty," we
yearn to get behind those words to erase any image of a patriarchal sense
of an elderly man with a white beard – a caricature rooted in art – to what
the meaning of paternity really is and how that paternity can also accommodate the sense of maternity, since God, obviously, is not constructed
by gender.

Second, the development of doctrine occurs when persons articulate
notions that seem to be at variance with the Gospel as well as the rule of
faith. Much of the development of doctrine that became crystallized in
the creeds came in reaction of heretical notions. Heresy is defined in the
Catholic Church in the code of canon law as obstinate denial of a baptized person about a truth "which must be believed with divine and
Catholic faith" (No. 751). Of course, a person may simply be mistaken
about a truth of faith and only materially in heresy. What the Church
formally considers a heresy is a belief that is contrary to the fundamental
truth of the rule of faith. Such an obstinately held belief removes one
from the community of believers.

Thus, doctrinal development is sometimes motivated by the need for
clarification: what is permissible and what is not permissible to say. Thus,
the great creeds we have already discussed were, in part, a response to
inadequate understandings put forth from people like Arius about the
relationship of the Son to the Father, or Nestorius, who, in the fourth
century, denied that Mary was the God-Bearer, etc. They taught things
that were either wrong on the face of it or their teachings led inevitably

to consequences that were at full variance with the rule of faith. Thus, to cite an example, when certain early Gnostics (Marcion, cited earlier, is a good example) held that Christ did not really have a body but only "seemed" to have had one, it was clear that such a position made a hash of the fundamental belief in the passion, death, and resurrection of Christ and, by extension, compromised the Catholic belief in our own resurrection.

Third, in order to preach the Gospel to "all nations" (see Matt. 28:19), it is necessary to articulate the faith in terms intelligible to people whose cultures are quite different from those in which Christianity first arose. One of the urgent tasks of the Church is to speak the Gospel truth in a fashion to make the Gospel intelligible. That means, among other things, that the way to speak to people must be adapted to levels of education, the culture in which they live, and so on. This process of articulating the faith must never compromise the fundamentals of the faith. This issue of inculturation will be taken up in greater depth in a later chapter.

Finally, the rule of faith functions to describe what the Catholic community believes in terms of its foundational theses. Most Catholics affirm the creed in the liturgy but "know" it only in the ways in which they have learned about its meaning in catechetical instruction and so on. They may or may not reflect on the meaning of creedal affirmations. It is only when they live outside the affirmations that they may be judged in some fashion as not orthodox, but, in reality, everyone, from prelate to the mythical person in the pew, reaches up to the full meaning of the creed without actually possessing it as a totality because, as Paul famously says, we all pray for that Spirit-given strength to comprehend "what is the breadth and length and height and depth and to know the love of Christ that surpasses knowledge" (Eph. 18–19). One does not have to be a trained theologian in order to be a good Catholic.

The Catholic Church teaches that all are called to the same holiness of life, although this fidelity to God's word may be experienced in different modes of life. In every age, people live out or perform the Gospel life in quite different ways. In doing so they plumb the mysteries of the faith, bringing forth both old things and new. In that process, they give new insights into the meaning of the Gospel. True living faith is not mere assent to abstract truths but the lived experience of what those truths convey.

It should be finally underscored that the rule of faith, as it is found in the historical creeds, is not an abstract list of propositional truths existing in a non-contextual fashion. The creed is most fundamentally important when it is said within the living life of the worshiping community. It is a central part of baptismal ceremonies and a regular part of the worship of Catholics at the liturgy on Sunday. Every great council of the Church, when the bishops gather together in solemn deliberation, makes the creed a part of their deliberations either by formulating a creed or by including it as a sign of their common faith. The creed, then, was not only a profession of faith but also a confession of praise and, in that sense, a prayer. It is that deep sense of "Confession" that Augustine alluded to in the title of his famous book the *Confessions*: It was a confession of his sinfulness, a confession of his faith, and a confession of praise.

In the ancient Church, it was common to teach adults who were preparing for baptism the words of the creed during the ceremonies leading up to the Easter vigil when they were to be baptized. This "handing over of the creed," as it was known, was a symbolic giving of the faith to the new Christians as part of their initiation into the new life of Christianity. Writing late in the fourth century, the great Saint Augustine of Hippo, as a bishop in North Africa, taught the creed to many new converts; he commented in an address he gave to his fellow bishops that

the Catholic Faith is made known to the faithful in the Creed and is committed to memory, in as short a form as so great a matter permits. In this way for beginners and sucklings, who have been reborn in Christ, but have not yet been strengthened by diligent and spiritual study and understanding of sacred scriptures, there has been drawn up in a few words a formula they must accept in faith, setting forth what would have to be expounded in many words to those who are making progress and are raising themselves up to attain the divine doctrine in the assured strength of humility and charity. (*Faith and the Creed*, I, 1)

It is essential to remember that from the Catholic perspective believers are always moving towards the full truth of revelation, are never in full possession of it and will not be until the end of time. In the eleventh century, Saint Anselm of Canterbury defined theology as "faith seeking understanding." Catholics affirm in faith the contents of the creed, but, as imperfect human beings, born, as Aristotle once observed, with a desire to know, we are also, individually and collectively, yearning to plumb the mysteries of faith ever more deeply. The great theologian of the Catholic Church, Saint Thomas Aquinas, once observed that our faith does not find its finality in the words of belief but in the realities beyond those words.

In the last analysis, one must hold in tension the articles of the creed, which are meaningful and coherent for the believer, and the conviction that the words we use are analogous and only point the way to the ineffable reality of God and God's life. When we utter the words "I believe" and, as a community, "We believe," Catholics are both affirming the truth of what is said as well as expressing that trust which is a part of faith. It has always been the experience of the great Christian mystics that in their experience of God in prayer the reality has always been greater than what they could express, which is why the mystics either resort to poetry or to the language of paradox.

Nor is it unimportant to note that the most common form of a profession of faith is the actual living out of the ordinary Catholic life. One of the most common Catholic gestures is making the sign of the cross; that common gesture is simultaneously a "little sacrament" (sacramental), a prayer, and an act of faith – it says, in gesture and word, that we are trinitarian believers. That is a small example of many in the ordinary life of Christians, which says, in essence, "I am a believer."

FAITH AND REASON

Catholics accept the teachings of Jesus proposed by the Catholic tradition in faith. The truths of Christianity are not propositions that can be "proved" by reason; they are accepted in faith, as a free gift of God. At the same time, the Catholic tradition has always maintained that through reason it is possible to come to some knowledge of God's existence even though that knowledge is not easily attained. The fact that a person might come to a knowledge of God through native intelligence is limited since it is the common belief of the Catholic Church that a knowledge of the triune nature of God and that God became flesh in Jesus Christ are revealed truths that come to us from God as sheer gift and would never have been ascertained through the use of reason alone.

The clearest conviction about the relationship of faith and reason was succinctly stated in the opening lines of the late Pope John Paul II's 1998 encyclical *Fides et ratio*: "Faith and reason are like two wings on which the human spirit rises to the contemplation of truth; and God has placed in the human heart a desire to know the truth – in a word to know himself – so that, by knowing and loving God, men and women may also come to the fullness of truth about themselves."

Catholicism has always tried to navigate between two extremes: fideism and rationalism. Fideism is the belief that humans can know nothing about God and must throw themselves, in blind faith, upon belief in God's revelation. The most extreme form of fideism is summed up in the old phrase (wrongly attributed to Tertullian): "I believe because it is absurd." The other extreme is rationalism, which affirms that nothing can be known certainly unless it passes the test of reason. The rationalist says, "in effect, prove it!"

It is not the case, however, that Catholics believe that faith is irrational; that reason has no role in the life of faith. Rather, it is Catholic teaching that faith, by which we assent to what God has revealed to us, is beyond reason. A well-intentioned person may investigate the claims of Christianity; that same person may come to a preliminary judgment that what the Church teaches has a certain plausibility, but, when the person is able to say, "I accept this as true in faith," there is always the intervention of God's help which is the gift of faith. That act of faith has both an intellectual component (I accept this as true) and a component of trust (God does not deceive).

On the other hand, it is possible to think about faith using one's intelligence to deepen faith; that is what, at a high level, theology does. Theology is "faith seeking understanding." It is also a worthy thing to do to articulate the grounds for one's faith for an interested person or to show to someone that what one believes is not stupid or mindless. That is the function of what is called apologetics. In the final analysis, however, the nexus between reason and faith is grounded in the conviction that one can know the truth and that all truths participate in the ultimate truth which is God. That God has been revealed by his Son, who, famously, said "I am the Truth, the Way, and the Life."

The deepest engagement of our human gifts with respect to God is in the experience of prayer; the turning to God in thanksgiving, praise, penitence, and praise is the most primordial form of "theology," because it is, as the word means, "discourse with God." The old monastic writer, Evagrius of Pontus, got it exactly right when he said that the person who prays is the true theologian.

Box 6   Catechism

Most Catholics who are raised in the faith have acquired their knowledge of the doctrines and practices of the Church through instruction in a catechism. Today, we think of catechisms as books of instruction frequently done in question-and-answer form. The notion of catechism, however, has a long history behind it.

The word "catechism" comes from the Greek "to echo," and, by extension, "to instruct." In the early centuries of the Church, when the vast majority were received into the Church as adults, the prospective converts were enrolled in a special class called the *catechumenate* in which they were instructed in the

Box 6 (cont.)

faith by degrees; we actually possess a fourth-century series of lectures given by the Bishop of Jerusalem destined for such converts; interestingly enough, twelve of those lectures were based on the creed used in Jerusalem. Such literature has come down to us in fair numbers. In fact, expositions of the articles of the creed have been a rather constant element in Christian writing.

In the early Middle Ages, when the formal process by which a person entered the Church came to be less formal, those to be baptized were required, as a bare minimum, to be able to recite the creed, to name the ten commandments and the sacraments, and to know from memory the Lord's Prayer. Throughout the Middle Ages, it was not uncommon for series of sermons to be preached on those core elements. Late in his career, for example, Saint Thomas Aquinas preached a series of sermons in Naples for ordinary people on the creed and the Lord's Prayer as well as some lectures on the petitions of the "Hail Mary."

As books became more available, it was common enough for written catechisms, based on creed, commandments, and the Lord's Prayer to be produced. We find such catechisms, usually in the form of questions and answers, written in the sixteenth century by Saint Peter Canisius, which were widely used in Germany as well as the *Roman Catechism* issued after the Council of Trent, which was to be used as a handbook for parish priests as an aid for the teaching of catechism for parishioners. It is worth noting that a catechism was also produced by Martin Luther in 1529 as a simple instrument for instruction (in its earliest format the *Kleine Katechismus* [the "Little Catechism"] was barely a dozen pages long), and a similar one is found in the *Book of Common Prayer* used in the Church of England.

In our own day, under the authority of the late Pope John Paul II, the Catechism of the Catholic Church was issued to be used by the bishops of the world as a template for the writing of catechisms for various age groups and different cultural needs. That catechism uses the traditional division of creed, commandment, and Lord's Prayer with an added section on the seven sacraments of the Church. Thus, the modern *Catechism of the Catholic Church* (published in 1994) has roots that go back more than a millennium and a half, even though, in addition to that authorized catechism, there are countless catechetical aids available within the Church for the handing down of the faith.

The use of catechisms, of course, is only one way in which the faith is handed down. It is a formal tool, which is aided by the good example and teaching that take place within families, the sermons preached in church, the acquaintance with the language of the Church that comes through worship, the development of the senses through art and music, and the other forms of sensory stimulation such as the now easily accessible mass media. We are also beginning to see basic catechetical instruction increasingly being produced for "on line" teaching via computers.

FURTHER READING

Ayo, Nicholas, *Creed as Symbol* (Notre Dame, Ind.: University of Notre Dame Press, 1989). A highly readable study of the development of the creed and its meaning.

Catechism of the Catholic Church (New York, N.Y.: Paulist, 1994). The Vatican's universal catechism which serves as the authoritative template for Catholic catechisms today.

DeLubac, Henri, *The Christian Faith* (San Francisco, Calif.: Ignatius, 1986). A classic study of the Apostles Creed and an exposition of it.

Johnson Luke T., *The Creed* (New York, N.Y.: Doubleday, 2003). A popular apologia for creedal Christianity and an exposition of the creed.

Kelly, J. N. D., *Early Christian Creeds*, (3rd edn, New York, N.Y.: McKay, 1972). The standard history of creeds.

Pelikan, Jaroslav, *Credo* (New Haven, Conn.: Yale, 2003). A masterful study of the creeds from both an historical and a theological point of view.

Pelikan, Jaroslav and Hotchkiss, Valerie, *Creeds and Confessions of Faith in the Christian Tradition* (New Haven, Conn.: Yale University Press, 2003). An exhaustive collection of creedal statements from antiquity to the present.

Ratzinger, Joseph, *Introduction to Christianity* (San Francisco, Calif.: Ignatius, 2004). An introduction to the Catholic faith based on the creed by the current pope, Benedict XVI.

Seitz, Christopher, *Nicene Christianity* (Grand Rapids, Mich.: Brazos, 2001). An ecumenical exposition of the creed known as the Nicene Creed.

Tanner, Norman, ed., *Decrees of the Ecumenical Councils* (2 vols., Washington, D.C.: Georgetown University Press, 1993). A collection of all the decrees of the ecumenical councils with the original language(s) of the councils and their English translation. Invaluable work.

Von Balthasar, Hanrs Urs, *Credo* (New York, N.Y.: Crossroad, 1990). A profound meditation on the articles of the creed.

CHAPTER 7

Catholic spirituality

INTRODUCTION

The word "spirituality" in our own time has come to mean something quite vaguely attached to feelings – thus, one commonly hears the phrase "I am spiritual but not religious." Historically, however, the term "spiritual" meant one who lived under the impulse of the Holy Spirit as a follower of Jesus Christ. The scriptural root for this usage derives from a classic passage in Saint Paul's Letter to the Romans (8:1–17) where Paul sharply distinguishes those who live "according to the flesh" from those who live according to the Spirit. For Paul, the contrast between "flesh" and "spirit" should not be confused with some kind of radical dualism, say, between, body and soul. For Paul, the word "flesh" (and Paul distinguishes "flesh" from "body") means those carnal impulses that degrade a human person and are further identified with death. By contrast, those who live "according to the Spirit" are those who have the Spirit within them and are further identified to be, according to adoption, what Jesus is by nature: "Children of God" who are able to cry out and call God "Abba" (see Rom. 8:15ff; and Gal. 4:4–6).

A person who lives in the Spirit is one who is linked to Christ through participation in his death and resurrection through baptism, by partaking in his body and blood through the eucharist, by being a part of his body in union with all others who make up the assembly of Christian believers, who follow his word, and await his coming in the final resurrection. Such persons listen to the word proclaimed and attempt to follow what Jesus has commanded us. They, according to Paul, live "in Christ." That phrase "in Christ" or a variant of it occurs over 160 times in Paul's letters so it is a root metaphor for the Pauline conception of being a Christian.

Christian spirituality is nothing else but following the way of Jesus in the Spirit. In fact, the earliest name for Christians, as the Acts of the Apostles makes clear, is that they were followers of the way (of Jesus). As a quick glance over the Christian history would show, however, the ways of following Jesus who is the way are varied. Saints Paul, John the Evangelist, and Peter are all followers of Jesus, but, it is clear, their approach to that following differ. The same, obviously, is true of any emblematic Christians who come later in the tradition. While certain constants are discernible, variations, while noting those constants, are multiple. Following Jesus is the way of the one whom the Early Fathers called the *pneumatikos* – the person who lives in the Spirit – and it is from that usage that we derive the word "spirituality." The discrete ways in which the person lives in the Spirit constitute the various spiritualities in the tradition. One could say that Christian spirituality boils down to following the one who says "I am the Way," but that there are various ways of following the way.

AN INTEGRATED CATHOLIC LIFE

In the first encyclical of his life as pope, *Deus caritas est,*[1] Benedict XVI wrote about Christian love. In the second part of that letter, the Pope says that the Church and its members are called to undertake three fundamental tasks called for in the New Testament itself. The proper balance of those three foundational tasks constitutes the integrative form of being a faithful Catholic Christian. They are:

> *Kerygma/martyria* The Greek word means "proclamation" and means, in its largest sense, that the Catholic believer is to accept the Word and then "proclaims" (*kerygma*) and witnesses (*martyria*) its truth both at an individual and communal level. Obviously, this task is practiced variously. Parents proclaim and are witnesses to their children; teachers to their pupils; parish priests to their congregations; public figures to their constituencies; etc. Some are called to proclaim the Gospel by explicit missionary work while others do the same at a more limited level through participation in the various pious works of the parish. It is almost a cliché to say that authentic Christians are the very best proclaimers and witnesses to the truth of the Gospel life.
>
> *Leiturgia* All Catholics are called on to worship God by participation in the prayer life of the Church. Under the rubric of worship we include not only the official worship of the Church but also those acts of "remembering God" by which our daily life is shaped: through

---

[1] All papal encyclicals take their title from the first words of the letter, in this case, "God is Love" (see 1 John 4).

prayers at table; through celebrations of feast days; and in the many other ways in which God's presence in the world is recognized. *Diakonia* All Catholics are called upon to that Christ-like love which we show to others. Works of charity and justice are not a by-product of the Catholic faith but are integral to it. The range of such service (*diakonia*) runs from the familiar to the care for the neediest of the world. It is a way to "perform" the Gospel.

It should be obvious that these three primordial functions of the Church and its members are not hermetically sealed off one from the other. They are, in fact, symbiotic. Worship is a form of proclamation, and service is inextricably tied to both. To serve the poor lovingly is a form of witness (*martyria*) just as worship overflows into concern for the Other. In other words, these are all parts of the larger whole that constitutes the way of Jesus within the Church. When the Acts of the Apostles describe the early community of believers as those who "devoted themselves to the Apostles' teaching and fellowship, to the breaking of bread, and the prayers" (Acts 2:42), they were not describing discrete activities but a sign of the whole of the community's life. Within the community, however, there are married persons, ascetic celibates, missionaries, scholars, artists, and so on who integrate themselves into the Church in their own ways while still being part of that larger reality of the Church.

To think of the Christian life "in the Spirit" as a working out of these three elements of witness, worship, and service is a useful way of thinking about spirituality in the broadest fashion free from any notion of elitism. It helps us to see that the Christian life is not something extra but a simple response to the call of every Christian. It is for that reason that the Second Vatican Council insisted that the call to holiness is universal: "It is quite clear that all Christians in whatever state of walk in life are called to the fullness of Christian life and to the perfection of charity and this holiness is conducive to a more human way of living even in society here on earth" (*Lumen gentium*, V.40).

SPIRITUALITY AND SOCIAL JUSTICE

Current writers on spirituality have been keen to deny that an interest in Christian spirituality is not to be construed as involving only and exclusively personal growth in holiness. There is an oft-repeated fear among the best Catholic spiritual writers that spirituality not be reduced to some kind of therapeutic strategy of personal development. This resistance to thinking of spirituality in any overly individualistic fashion derives from two basic insights in Catholicism. The first is that our growth in the Christian life is inextricably tied to our conviction that we are members of the Body of Christ. As a consequence, it is also the case, as the contemporary liberation theologians have pointed out, that growth in the Christian life has, as we say above, a necessary nexus between our Christian life and the demands of the poor.

The contemporary liberation theologian, Jon Sobrino, has understood the term "spirituality" to mean living in the Spirit; that understanding is, as we have seen, the very traditional one. Sobrino goes further to say that this living in the Spirit is to give sense to what it really means to be authentically human. He can conclude from this, if we take history and culture seriously, that the

theology of liberation has sought to be a creative synthesis of what it means to be human and to be Christian in the real world of today, specifically in the world of the hoping, suffering poor, whose sudden appearance on the scene has been what has unhinged the old world and its theology, while at the same time giving the new synthesis its meaning and thrust.[2]

While the liberation theologians still work on a full theology of liberation under the aspect of spirituality, their emphases are easy enough to discern. They propose a vigorous synthesis of action and contemplation, an insistence that spirituality must be holistic, and that we "encounter the spiritual not outside ourselves through the concrete, historical and the natural. Consequently, knowledge of the spiritual comes, not through a withdrawal from society, but through an ever greater immersion in the vicissitudes and struggles of our time [. . .]."[3]

SCHOOLS OF SPIRITUALITY

The Catholic Tradition has recognized retrospectively that certain historical "ways" of Christianity have emerged at various times in history and have been found to be so attractive and possessed of such longevity that they remain within the Tradition. These "ways" have become known as schools of spirituality. The term "school" in the sense we will use it in

---

[2] Jon Sobrino, "Spirituality and the Following of Jesus," in Ignacio Ellacuría and Jon Sobrino, eds, *Mysterium Liberationis: Fundamental Concepts of Liberation Theology*, ed. Ellacuria and Sobrino. (Maryknoll, N.Y.: Orbis, 1993), p. 679.
[3] Roberto Goizueta, "Liberation Theology," in Michael Downey, ed., *The New Dictionary of Catholic Spirituality* (Collegeville, Minn.: Liturgical/Glazier, 1993), p. 600.

this chapter is to be understood as a broad communal tradition within which there is a kind of pedagogy of Christian living. Schools of spirituality emerge according to a loose but discernible pattern of development. A person or a small group of persons discover a certain way of living the Christian life. That "certain way" may constitute over time a series of models in the person of holy people who have lived the way, a body of instructional literature in the form of rules, treatises, and other texts, as well as a tradition about how the life is to be lived. Finally, this way of living is attractive enough to constitute a gift which the Church accepts as part of its heritage and receives the gift as a grace or charism for others to accept if they find it equally attractive.

Certainly, the emergence of what today we call monasticism would constitute a certain school of spirituality (obviously not the only one) within the Catholic Tradition. It has certain emblematic figures – one thinks of Saint Anthony, the Desert Fathers and Mothers, Founders such as Basil the Great and Benedict as well as other foundational leaders. From them and others have come, as well, a large literature of biography, sayings, rules, ascetical texts, sermons, and so on. Those who follow the monastic life today draw on these ancient sources and produce a literature of their own to adapt monasticism to the age in which we live. Benedictine monks and nuns, for example, have followed the Rule ascribed to Benedict for over 1,500 years. The presence of the monastic life in Catholic Christianity can trace itself back to the late third century. This particular way highlights certain Christian virtues and values: common prayer, the sharing of goods, the value of work, a certain ascetic distance from the world, the desire for personal conversion, and so on. The monastic school then also shows longevity in that it has never lost its attractive power for some Christians. It is one way of being a Christian, but, obviously, not the only way.

More generally speaking, we can determine certain constants that shape a school of spirituality. At the very least, they would include the following:

A canon within the canon of biblical texts Every school of spirituality tends to privilege certain texts from scared scripture as central to their way of understanding the Christian life. They tend to have a kind of a "canon within the canon" from which they draw particular inspiration. Such a school, of course, does not ignore the entire scriptures; it is the case, rather, that they find a certain attraction for some texts. Those texts become particularly "performative" in the sense that they draw from those texts a manner of living and acting. Thus, to cite a few examples, the monastic tradition constantly harkens back to the picture in the early chapters of the Acts of the Apostles about how the primitive Church lived by sharing all things in common. By contrast, missionary schools of spirituality take their clue from the great mandate to evangelize all peoples found in Matthew 28, while the deeply contemplative orders (for example, the Carmelites) draw much from the mystical reading of the Song of Songs just as the Franciscan School is attracted to the evangelical poverty described in Matthew 5–7.

A pedagogy of prayer Each school of spirituality has a preferred way of praying and a "theory" about how best to attain a more perfect life of prayer. Again, the Ignatian tradition models its prayer on the *Spiritual Exercises* of Saint Ignatius of Loyola in a way quite different to the form of scriptural prayer (*lectio divina*) found in the monastic tradition although the former has some echoes of the latter. Prayer is "taught" by initiating a follower of a particular school through a pedagogical system that usually comes from the experience of someone who is already shaped by the school, for example, a novice master or an elder or a spiritual guide. This pedagogy of prayer presumes the ordinary exercises of the life of the liturgy.

Experience of conversion We have used the word "school" and "pedagogy" in this section but it would be wrong if anyone thought that a school of spirituality has as its aim intellectual formation alone. Schools of spirituality have as their final end changing a person or, to use the traditional vocabulary, to conversion or change of heart. Schools of spirituality want to bring about that kind of person who lives "according to the Spirit" even though the vocabulary of what this change or conversion entails. It is clear from the words used that what is desired is to make a person – here, I use just some of the vocabulary – conformed to Christ; pure of heart; transformed; living in the Spirit; etc.

When we look back over the Christian tradition, it is clear that these schools of spirituality almost always derive from the inspiration of individuals or small groups who conceived of them in tandem with what we would call the founding of "religious orders" which have been the vehicle for representing these schools over the course of time. Thus, it is common to speak of the monastic school as well as the Franciscan, Salesian, Ignatian, etc. It was the religious community itself that guarded and passed on the teachings of its school, but the distinctive spirituality associated with the school was available to all. Thus, to cite again an obvious example, all members of the Society of Jesus (the Jesuits) are shaped by the tradition of Ignatius of Loyola but in their ministries over the centuries the Jesuits have "given" the Spiritual Exercises to countless people, ranging from the students who attended their schools to those who make retreats (they seem to have originated the practice of the retreat – a period of days set aside for spiritual renewal) under their direction.

The final test of whether a given Catholic practice solidifies into a school is the test of time; it has an ancestry that endures in the tradition. If the teaching of a potential school does not adapt itself to the circumstances of history, it becomes stagnant and passes from the picture. Thus, new movements in the Church (like the Spirit-moved Catholic Charismatic Movement) will become recognized (not by authority but by the consensus of history) as a distinct school based on its power to attract people to its teaching and practice over the generations. Certain spiritual movements, on the other hand, may have their moment in history but fail to have a sustaining power that carries them over to subsequent generations; thus, they have not attained the title of being a "school" of spirituality.

The beauty of diverse schools of spirituality within the larger Catholic tradition is that these schools provide a Catholic a way of being Catholic amenable to the personality of the individual. If a person is of a retiring contemplative bent, there are practices to encourage that; if another is more activist, there are schools that encourage such desires. In a broad sense, the various schools of spirituality that exist under the broad umbrella of Catholicism function rather like denominations within Protestantism. Liturgically minded Protestants do not become Quakers, but those who love the silence and simplicity of the Quakers provide that option. Within Catholicism, the various schools function in a somewhat analogous fashion. The presumption always is that the person would do all the things expected of any practicing Catholic but would enrich their faith by an intensification of the spiritual life by participating in the accumulated wisdom of a given school of spirituality.

Historically speaking, the various schools of spirituality have been identified with religious orders. Until recently, these traditions have had an enormous impact on Catholic spirituality even though they are modified for prayer practice. The Second Vatican Council insisted, however, that every Christian has been called to holiness so that one of the urgent tasks of the contemporary Catholic Church is to think through questions such as these: How does one draw upon the inherited wisdom of these traditional schools or reimagine new ways to assist those who are not vowed religious to develop appropriate ways of holiness and spiritual living? A recent lay theologian has put it nicely: "The call to holiness for laity is lived precisely in and through our relationships at home, at work, and in the marketplace. The challenge [. . .] is for us to discover extraordinary grace ever active in our ordinary lives."[4]

The Gospels outline traditional elements of the Christian life of holiness, and these deserve special consideration. They are important because over the centuries they have been a sort of launching pad for whole trajectories of spiritual practice.

ASCETICISM

Asceticism derives from the Greek word *askesis,* which means the training undertaken by an athlete. The training was not an end in itself but a means towards an end as is true even today. In religious discourse, asceticism is also a means towards a greater end. All religions enjoin on their members some kind of ascetic practice. In the religions of the East, persons master their bodies in order to attain greater mindfulness; in fact, the word *yoga* (from the same root we get the English word "yoke") is a mastery of the body for that precise purpose. Many religions demand a dietary discipline as a sign of fidelity to that tradition; hence, pious Jews keep a kosher diet and observant Muslims abstain from alcoholic beverages. All religions have their ascetic practices.

Asceticism from a religious perspective may be defined as a "voluntary, sustained, and at least partially systematic program of self-discipline and self denial in which immediate, sensual, or profane gratifications are renounced in order to attain a higher spiritual state or a more thorough absorption in the sacred."[5]

Catholicism has a set of ascetic practices, some of which are found in other faith traditions while some are peculiar to its own tradition. Some of them are voluntary, such as the practice of celibate living for members of religious orders and priests of the Roman Rite. Traditionally, the Catholic Church has seen, in the witness of the New Testament, counsels of perfection which may be undertaken as a way of following Jesus. Three

---

[4] Donna Orsuto, *Holiness* (London and New York, N.Y.: Continuum, 2006), p. 166.
[5] Walter O. Kaelber, "Asceticism," in Mircea Eliade, ed., *The Encyclopedia of Religion* (New York, N.Y.: MacMillan, 1987), Vol. I, p. 441.

such counsels are traditional: the renunciation of personal possessions or the communal sharing of them; a life of chastity or renunciation of marriage; obedience to a lawful authority by the submission of one's will. The earliest ascetics followed these counsels without much in the way of a formal structure, although, in time, and certainly by the Middle Ages, they became the formal vows for anyone joining a religious community.

Other ascetic practices derive from the tradition of the New Testament itself; chief among these are the three ascetic practices urged by the Gospel of Matthew (Matt. 5–7) in the New Testament: fasting, the discipline of prayer, and almsgiving. About these, some words need to be said.

Fasting

Understood as abstaining from eating, eating sparingly or abstaining from certain foods, fasting has been a practice, inherited from Judaism, that goes back to the very beginnings of Christianity. While the New Testament reflects the custom of fasting in the Early Church (see Acts 13:2, 14:23; 2 Cor 11:27), it is only in the second century that there are mentions of weekly fasting (the very ancient text called the *Didache* mentions Wednesdays and Fridays), and, by the fourth century, there are mentions of forty days of fasting (only one meal a day) in preparation for Easter. From the early days of the Church, meat was not eaten on Fridays (in honor of the crucifixion), and, until recently, Catholics would abstain from all eating and drinking on the day prior to receiving holy communion; today, that obligation has been radically modified. Current practice in the Roman Catholic Church enjoins two obligatory fast days (Ash Wednesday and Good Friday) for all except the ill, children, and adults over sixty.

The rationale for fasting included a belief that to give up a good (eating) for a greater good (focus on the mysteries of faith) or as an act of penance was a way to serve God by following the example of Jesus himself. While it is not obligatory, some Catholics, especially during the season of Lent or on some special occasion, will restrict their food intake as a sign of solidarity with the poor while giving the equivalent amount of money saved by not eating to some organized charity for the aid of the poor.

The discipline of prayer

While worship, as we have seen, is one of the foundational elements of being a Christian, prayer is also a form of asceticism in the sense that observing a discipline of personal prayer is a strategy for "remembering God." Early Church documents ask that people pray at specific hours every day. Origen of Alexandria, in his treatise on prayer, suggests that the Lord's Prayer be said at morning, noon, and night. What has become most customary, however, is for the practice of praying on rising and retiring, while offering a word of blessing and thanksgiving before meals. The Catholic spiritual tradition has added refinements to those simple temporal activities by more particular pious practices such as recalling the presence of God during our daily activities or the insistence that families pray together as a sign of family solidarity.

The asceticism of prayer consists of "framing" the day in a regular way by the practice of prayer either individually or as a family. It is clear, of course, that there is a relation between fasting and prayer since the former is designed to create a kind of "alertness" that makes us more conscious of breaking out of a routine for the purpose of prayer.

Almsgiving

Almsgiving can be understood as a shorthand way of speaking about all of the acts of charity that oblige the Christian. The Catholic Church has a traditional way of describing such activity by referring to the seven corporal works of mercy. Based on Matthew 25, they are:

1. feeding the hungry;
2. giving drink to the thirsty;
3. sheltering the stranger;
4. visiting the ill;
5. ministering to the imprisoned;
6. clothing the naked;
7. burying the dead.

This form of giving (with all of the various forms that go beyond the traditional seven) obligates both the individual and the community.

We know that within decades of the end of the Roman persecutions in the early fourth century the Church had set up institutions for the care of pilgrims, abandoned children, hospitals, the elderly or orphaned, and others in need. Deacons administered these charities (there were seven such decanal stations in Rome by the end of the fourth century), and, later, monks did the same from their monasteries. In the course of history, lay fraternities and specific religious communities were founded for such charitable aims. In contemporary society, there are a myriad of organizations who work both locally and internationally in direct service to the poor.

These institutional organizations are sustained by the self-giving of the ordinary Catholic either by direct service or through goods. When one examines the activities of any large typical parish, it is easy to see sustenance given to the needy in everything from food pantries to clothing depots for the poor or disadvantaged. Within a three-mile radius of where this author writes, there is, under Catholic auspices, a hospital, a center for the homeless, a shelter for abused women and children, a respite center for care-givers, an agency that ministers to unwed mothers, a Catholic Worker House, and a large store maintained by the Saint Vincent de Paul Society. Each of these agencies depends on the "almsgiving" of parishes and individuals who perform the ascetic practice of outreach in charity. Participation in the charitable Church should radiate out from the local community to the larger world. That imperative constitutes the deepest meaning of what it means to be a Catholic: to be part of the larger whole.

The seven corporal works of mercy were tabulated from texts in the New Testament. The Catholic tradition understands them to be oriented towards the bodily needs of the neighbor. As an act of symmetry, the tradition developed a corresponding list of spiritual works of mercy. Like the former list, they number seven, and their symmetry was undoubtedly a pedagogical device to help people remember some fundamental duties of the Christian. The seven spiritual works are:

1. Convert the sinner.
2. Instruct the ignorant.
3. Counsel the doubtful.
4. Comfort the afflicted.
5. Bear afflictions patiently.
6. Forgive the sinner.
7. Pray for the living and the dead.

MYSTICAL PRAYER

The ways of Catholic prayer are many. We have the formal prayers of the public liturgy; people pray meditatively with the scriptures; we recite "set" prayers and also raise up our hearts to God in our own language. Treatises on prayers are too many to enumerate, and "methods" of prayer are countless. One adjective that often gets attached to prayer is "mystical." To that form of prayer some explanation is required if only to disabuse those who think that the word "mystical" is esoteric.

The much abused and quite modern word "mysticism" derives from the older adjective "mystical," which, in the Catholic tradition, simply means "hidden." It is a word that derives from the same Greek root from which we get the word "mystery." The Early Church used the term to describe, among other things, the Church, the eucharist, and the scriptures in the sense that it is possible to "see" the eucharist, for example, as bread and wine, but, through the eyes of faith, one can more deeply "see" what is hidden – namely, the true presence of Christ. Similarly, we may "see" the Church as a visible reality but only through faith can we recognize it as the "Mystical Body of Christ." The tradition also speaks of "mystical theology" (a term coined by the Syrian monk Dionysius around the year AD 500). Mystical theology signifies those hidden things of God which we cannot express as opposed to those things which we can say of God: God as father, rock, savior, etc.

Fundamentally, the Catholic spiritual tradition has said that those persons of deep prayer, nourished in the liturgy and the Word of God, may become aware (here I am using the language of the distinguished scholar Bernard McGinn) in some direct but obscure fashion the presence of God. This awareness is wordless in such a manner that after the experience, the person may only be able to describe it through the use of analogous language or by poetic metaphor. Such experiences are often also called "contemplative" experiences because at their root is the simple act of "gazing" without the use of language.

It has always been the conviction of the Catholic tradition that such experiences are a free gift of God, open to anyone who is open to God. Such moments of intense personal encounter of God through Christ in the Spirit presuppose a life lived in grace and the ascetic discipline of living in the Spirit.

The Catholic spiritual tradition has an ancient lineage of spiritual writers, male and female, who have described the life of prayer.[6] While they write from somewhat different perspectives and emphasize different approaches, they all agree that fidelity to prayer and meditation allow us to have some hidden sense of God's presence in our lives. It is probably the case that many faithful Catholics have had those experiences but do not possess the vocabulary to express them. They may say something like having experienced an overwhelming sense of the presence of God

---

[6] The series published by the Paulist Fathers since 1978 under the rubric "The Classics of Western Spirituality" has given us over sixty volumes of primary sources newly translated and wonderfully introduced to help unlock this rich tradition of spirituality.

or being enveloped in a sense of the love of God or something similar. It is only after the experience itself that they reach for language to express it.

The language of the mystics

In the prologue to his treatise *The Spiritual Canticle,* Saint John of the Cross explains why he expresses his deepest experience in prayer in poetry. People who have such experiences let something of their experience "overflow in figures, comparisons, and similitudes, and from the abundance of their spirit pour out secrets and mysteries rather than rational explanations." John goes on to say that if people do not read such things in the spirit of knowledge and love which they contain, they will seem to be absurdities.

John draws an analogy from sacred scripture, where, as in places such as The Song of Songs, the Holy Spirit is "unable to express the fullness of his meaning in ordinary words." John goes on to note that the doctors of the Church, no matter how much they explain these passages, "can never furnish an exhaustive explanation of these figures," since, as he concludes, the abundant meanings of the Holy Spirit cannot be caught in words."[7]

THE DEVOTIONAL LIFE

Throughout this book we have mentioned many practices that grew up over the long history of the Church, which were part of the armory of the pious Catholic but which are not part of the formal worship of the Church. Such practices, and they are numerous, are known as devotional practices. Pilgrimage would certainly be one of them, and listening to stories or reading about saints or other edifying works would be another. Pious practices, such as making the stations of the cross – a symbolic walk before images depicting events connected to the Passion of Christ – would be still another. Every Catholic church marks such stations, even though the fourteen traditional ones only date back to the early modern period. The wearing of religious medals, the custom of keeping sacred pictures in a home, the making of the sign of the cross upon one's person, the habit of stopping in a church or at a shrine site to pray privately, or attending communal devotional services are all part of ordinary Catholic experience.

---

[7] I borrow from the translation in *The Collected Works of John of the Cross,* edited by Kieran Kavanaugh (Washington, D.C.: ICS Publications, 1992), pp. 469–70.

These devotional practices, deriving from customs which go back centuries or which may be of a more recent date, are all options available to the Catholic for the enrichment of the life of piety. They are practices that can suit the individual but they can also call forth communal responses. From the Middle Ages on, for example, there have been confraternities of both men and women who have had a particular devotion to Mary or one of the saints, who banded together not only for prayers but also for public social services ranging from aid to the poor to comforting condemned prisoners. In the nineteenth century, a French professor at the Sorbonne, Frederic Ozanam (1813–53), began a little circle of devout men who would work for the extremely poor of Paris. They did this under the patronage of the seventeenth-century priest, the beloved Saint Vincent de Paul, who gave his life for the disadvantaged. The Society of Saint Vincent de Paul is still one of the largest charitable organizations in the Catholic Church even though its deep roots are to be found in its prayer life.

The number of lay groups who bond together to engage in devotional activities are so numerous that they could not even be named, but what they all share in common is that they are subsets of the larger life of the Church suited to the needs and aspirations of the people. The Church recognizes the right of all Catholics to form such groups as long as their practices and beliefs are not alien to the teaching and practice of the Church. Such groups wax and wane so they are not as established as the historic schools of spirituality and had no intention of becoming so. Often, they fed from the wisdom of those schools and were active as long as they served a need. It is also the case that devotional practices vary from country to country.

While, as we have seen, most Catholics find the parish to be the focal point of their Catholic life it is also true that within or even beyond the parish many people look for more intimate community experiences. It is quite common today for people to join small Christian communities for more intense experiences of prayer and Bible study. In large parts of Latin America there has been an explosion of these communities (called *communidades di base*), which are, at least indirectly, the result of a priest shortage. Many similar communities exist in other parts of the world, sometimes within a parish. Similarly, large numbers of Catholics go on periods of retreat for longer or shorter periods of time (retreats can be traced back to the Jesuits who recommended such periods of withdrawal in order to do the Spiritual Exercises of Saint Ignatius) at religious houses or monasteries. Similarly, others find their need for more intense community by joining prayer groups or interest groups which cater, for example, to married couples, young people, students, and so on.

THE STUDY OF SPIRITUALITY

As one looks back over the history of Catholicism, it is easy to see how certain spiritual practices grew in response to certain cultural pressures. We have already noted this in our discussion of schools of spirituality. A person has a certain kind of way of living the Christian life. That person's practice and example draw other people to that way of living, and a certain tradition grows up and is handed on and remembered by subsequent generations. There emerges, then, a recognizable body of literature and practice which can be reflected upon. The study of Catholic spirituality is a second-order phenomenon: Those interested can reflect critically on the various "ways" of the schools, movements, and personages that have been recorded in history. Such a study is of interest both to the historian and to the theologian.

This kind of study has a long history behind it. Since the late 1930s, scholars, writing mainly in French, have studied every aspect of Catholic spirituality, publishing their results in the multiple volumes of the encyclopedic *Dictionnaire de Spiritualité*. Along with that massive work of scholarship there has been a cascade of other studies and monographs ranging from the recuperation of spiritual classics of the various schools as well as more targeted monographs on specific issues.

One purpose of such scholarly writing, of course, is pure scholarship, but there is the added necessity of discerning within studies what is perennial and what is culture-bound, and adjudicating what is dangerous or peripheral or possibly heterodox. A sure grasp of the authentic roots of spirituality is a safeguard against canonizing the spiritual impulses of one whose own experiences are then purported to be somehow normative.

It is obvious that certain ways of acting out the Christian life are not in conformity with the larger understanding of the faith or of the moral life proper to a Christian. History is replete with such examples. Many heretical movements in the history of Christianity had their origins not in strict doctrinal pursuits (although there have been those also) but in certain ways of behavior that, in the long view of things, had doctrinal consequences. Certain reforming groups in the Middle Ages, to cite an example, were so determined to reform the Church that they embraced notions and patterns of behavior which simply were not in conformity with the Great Church. Attempts to live a "strict" Gospel life led some, such as the Poor Men of Lyons, the Patarines, and others, to deny the efficacy of the sacraments, to resist Church authority, and so on, in a fashion that turned them into sectarians. In the early modern period, people who so emphasized the working of grace turned themselves into passive instruments of God (think of the Quietists) that they become alienated from the ordinary workings of Catholic life. In these – and many other instances can be noted – what happened was that a desire to live in the Spirit ended up in sectarian separation. These heterodox movements have been of keen interest to historians of ideas.

It is for that reason that the tradition of spiritual writings, from the earliest monastic literature through the long history of the Church down to the present day, have constantly insisted that part of being a spiritual person demands some sort of discernment to sort out the authentic from the illusory. The practical working out of that discernment takes a number of forms. Sacramental confession has been one form of discernment because historically that process involves a manifestation of conscience to a confessor who can serve as both a teacher and a judge about whether one's actions, intentions, and desires are wholesomely leading to a better Christian life. The tradition also encourages a spiritual director, or what the Irish tradition called a "soul friend," to serve as a guide on the spiritual way. Finally, the community itself can serve as both a support and a director to help people in their Christian lives. One way to think about this process is to see it as participation in the received wisdom of the tradition within the Christian community.

Such discernment, of course, does not preclude the impulse of the prophetic spirit by which a person feels a need to try something hitherto untried. As the late theologian Karl Rahner noted, the story of the saints illustrates the fact that even in *this* new way it is possible to be a Christian. The great saints of the Church either demonstrated the perennial value of the Christian life or, in some instances, developed new ways of being a Christian.

Studies in spirituality have been a rich resource for the ongoing reform of the Church. It has been a hallmark of modern Catholicism to go back, for instance, into the early history of various schools of spirituality in an attempt to understand the primary impulses for such schools, what is of perennial value in them, and how to learn from such considerations for contemporary needs. This process is one of the essential parts of that reforming impulse we have considered before in this book; it goes under the name of *ressourcement*.

THE BLESSED VIRGIN AND THE SAINTS

One of the characteristics of Roman Catholic (and Orthodox) spirituality is a strong devotion to Mary, the Mother of God, and the saints. That devotion is expressed in its eucharistic liturgy and in its prayer life more generally. Such devotion is strongly connected to the broad understanding that Catholicism has concerning the Church which it sees as a continuity between all believers both living and dead. The *Catechism of the Catholic Church* satisfies itself on this point by simply quoting the Second Vatican Council: "Exactly as Christian communion among our fellow pilgrims brings us closer to Christ, so our communion with the saints joins us to Christ, from whom as from its fountain and head issues all grace, and the life of the People of God itself" (No. 957; see *Lumen gentium,* 50).

The singular place of Mary in the thinking and devotional life of the Catholic Church derives from its understanding of Christ. Already in the fifth century, when certain Christians attempted to call Mary only the mother of the human Jesus, the Catholic Church, at the Council of Ephesus in 431, rejected any such bifurcation by understanding Mary as the mother of a person, not a nature, thus giving her the right to be called, in Greek, *Theotokos* (Latin, *Deipara*), the one who bears God. That title was already in use, centuries before Ephesus made it a canonical phrase in the Catholic vocabulary. By extrapolation, the Church believes that Mary is the human link, who, by reason, of her free choice to bear the Savior (see Luke 1:38) was the human agent through whom salvation came into the world. Just as the Church now brings forth Christ to the world, so, in the beginning, Mary did the same – thus initiating the whole plan of salvation. This plan came into being not at any old time but in what Paul calls this "fullness of time" when Christ was born under the law and born of a woman (see Gal. 4:4). It is for that reason that Mary's place in the plan of salvation is mentioned in the rule of faith, the creed.

The doctrinal reality of Mary's place in salvation has been preserved in creed and liturgy but, along with that dogmatic assertion about Mary, there has grown up over time a deep-seated devotional love for the Blessed Virgin Mary expressed with varying degrees of intensity in different eras of the Church's life. Surely, the flowering of the medieval cathedral dedicated to the Virgin Mary was one high point of such devotional expression when, it could be said, there was a happy confluence of architecture, art, music, and literature dedicated to the Virgin. Such a strong devotional appeal was reinforced in the period of the Reformation when many of the Reformers, in reaction to what they saw as Marian excesses, turned against a whole range of devotional practices as superstitious and idolatrous. For every action, there is always a reaction, so the Catholic Reformation not only reaffirmed its devotion to Mary but also refined its thinking, found new forms of devotion, and advanced certain elaborations of Marian doctrine.

There is a sense in which devotion to Mary wells up from a deep intuitive reserve found in the Catholic faithful. The apparitions and their annexed pilgrimage sites of the nineteenth and early twentieth century (Lourdes, LaSallette, Fatima, etc.) were all rooted in lay experience coinciding with vigorous reactions against the Church in social society so that the faith of the laity became encouraged in time by the hierarchy. Such popular manifestations of piety frequently acted as a counterbalance to loss of courage in the Church. Such traditional piety has had a long history in the Church itself, and it is often oriented towards devotion to the Blessed Mother and the saints.

The forms of non-liturgical devotions to the Blessed Mother may be handily summarized as follows.

Prayers and hymns to the Blessed Virgin

There is a vast corpus of such prayers ranging from earliest prayer that we have dating from the late second century: "Under thy patronage, we fly to thee, o holy Mother of God" to prayers written in our own time. Equally, hymnody has a long history, with the "Salve Regina" written by the monk Herman the Cripple in the late eleventh century being one of the most famous. The standard "Hail Mary" is taken directly from Luke's Gospel and appears in liturgies from the fourth century on; the second part ("Holy Mary [. . .] pray for us sinners," etc.) appears to have derived from litanies first developed in the seventh century.

Special devotions

Over the course of the centuries, special focus has been placed on one aspect or other of the Virgin's life, which, in turn, gave rise to the invocation of Mary under a particular rubric: the sorrowful mother; the seven sorrows of Mary; the Virgin as queen, etc. Many such devotions developed in the Middle Ages as a result of the affective piety which was preached by monastic orders such as the Cistercians and the mendicant friars such as the Franciscans.

Pilgrimage shrines

From the Middle Ages down to the present day, people have made pilgrimages to places associated with the Blessed Virgin Mary. Some of these locations reflect deep religious and cultural sentiments. The great cathedral of Chartres in France, with its emblematic Virgin, is often regarded as a shorthand symbol of French Catholicism just as Mexican identity is closely aligned to devotion to the Virgin of Guadalupe. To this day, hundreds of thousands of pilgrims travel to Fatima in Portugal, Lourdes in France, Loreto in Italy and other places in honor of Mary, the mother of Jesus.

Titles

Over the centuries, Mary has been associated with various honorary titles. Some of these are associated with biblical symbols (Ark of the Covenant, tower of ivory, etc.) while others are honorifics that have entered into the pious vocabulary of Catholics. The most common list of such titles may be found in the so-called "Litany of Loreto", a sixteenth-century list of supplications derived from an earlier litany and subsequently added to in more modern times. The titles of the Virgin (for example, "Queen of Peace") are called out with each receiving the response "Pray for us." This litany is frequently recited in churches around the Catholic world.

Feasts

Although there are many regional feast days dedicated to the Blessed Virgin, the reforms following on the Second Vatican Council have reduced the feast days in the universal Roman calendar to the following:

January 1	Solemnity of Mary, the Mother of God.
March 25	The Annunciation of the Lord to Mary.
August 15	The Assumption of Mary into Heaven.
September 8	The Birthday of the Virgin.
September 15	Our Lady of Sorrows.
October 7	Our Lady of the Rosary.
November 21	The Presentation of Mary in the Temple.
December 8	The Immaculate Conception of Mary.
December 12	Our Lady of Guadalupe (in Mexico and the USA).

The oldest core of these feast days are four in number: the Annunciation, the Assumption (known in the East as the "Falling Asleep of the Virgin"), the birthday of Mary, and her presentation in the Temple. Those feasts were established in Rome to be celebrated with solemn processions by Pope Sergius I (d.701). Sergius was of Syrian background but born in Palermo (Sicily), and his highlighting of those feasts was most likely due to his knowledge of liturgical customs in the East where these feasts had a long history.

THE BLESSED VIRGIN MARY AND VATICAN II

A great deal of piety and pious practices relative to Mary and the other saints were part and parcel of the popular piety of common people. It was widely recognized that many practices, separated from the doctrinal and formal liturgical practices of the Church, were open to abuse and exaggeration. At the dawn of the Reformation, Catholic writers such as Erasmus of Rotterdam, protested against the abuses in the cult of the saints. In the period after the Reformation, and, as we have seen, in reaction against the reformers, many claims were made on behalf of the intercession of the saints, and increasing honors were paid to the Blessed Virgin. It is no accident that a separate tract in theology known as "mariology" first began to appear only in the late sixteenth century.

When the Second Vatican Council convened, there was a sense that certain aspects of Marian devotion and ideas connected to that devotion had run too independent a course over the previous centuries. Such an independence could be seen as a distorting feature of Catholic theology as a whole and, further, as an obstacle in one of the most important topics facing the Catholic Church in the twentieth century, namely ecumenical discussion and dialogue with other Christian bodies. Accordingly, there was a decision, not without lively debate, to do two things that would refocus Catholic thought and practice into a more organic whole. To accomplish this end, the Council made two important decisions.

The first decision was not to have a separate document on the Blessed Virgin Mary promulgated at the Council despite some early indications that some wished for such a document to be written. The second decision was to incorporate the Church's thinking about the Blessed Virgin Mary within a larger context in order to reorient the direction of theology towards a more holistic vision of Mary within the larger doctrinal tradition of the Church.

Accordingly, the eighth chapter of the dogmatic constitution on the Church (*Lumen gentium*) was devoted to Mary. Early in that chapter, the Council asserted that it did not intend to "give a complete doctrine on Mary, nor does it wish to decide those questions which the work of theologians has not fully clarified" (*Lumen gentium*, 54). In that same paragraph, however, it describes what it does intend to do: "to set forth diligently both the role of the Blessed Virgin in the mystery of the Incarnate Word and in the mystical body, and the duties of the redeemed towards the Mother of God, who is mother of Christ and mother of humanity, and especially of those who believe" (*Lumen gentium*, 54).

In the subsequent sections of Chapter 8 are outlined the historic belief of the Church about the role of Mary in the economy of salvation, her rightful role as the one who brought Christ into the world, and, following on an analogy that goes back at least as far as Saint Ambrose of Milan, that Mary is a type of the Church itself which constantly brings forth Christ to the world. Thus, Saint Augustine would write commenting on the creed in his *Enchiridion*, while affirming that the virginity of Mary cannot be impugned because it would mean that the Church was wrong and "in acknowledging him as born of the Virgin Mary, the Church which in imitation of his mother daily brings his members to birth and remains a virgin."

Towards the end of the section on Mary, it also takes cognizance of certain tendencies to separate the cult of the Virgin from the larger picture of the Christian mystery by reminding Catholics of the historic canons about the proper use of images of Christ, the Virgin, and the saints while strongly urging theologians and preachers

to refrain as much from all false exaggeration as from too summary an attitude in considering the special dignity of the Mother of God. Following the study of sacred scripture, the Fathers, the doctors and the liturgy of the Church, and under the guidance of the magisterium, let them rightly illustrate the offices and privileges of the Blessed Virgin, which *always refers to Christ, the source of all truth, sanctity, and devotion.* (*Lumen gentium*, 67; emphasis added)

The Catholic understanding of Mary has hardly diminished since Vatican II. The late Pope John Paul II was a keen supporter of devotion to Our Lady albeit in a deeply traditional vein. The liberation theologians of Latin America have emphasized another element in the life of Mary: that of an unwed mother who fled into exile and whose hymn in Luke 2 (the so-called Magnificat) provides hope for the poor as well as a prophetic challenge to the rich. At the same time, due to serious and respectful dialogue with other Christians, the Protestant world has come to a deeper appreciation of Mary without, however, accepting some of the doctrinal formulations so characteristic of Catholicism. Recent documents from the Lutheran/Catholic, the Anglican/Catholic, and others on the role of Mary are fair proof of this new dialogue.

CATHOLIC SPIRITUALITY AND WORLD RELIGIONS

Roman Catholicism is not only committed to ecumenical dialogue within the Christian family but also to dialogue with the great religions of the world. Such dialogue received its seal of approval with the adoption of the *Declaration of the Relationship of the Church to Non-Christian Religions* (*Nostra aetate*) at the Second Vatican Council. We will discuss this important document in other places in this book, but it is pertinent for our discussion of spirituality for one simple reason: Relations between Christians and Buddhists, Hindus, and, to Jews and Muslims have gone apace over the past decades at two levels: intellectual discussion and, where possible, joint cooperation in the area of charity and social justice. However, two of the great religions of the world, Hinduism and Buddhism, have a long millennial history of ascetic practice organized into monastic traditions.

It has been recognized that this long contemplative tradition offers an opportunity for Catholic contemplatives to engage in a dialogue of practice with the other contemplative traditions of the world. What can Catholic monastics learn from the contemplative tradition of the other religions of the world? Such a dialogue does not mean adopting wholesale practices from other religious traditions, but it does mean that it is possible to learn from these practices. Do Zen techniques have anything to say to the meditative practices of Catholic monastics? What similarities exist between the search to experience the love of God, as happens in the Sufi tradition of Islam, and the interior search which is so central to the Christian mystical tradition?

Such exchanges have gone on (even before Vatican II) for a long time even though anyone who has participated at a very deep level knows well that superficial similarities (Buddhists meditate, we meditate; Hindus fast, we fast; etc.) do not get to foundational levels of belief. The many exchanges that take place at a deep level of conversation have the benefit of lessening religious tensions, increasing fraternal cooperation, and deepening understanding. In a talk the American monk Thomas Merton gave in Calcutta, India in 1968, just weeks before his untimely death, he opined that

we have now reached a stage of (long overdue) religious maturity at which it may be possible for someone to remain perfectly faithful to a Christian and Western monastic commitment and yet to learn in depth from, say, a Buddhist or Hindu discipline and experience. I believe that some of us need to do this in order to improve the quality of our own monastic life and even to help in the task of monastic renewal which has been undertaken within the Western Church. (From his *Asian Journal*)

Thirty years later, the Dalai Lama came to visit Merton's monastery to pay tribute to his vision and to encourage such exchanges as those he had with Merton shortly after his talk in Calcutta.

While it has become somewhat common today for Catholics to use certain techniques for religious meditation, adopted, mainly, from Buddhist sources, Merton was quite clear that such adaptations must never sink into a kind of facile syncretism. It is for that reason that the Church insists such dialogue and exchange be done with care and with a clear understanding that, as all scholars know, there are many radical differences between Catholic beliefs and those of other religions. These incommensurabilities must not be brushed off as being of little consequence.

It has been increasingly recognized that perhaps the most fruitful place for interreligious dialogue will be among contemplatives of the various traditions. The mutual exchange of insights and practices at this contemplative level involves both ideas and experiences. These contemplatives, after all, are the most committed practitioners of their respective faiths and are most ready to explain their practice. Such dialogues already take place and are an important part of the Catholic practice of dialogue – a practice encouraged by the Second Vatican Council.

The reason why interreligious dialogue might best be undertaken among contemplatives is because the contemplative tradition puts a high priority on religious experience as flowing from a disciplined life of faith and practice. The contemplative speaks with an authenticity that runs deeper than merely "knowing" at an intellectual level. The contemplative is one who is able to say to another, "Here is what my experience has been – does this experience strike you as something you recognize?" Such an exchange does not satisfy itself with superficial similarities. Done at a properly mature level it is critical that each participant remain faithful to his or her own tradition while exchanging experiences in the search for the Transcendent. Again, Thomas Merton got it right when he said, in

1968 just a few years after Vatican II, that the contemplative dialogue must be reserved for those who have been seriously disciplined by years of silence and by a long habit of meditation, it must be reserved for those who have entered into full seriousness into their own monastic tradition, and are in authentic contact with the past of their own religious community (*The Asian Journal*).

Box 7   The rosary

In our discussion of Catholic spirituality, we have not yet considered one feature of Catholic devotional practice which is almost identified with Catholicism: the recitation of the rosary. The use of a stringed counting device is not peculiar to Catholicism. Orthodox often use a rosary as an aid when reciting the Jesus Prayer, and some Protestants are devising rosaries which are used for the recitation of biblical verses. Of course, in the other religions of the world, similar beads are used; in Islam, the pious can recite the ninety-nine beautiful names of Allah using a type of rosary.

In Catholicism, the predecessor of the rosary was the custom of reciting the Lord's Prayer (the *Pater* as it is known in Latin) 150 times by those who could not read the psalms at common prayer. This custom was often called the "poor person's psalter." Sometime in the early Middle Ages the prayer that substituted for the *Pater* was the Hail Mary (*Ave Maria*). Beginning in the fifteenth century, it became customary to add mental reflections on the mysteries of faith for each ten (decade) of the rosary. In time, these solidified into the sorrowful, joyful, and glorious mysteries. These three groups of five mysteries are often called the Dominican rosary because this devotion spread largely though the missionary preaching of the Dominican order. The late Pope John Paul II added to the three sets of meditation what he called the "luminous mysteries" in order to recall great events during the early life of Jesus.

The general shape of the standard rosary, with an attached crucifix and the five sets of ten beads separated by a single bead, was only standardized in the sixteenth century, but rosary forms of diverse kinds go back centuries earlier. The custom of providing meditations for each of the decades seems to have originated in Carthusian monasteries in the fifteenth century.

In the period after the Second Vatican Council, the ubiquity of the use of the rosary abated somewhat, but it is still very popular among Catholics. Its communal recitation takes place in many churches especially during times where an emphasis on Marian devotions is encouraged as in the months of May and October. The rosary is often recited on the evening before a person's funeral at the wake – a custom that seems to have begun in Ireland.

FURTHER READING

Barton, Stephen, ed., *Holiness Past and Present* (London: T & T Clark, 2003). Valuable essays on holiness in an ecumenical context.

Casey, Michael, *Towards God: The Ancient Wisdom of Western Prayer* (Liguori, Miss.: Triumph, 1996). A useful survey of the history of prayer in the West.

Cunningham, Lawrence and Egan, Keith, *Christian Spirituality: Themes from the Tradition* (New York, N.Y.: Paulist, 1996). A basic introduction.

Dreyer, Elizabeth and Burrows, Mark, eds., *Minding the Spirit: The Study of Christian Spirituality* (Baltimore, Md.: Johns Hopkins University Press, 2005). Important methodological essays.

Downey, Michael, ed., *The New Dictionary of Catholic Spirituality* (Collegeville, Pa.: Glazier, 1993). Comprehensive resource from a Catholic perspective.

Gutiérrez, Gustavo, *We Drink from Our Own Wells* (Maryknoll, N.Y.: Orbis, 1983). Spirituality from the perspective of liberation theology.

Harmless, William, *Mystics* (Oxford: Oxford University Press, 2007). A valuable book on how to understand and read mysticl texts.

Graef, Hilda, *Mary: A History of Doctrine and Devotion* (2 vols., London: Sheed & Ward, 1965). An old but useful survey.

Orsuto, Donna, *Holiness* (London and New York, N.Y.: Continuum, 2006). A useful overview of Catholic spirituality written by a lay theologian.

Sheldrake, Philip, *Spirituality and History* (New York, N.Y.: Crossroad, 1992). A useful study of how spirituality has an historical shape.

Sheldrake, Philip, ed., *The New Westminster Dictionary of Christian Spirituality* (London and Louisville, Ky.: SCM and Westminster, 2005). Highly informative and ecumenical in scope.

Waaijman, Kees, *Spirituality: Forms, Foundations, Methods* (Leuven: Peeters, 2003). Massive study done from a Catholic perspective with a phenomenological orientation.

Wimbush, Vincent L. and Valantasis, Richard, eds., *Asceticism* (Oxford: Oxford University Press, 1995). A collection of essays from a comparative perspective.

Zaleski, Philip and Zaleski, Carol, *Prayer: A History* (Boston, Mass.: Houghton Mifflin, 2005). An excellent survey of prayer in cross-cultural perspective.

CHAPTER 8

The missionary character of Catholicism

INTRODUCTION

As we noted in the opening chapter of this book, Catholicism has always understood its universality as a call to reach all people. As a consequence, the Catholic Church has always manifested a strong missionary character as one of its defining characteristics. That missionary impulse means that it is a mandate to reach the Gospel everywhere and at all times. The universal character of Catholicism is both a fact and an urgent necessity.

That Christianity spread from its Jerusalem center rapidly after the earthly life of Jesus is a fact. Indeed, it is clear from the New Testament itself that the first Christians had a conviction that they were inspired by God to spread their faith universally. Catholics have always invoked the "great mandate" found in the Gospel of Matthew as their missionary watchword: "Go therefore and make disciples of all nations, baptizing them in the name of the Father and of the son and of the Holy Spirit" (Matt. 28:19). According to the Acts of the Apostles, the disciples, shortly before the ascension of Jesus into the heavens, heard him stipulate something quite similar: "But you will receive power when the Holy Spirit comes upon you; and you will be my witnesses in Jerusalem, in all Judea and Samaria, and to the ends of the earth" (Acts 1:8).

There was one crucial problem in those primitive days of preaching the Gospel and it was this: Did the new followers of Jesus have to observe the demands of the Jewish law? The reasons why this question was crucial is simple: Jesus and all of his followers were, themselves, Jewish, and, further, they tended to identify themselves with both the synagogue and the temple in Jerusalem. As Gentiles became attracted to Jesus and his life and message, the question of Torah observance became important. Were male converts to undergo circumcision? Were all those who joined the Christian *ekklesia* to observe the dietary laws? Again, it is clear from the New Testament (and especially the letters of Paul, and, most particularly, his letter to the Galatians) that this was an enormously vexatious issue that pitted the Jerusalem Church against the missionary communities identified with Paul. As is clear historically, Paul won that battle even though Jewish Christian groups existed for centuries after the New Testament debate. The important point, of course, is that had Paul not prevailed, nascent Christianity could well have ended up as a somewhat heterodox movement within the larger world of Judaism itself. It is not without significance that Paul is sometimes called the Apostle to the Gentiles.

Although the issue of Jewish law as obligatory had been solved in favor of Gentile converts, early Christianity never saw itself as severing its roots from its Jewish matrix. The earliest Christian communities had a mixture of Jewish and Gentile members within it. Indeed, it could be fairly said that if one does not understand the profound Jewish roots of Christianity one does not understand Christianity at all. Jesus was Jewish as were all of his disciples. Even though Paul broke the impasse over Jewish observance, he still proudly cried out: "Are they Hebrews? So am I! Are they Israelites? So am I! Are they descendants of Abraham? So am I!" (1 Cor. 11:22). Even with the growth of the gentile presence in the Early Church, it never rejected the revelation found in the Old Testament; indeed, it reacted negatively to an attempt in the second century in Rome to reject the Old Testament when such a proposal was made by Marcion. In fact, any close reader of the canonical New Testament knows, among other things, that it is a vast gloss on the Hebrew scriptures.

It is also clear that, at its earliest stages, the point of contact for Christian missionaries in the generation or so after the life of Jesus was the synagogues of the diaspora which were dotted all over the Roman Empire. It is also the case that as the Christians found unwelcome audiences in the Jewish diaspora they were also attracting Gentile converts. Paul himself mentions his fellow missionary Titus as one of these.

While, as the sporadic persecution of Christians under Rome law demonstrates, the message of Christianity was not always received enthusiastically, it is also true that the Christian message was spreading around the Mediterranean littoral. The question is, why? Of course, the Christian answer was that its success was due to the power of the Holy Spirit, but it is also the case that there are some plausible empirical reasons for Christian success.

In the first place, despite the persecutions directed at the early Christians, the Roman Empire was at peace, it was powerful, and it was stable. Rome had a usable series of trade routes both by land and sea; the Mediterranean was mostly free of brigands and pirates. There was a common language for commerce, Koine (Greek). Despite the sporadic outbreak of persecutions, the Romans typically exhibited a fair tolerance towards all religions as long as any given religion was not hostile to Roman authority or resisted the minimal obligation of honoring the Roman pantheon and acknowledging the divinity of the emperor. Christianity, also, from its very beginnings looked after the widows, orphans, travelers, sick, infirm, and other needy persons, thus providing within its community a social net for those who might have otherwise ended up destitute. Christian communities received women as converts (unlike some of the mystery religions such as Mithraism) as well as members of different classes. Nor were the doctrines of Christianity without appeal. They offered a high moral code, a belief in one God, and a view about assuaging guilt as well as a sense of common bonds within their fellowship.

In a period of religious yearning, these factors had attractive power. As has often been pointed out, Christianity's biggest competitor in the early centuries of its existence were the various forms of the mystery religions, but it did not have their liabilities. The Mithraic Mysteries, for example, did not permit women to be initiated. Finally, as scholars such as Robert Wilken have pointed out, the Christian faith could offer to its converts a new vocabulary that enhanced pagan discourse. To justice they could speak of love; to duty, they added the concept of grace; to earthly pessimism they offered eternal salvation, etc. The Christian apologists made full use of these doctrinal points in their dialogues with Roman intellectuals.

It seems fair to say that, based on the evidence that we have, in the period of the persecutions, the Church grew by something akin to cell division. A small community of believers would meet in a house church; when that house church reached a certain size, it would necessitate another place of worship. Alternatively, a number of house churches would exist simultaneously in a city started separately by different groups (predominantly Jewish or Gentile or of a different language group), which, in turn, would multiply. It is important to remember that, generally speaking, churches grew basically within cities; in fact, our modern word "pagan" means someone who lived not in the city, but in the countryside (Latin *pagus*). It would take a long time for the countryside to be Christianized, and often then, on the face of it, the Christianity was often mixed with folk religion. The one thing that does seem clear is that Christianity grew by increments and, judging from the scanty evidence that has been preserved, drew its membership from various classes. If we can take the early second-century Roman text *The Shepherd of Hermas,* as witness, the relationship between the rich and the very poor was not always harmonious even though the author of the *Shepherd* makes it clear that the rich who were Christians were not permitted to be indifferent to the needs of their poor counterparts.

While we tend to think of the expansion of Christianity towards the West – from Jerusalem towards Rome – it is also important to remember that Christianity also had a stronghold in Roman Africa – the southern side of the Mediterranean littoral – and to the East through Western Syria and beyond. There was a Syriac-speaking Church in that part of the world before the time of Constantine, while Armenia was the first country officially to declare itself Christian in 301, after it had been evangelized by Gregory the Illuminator (d.332), who had come from already Christian Cappadocia (modern-day Turkey) for that purpose. We also know that Constantine himself congratulated the King of Persia (present-day Iran) because some of the finest provinces of his kingdom were hospitable to Christians living there. The thrust of Christianity eastward has often been overlooked in histories of the Church, but it was an area replete with Christian communities.

CONSTANTINE AND BEYOND

When Emperor Constantine granted toleration to the Christians in the early fourth century, it is estimated that about 10 percent of the 50 million people in the Roman Empire were Christian. Much of that growth came through the multiplication of house churches, but the rest of it was the fruit of the work of traveling evangelists. Writing in the fourth century, the church historian Eusebius (d.340) said that these itinerant preachers would lay the foundations of a Christian community in a place, appoint pastors to oversee the community, and then move on to another location. By the time of Eusebius, these itinerants were fewer in number, being replaced by stable bishops who assumed the task of evangelizing in his local area. The spread of Christians typically expanded out from town to countryside and not vice versa. It is a safe generalization to say that Christianity in the period after Constantine extended west to the present Iberian peninsula (present-day Spain and Portugal), north into Roman Britain, south along the Mediterranean coast of North (Roman) Africa and east to the area nominally under Roman jurisdiction east of the Euphrates river.

Constantine, of course, had moved his capital city to the east, founding a new city, named after him, Constantinople (present-day Istanbul). Constantinople would become the "Second Rome." Even though the rival Persian Empire to the east looked skeptically at Christianity because of its identification with the Roman Empire, there was a flourishing missionary activity in the Syriac-speaking world, with missions reaching all the way to China in that period. The Syriac Church has given us a vast literature, and a living Church still existing in the Middle East.

The great shift in the religious situation came, of course, with the rise of a new religion, Islam, which was as aggressively missionary as was Christianity although its expansion was more often than not accomplished by invasion and the sword. In the Carolingian period, however, there was ample evidence that Christianity was also imposed by the military power of the emperors. By the middle of the eighth century – say around 750 – half of the old Christian lands in the Roman Empire had become Islamic: all of North Africa, parts of the Iberian peninsula, and the present-day area covering the Middle East especially in ancient Palestine with its all-important city, Jerusalem. Islam, generally, grew not by the slow spread of Islamic communities but by a policy of conquering lands and "Islamicizing" the local inhabitants. Many countries that had been largely Christian ended up as small communities under Islamic rule.

Christian missions looked in other directions during the period of the rise of Islam, and they did so largely under the impulse of the rise of organized monasticism. There were several fronts for this missionary activity.

Ireland

Although there was a Catholic bishop in Ireland in the early fifth century, it was Saint Patrick who was the first great missionary to Ireland. It has been often said that Patrick was the first Christian missionary who actually evangelized a pagan population. Although by Patrick's time there was a small enclave of Christians on the coast, it was left to him to move into pagan areas to preach Christianity. Throughout the middle of the fifth century, Patrick evangelized in Ireland, teaching and establishing communities of monks and nuns. We have some sense of his life from his *Confession,* written late in his life, and a letter he wrote to a certain "Coroticus" protesting the enslavement of Irish Christians. Patrick does refer to himself as a "bishop in Ireland."

Patrick was not a monk himself (although he probably had been shaped by monasticism in France), but, in the generations after him, monasticism of a definite Celtic type was characteristic of the Irish Church. One form of asceticism peculiar to Irish monasticism was the practice of wandering or self-exile as a form of penance. One such wanderer, Columba (d.597), left Ireland for Scotland and evangelized that people. Another,

Columban (d.615), headed south and, through his labors, evangelized in France and even down into Italy.

Britain

Even though there were pockets of Christians in Roman Britain, it was Pope Gregory the Great who, in 590, sent a body of monks from Italy under a monk named Augustine to convert the English. This missionary enterprise, centered around Canterbury, was responsible, over a long period, for the conversion of the Anglo-Saxon population of Britain. The story of the spread of Christianity there has been beautifully described by the Venerable Bede (d.735) in his *Ecclesiastical History of the English Nation* completed four years before his death – a work which still provides us with a fundamental knowledge of the growth of Christianity in England even though it may be a bit romanticized through Bede's presuppositions about the provident will of God.

The English mission

Pope Gregory I asked Augustine and some monks to go England as missionaries. The monks, fearful of what they might find there, asked Augustine to petition the pope to cancel the mission. Gregory encouraged them to proceed and sent a letter to the monastic group; the letter is found in the Venerable Bede's *Ecclesistial History*:

GREGORY, Servant of the servants of God, to the servants of the Lord. My very dear sons, it is better never to undertake any high enterprise than to abandon it when once begun. So with the help of God you must carry out this holy task which you have begun. Do not be deterred by the troubles of the journey or by what men say. Be constant and zealous in carrying out this enterprise which, under God's guidance, you have undertaken and be assured that the greater the labor, the greater will be your eternal reward. When Augustine, your leader returns, whom We have appointed your abbot, obey him humbly in all things, remembering that whatever he directs you to do will always be to the good of your souls. May almighty God protest you with his grace and grant me to see the results of your labors in our heavenly home. And although my office prevents me from working at your side, yet because I long to do so, I hope to share in your heavenly reward. God keep you safe, my dearest sons.

The planting of monasteries in Britain allowed the monks there to extend the outreach of the Church. One of the most famous of these was a monk from Crediton in southern England named Boniface (d.754), who left England for Germany and, by planting monasteries, evangelized, especially from a large monastery in Fulda. Boniface eventually pushed into the land of the Frisians, where he was martyred along with a number of his companions. Interestingly enough, he utilized the labors of monastic women in his missionary enterprise, bringing to Germany a nun named Lioba (or Leoba), who established convents as centers of religious instruction and conversion.

Tribal conversions

The slow penetration of Christianity into Eastern Europe ran apace through the tenth century either through the influence of monastic pioneers (as was the case in Poland, Hungary, Scandinavia, and Bohemia) or by the aggressive conquering of peoples by Christian kings who forced conversions on subject peoples, as was the case with Charlemagne who conquered the Saxons on his eastern border.

The Slavs

Outreach to Slavic peoples inevitably calls to mind two extraordinary brothers Cyril (d.869) and Methodius (d.885), natives of Thessalonica in Greece, who were sent by the Emperor in Constantinople to Moravia where they preached the Gospel, translated the liturgy into Slavonic, and invented a new alphabet (now known as Cyrillic) in order to translate Christian texts adequately. Using Slavonic, they translated both the liturgy and a version of the scriptures into that language. That language is still used in the Russian Orthodox liturgy. Many of their innovations were contested by German missionaries. The brothers had papal support for their efforts despite resistance in some quarters to a vernacular liturgy. Cyril died in Rome, but Methodius was ordained a bishop and labored in the eastern part of Europe until his death in what are the present-day Czech and Slovak Republics. Today, the brothers are seen as pioneers in cultural adaptation, and the late pope, John Paul II, nominated them as co-patrons of Europe for their pioneering efforts to bridge East and West. They are honored as saints both in the East and in the West. It has been common in the Catholic Church to refer to the various bishops who evangelized in this period as the "Apostles" to those countries. Hence, Saint Augustine of Canterbury is the Apostle to the English; Patrick to the Irish; Boniface to the Germans; Cyril and Methodius to the Slavs, etc.

THE HIGH MIDDLE AGES

If there is any one thing that occupied the attention of Christian missionaries as well as the general population in the Middle Ages it was the looming presence of Islam at its borders. Dante described the walls of Hell itself as being crowned by fiery mosques, and, centuries earlier, *The Song of Roland* demonized the Muslims. The response to the world of Islam was various. One strategy, beginning in the late eleventh century, was to send armies in a series of crusades against the Muslim-controlled Holy Land where their presence was seen as an unpardonable affront to the Christian religion. Those various crusades had varying degrees of success (there was for a period a crusader state in the Holy Land), but the one persistent fallout from these military adventures was an unremitting hatred for the Christian West in the Muslim world. To this day, Islamic polemicists and preachers describe Christianity in terms of the crusades. One other by-product of the crusades was the sacking of Constantinople by a crusading army from the West, which also brought a long history of bitter distrust between the Orthodox Christians and their Western counterparts. The medieval sack of Constantinople by the Crusaders has been retained as an unhappy memory in the Orthodox world and is often an implicit cause of tension between the Churches of the East and the West. The weakness of the Byzantine culture left in the wake of the Crusader sacking of the city is still mentioned by Eastern writers as a contributing cause of the fall of Constantinople to the Ottoman Turks in the mid-fifteenth century.

Another, more benign response, was the sending of missionaries to Muslim lands. Conspicuous in this effort was the rise of the so-called mendicant friars such as the Franciscans and the Dominicans. Francis of Assisi, in his own lifetime, crossed crusader lines around 1218 to speak with Harun al Rashid, the leader of the Muslim army in Egypt, but to no lasting avail. Within his lifetime, five Franciscans were martyred in Morocco as a consequence of their missionary efforts. The only long-term success the Franciscans had was that they managed to stay in the Holy Land as caretakers to the Christian holy sites and in service to pilgrims, a pastoral duty that they exercise to this day.

A third strategy was to study the world of Islam in an effort better to understand Islamic thought in order to write apologetic literature against its ideas. In places where there was something like peaceful coexistence between Muslims and Christians (in Sicily, parts of Spain, etc.), there was, in fact, some exchange between Muslim and Christian intellectuals.

Peter the Venerable (1092?–1156), Abbot of the influential monastery of Cluny, was keenly curious about Islam. He traveled to Spain to get Latin translations of Islamic works, including commissioning a translation of the Qur'an. A century later, Thomas Aquinas, for example, learned much of his Aristotle from Latin translations provided by William of Moerboke, who got his texts from Islamic sources in Spain. Aquinas's *Summa contra gentiles* is often designated as a Dominican handbook to be used in conversation with the Muslim world. Probably the most famous attempt to enter into this discussion was done by the polymath Spaniard and lay mystic Raymond Lull (also spelled Llull; died *c.*1315), who devoted his life to mission efforts (he died a martyr in North Africa) but took the time to learn what Muslims and Jews actually taught. Lull was aided in his acquisition of languages through Dominicans who worked in his native Majorca. He wrote passionately about the unity of all religion, studied Oriental languages, and established a training school for Franciscan missionaries on the island of Majorca. The one practical result of his efforts was the decree at the Council of Vienne (1311) to establish university faculties for the study of Oriental languages.

THE AGE OF EXPLORATION

Some in the Middle Ages assumed that the Christian message had reached pretty much all of the known world. A consequence of this comfortable idea was that those who were not Christian were so because of willfulness, and, as a consequence, they were outside the Catholic faith by some lack of grace. The explorations carried out to the hitherto-unknown world came as something of a shock, and, as a consequence, exploration and missionary efforts went hand in glove. It also raised the theological question of the salvation of those who were inculpably ignorant of salvation in Christ – a question, as we shall see later in detail, that has been discussed from various angles right down to the present day.

Sporadic attempts were made through the mendicants to reach the outer limits of exploration in the Middle Ages. Franciscan missionaries had made incursions among the Mongols and had even reached China during this period. However, the year 1492 was a crucial moment for the expansion of Christianity. It was in that year that the Catholic Monarchs of Spain (Ferdinand and Isabella) finally unified Spain into a country by defeating and expelling the Muslims from their traditional stronghold, in the process also expelling the Jews. This event is still known as the age of the *Reconquista*.

In the same year, of course, the Italian mariner, Christopher Columbus, made landfall, under the Spanish flag of Ferdinand and Isabella, in the so-called New World, bringing with him missionaries who, over the course of the next century or so, would spread Christianity over all of Central and Latin America as well as along the Santa Fe trail from what is present-day Florida westward, while in the eighteenth century friars also came north from Mexico along the California coast.

The history of the rise of Christianity in the Southern Hemisphere of the Americas is too complex to trace out in this work, but a few details need to be discussed. First, the Spanish system of allotting territory to the settlers from abroad with the concomitant obligation to care for the indigenous peoples was widely abused. This system of the *encomienda,* as it was known, soon led to the virtual enslavement of the native peoples; it is an unhappy part of this history. Already in the early sixteenth century, Dominicans such as Bartoleme' de las Casas (1484–1566), a bishop in the Mexican state of Chiapas, raised their voices against this system giving occasion to a fresh discussion about human rights for all peoples. Others, mainly from missionary religious, attempted to build model villages around the Church and to organize the peoples into small communities. They were well intentioned but, in fact, more or less kept the native population in some form of civil bondage. Perhaps the most famous of these were the Jesuit "reductions" in what is present-day Paraguay. These missionaries would lay out a town in a patterned order with church, school, workshops, housing, etc. There was to be some leadership from the native peoples, although ultimate authority rested in the Spanish themselves. This system of establishing settled towns under clerical supervision was also found in what is present-day California along the so-called "Royal Highway" (*El Camino Real*). Many of the cities of California, from San Diego in the southern part of the state to its present capital Sacramento, take their names from Franciscan settlements in this period.

By the eighteenth century, Catholicism was the main religion in all of Latin America with the exception of the small enclave of British who ruled along the west coast in what is present-day Guyana. Similarly, Catholicism was also the religion of Central America and Mexico as well as Spanish California in the west to Florida in the east and the Caribbean islands (Cuba, Santo Domingo, etc.). The Catholicism found in these countries was almost always touched by the residue of native religious practices, which resulted frequently, as we see today, in Catholicism mixed with folk religion.

The missionary expansion in the north of the New World derived mainly from the French exploration of what is present-day Canada. The style of missionary activity was twofold: the planting of the Church in colonial settlements and the work of missionaries (mainly Jesuit) who evangelized native peoples in Canada and what is present-day northern New York. By the late eighteenth century, there was a substantial Catholic presence in the province of Quebec, some Catholic presence in the Indian territories (which extended along the borders of the thirteen colonies that would make up the future USA). When looked at overall, Catholicism was like a vast parentheses with the south (Spanish- and Portuguese-speaking America) and north (French-speaking Canada) being Catholic and the emerging USA largely Protestant (due to English colonial strength).

During this age of exploration, the Portuguese had successfully traveled down the coast of Africa and around the horn, which put Europeans in a position to explore, by sea, both the Indian and the Asian world. Along with exploration and mercantile activities, the missionaries also came so that the more intrepid of them began to evangelize in hitherto inaccessible places. The most successful of these enterprises was the evangelization of the Philippines after the Spanish conquered that area. The work of the missionaries there, mainly by the Franciscans, Dominicans, and Augustinian friars was very traditional, but the long-term results were favorable since the Philippines today constitute the most Christian country in the Far East.

The Jesuits, however, attempted to adapt their missionary strategy to take account of the ancient cultures of India, Japan, and China. The pioneer in this regard was Francis Xavier, who had been one of the first members of the Jesuits. He left Europe in 1541 for Goa on the west coast of India, where there was a large Portuguese settlement. He later worked along the coast of India. He went on to the Malay peninsula and into what is present-day Indonesia and, from there, in 1549, to Japan, where he had a modest success in planting a Church. His last goal was to reach China, but he died off the coast in 1552.

Those who came after him were more adventuresome in their approach to their missionary work. The Italian Jesuit Matteo Ricci went to China, became expert in Mandarin Chinese, identified himself with the elite class of mandarins, and, in 1598, entered Beijing, where he ingratiated himself to the royal house due to his great skill as a clockmaker and scientist. Ricci wanted the Catholic mass to be celebrated in Mandarin; he thought it permissible for Christians to venerate the ancestors; and he attempted to show some degree of harmony between Christianity and the ethical ideals of Confucianism. One of the saddest events in missionary history was Rome's ultimate refusal to accept Ricci's ideas for adaptation – a refusal he never lived to see since he died in 1610 honored in China as the Wise Man from the West.

Ricci's strategy was adapted by the Jesuit Robert de Nobili, the seventeenth-century missionary in India. De Nobili adopted the way of life of an Indian holy man by wearing saffron robes, begging for his sustenance, eating a vegetarian diet, and devoting his time to meditation. He saw no problem in allowing certain cultural customs such as wearing the Hindu sacred thread, and he did not fight the notion of a caste system. De Nobili learned the native languages and became a keen scholar of ancient Sanskrit. Although Rome first gave its approval to his methods, his ideas eventually lost favor in the so-called "rites controversy" over Ricci's ideas. De Nobili's approach never made much headway among the high-caste Brahmins. Most Christians in India today belong to the lower castes.

The most successful of the innovative Jesuit missionaries of the period was Alexandre de Rhodes who actually developed the Vietnamese alphabet which is used to this day. The solid minority of Vietnamese Catholics today can trace their spiritual genealogy back to the missionary work done by Rhodes. He was expelled from Vietnam in 1645, but, true to his missionary impulse, he eventually went to Persia (present-day Iran), where he died in 1660. A substantial minority of Vietnamese remained Catholic, and, in a true instance of irony, the Vietnamese community in the USA, established as a result of refugees in the 1960s after the disastrous war in Vietnam, has been a precious reservoir of new priests and religious in that country.

In the period after the Protestant Reformation, the popes took a keen interest in missionary activity both within the historical boundaries of Christianity and in missionary expansion. Pope Gregory XV instituted a separate Roman congregation, De Propaganda Fide, to coordinate the missionary work of the Catholic Church in 1622. Five years later, Gregory's successor, Urban VIII, established a college (later a university) for the training of missionary clergy. In 1988, Pope John Paul II renamed, appropriately, the Congregation De Propaganda Fide the "Congregation for the Evangelization of Peoples."[1]

The present-day Congregation for the Evangelization of Peoples houses four missionary societies that concern themselves with the missionary

---

[1] The word "propaganda" originally meant "spreading" or "propagating." Today, it has a less affirming sense.

outreach of the Catholic Church. They are the Society for the Propagation of the Faith, which was originally founded in France in the nineteenth century by the Catholic laywoman Pauline Marie Jaricot (1799–1862); the Society of Saint Peter the Apostle, which supports the education of priests in developing countries; the Missionary Union of Priests and Religious, which attempts to foster formation, spiritual development, and education for the clergy and religious; and the Holy Childhood Association dedicated to make children around the world "mission conscious." These societies, located in and governed by the Roman Congregation, have branches around the world.

THE NINETEENTH CENTURY

Despite Roman support and the zeal of many missionaries, missionary efforts flagged in the late eighteenth century but would take on a new life in the nineteenth. Not only was there a proliferation of religious communities of both men and women established in various countries (recent historians of missions list dozens of them [see Bevans and Shroeder, details in "Further Reading below]) but older established religious orders took a renewed interest in foreign mission work. The greatest colonial impulse of the nineteenth century targeted the continent of Africa. The British, French, Belgian, German, Italian, Spanish, and Portuguese all "carved out" parts of Africa to keep under their own control. The French, for example, had a colonial empire that included Morocco and Algeria in the north and a large part of West Africa, while the British had a complementary swatch of the continent in the east from Egypt down into what is present-day Uganda, Kenya, and Tanzania. Their possessions Rhodesia (now Zimbabwe) and South Africa were separated from the others by the vast Belgian control over the Congo. Along both coasts, there were smaller enclaves of colonial powers.

The colonial presence brought with it the missionary presence of Christians, and, in those countries with historic ties to Catholicism, this meant Catholic missions: French, Belgian, German, Portuguese (in Mozambique), and Italian and Spanish priests, brothers, and sisters. In the north, which was predominantly Muslim, the missioners labored mainly to the benefit of colonial settlers with some, usually not successful, efforts to evangelize the Muslim majority.[2]

---

[2] Lamin Sanneh's *Disciples of All Nations: Pillars of World Christianity* (Oxford: Oxford University Press, 2008) is a brilliant work on mission seen not from the colonial powers of the West but from the perspective of those colonized and evangelized.

In this expansive missionary outreach (the burgeoning Catholic Church in Africa today is the fruit of the labors, mainly, of nineteenth-century missionary efforts), there were several assumptions deeply rooted in the culture of the missionaries themselves. First, they were convinced that they were bringing a superior culture to Africa; hence, they tended to assume a somewhat superior air vis-à-vis the native population. It was not uncommon in French colonial circles to speak of a *mission civilitrice* – i.e. that colonial supervision was bringing "civilization" to the countries where the colonial power was exercised. Second, however, they did bring schooling, healthcare and other social services which began an infra-structure that would serve in the post-colonial period. Third, apart from some pioneering efforts, the "style" of Catholicism tended to reflect European cultural norms. That "style" was also assumed because of the fact that Catholicism, still largely under the influence of the Catholic Reformation, put uniformity in pride of place. Finally, the spread of the faith was often accomplished by the training of lay catechists who extended the work of the ordained missionaries and formed the basis from which, in time, a native clergy and (more slowly) a native hierarchy would be developed. That development would slowly take hold in the twentieth century.

One last nineteenth-century development needs a comment. While the American colonies received their independence from Great Britain in the late eighteenth century, the growth of the Catholic population in the expanding USA was rather sporadic until the middle of the nineteenth century when an explosion of immigration began which lasted until the eve of World War I. The waves of immigrants from Ireland (especially after the famine year of 1848), Poland, Germany, Italy, and other Catholic countries brought with them an enormous need for pastoral care which was taken care of by a largely immigrant clergy and religious sisters. Every major American city had parishes which were self-consciously ethnic in their makeup. In the middling-sized city in which this writer resides, there are Irish, Polish, Hungarian, German, Lithuanian, and Belgian parishes all built in the center city in the nineteenth century.[3] That demographic could be duplicated in almost every city in the Northeast and Midwest of the USA as the country grew westward. The American Catholic Church was mature enough, on the eve of World War I (1911), to found its own missionary society, Maryknoll, which began sending missionaries both

[3] Many of these parishes are now becoming predominantly Hispanic as new immigrants flow north from Mexico.

male and female overseas, at first to China. In the twentieth century, most communities of religious women sent missionaries to various parts of the world.

THE TWENTIETH CENTURY AND VATICAN II

In the immediate aftermath of World War I (1919), Pope Benedict XV issued an encyclical *Maximum illud,* which encouraged the conversion of all peoples to Christianity and the importance of "planting" churches in hitherto unevangelized areas. To illustrate the need for a robust Church outside of the confines of traditional Christianity, Pope Pius XI ordained six Chinese bishops in 1926, a Japanese bishop in 1927, and a Vietnamese bishop in 1933. Despite these shows of support, the Catholic Church was hobbled in its missionary efforts by a large number of factors outside of its own control in the aftermath of World War I including, among other things, the turmoil caused by the rise of Nazism and the looming fear of Russian Communism. Despite these difficulties (as well as the economic turmoil caused by the worldwide depression in the 1930s), missionary efforts went apace. On the eve of World War II, the US Church was supporting just under 3,000 missionaries abroad with a fifth of them in China itself.

World War II resulted in more obstacles to foreign mission work including, in 1948, the triumph of Chinese Communism resulting in first the suppression and later the expulsion of foreign missionaries with the beginning of the persecution of the Church in China. In the 1960s, independence movements in Africa were a further disturbance to missionary work to the degree that many saw the missionaries as symbols of colonial oppression. Just before the opening of the Second Vatican Council by Pope John XXIII, his predecessor Pius XII contributed a new impetus to future missionary activity when, in new encyclicals (*Evangelii praecones* [1951] and *Fidei donum* [1957]) he encouraged the participation of lay missionaries to work, in tandem, with what had hitherto been a clerical and religious monopoly.

The Fathers of the Second Vatican Council did publish, in fact, a decree on the Church missionary activity on December 7, 1965, the last day of the final session, although it had been worked on during the three sessions before a satisfactory text had been written. Obviously, the Council had to take into account the newer realities of the world in everything from the rise of anti-colonialism to the regnant fact of Communism with its militant resistance to overt Christian work as well as the encouragement of the popes to incorporate laypeople into the missionary activity of the Church. Over and beyond those facts is that there was a substantial number of native bishops from the so-called "Third World." As the late Karl Rahner noted, in a famous essay published after the council, Vatican II was singular in that, for the first time, the participants represented a world Church (*Weltkirche*) with all that implied not only for missionary strategy but also for Christian pedagogy, liturgy, and doctrinal as well as moral formulations.

Ad gentes divinitus, as the decree is known, consisted of an introduction and six substantial chapters. The document makes clear that the Church is, by its nature, a missionary enterprise because it continues to radiate the very mystery of the Trinity in its sending forth. It makes the crucial point that every baptized Christian is called to mission and not only those who are professional. Thus, the Council tried to erase the notion that "missionary" only meant a professional; all baptized Catholics are, by baptism, missionaries. It further makes a critical distinction between the essential missionary character of the Church and the different way(s) in which mission is to be exercised. The differences which must be recognized in this activity of the Church do not flow from the inner nature of the mission itself but "from the circumstances in which it is exercised" (*Ad gentes divinitus,* I, 6). In other words, one mission with many missions. These missions may be various from preaching and "planting" Churches to situations where, for now, there is no possibility for direct missionary activity in which case some ought simply to be present and bear witness to Christ in love and service and "thus prepare a way for the Lord, and in some way to make Him present" (*Ad gentes divinitus,* I, 6).

In subsequent chapters, the decree encourages missionaries to involve themselves in the temporal needs of people, in education, healthcare, and other forms of social amelioration. Furthermore, and this is a tribute to the open spirit of Vatican II, the Council encourages "after due deliberation," collaboration "in projects initiated by private, public, state or international bodies or by *other Christian or even non-Christian communities*" (*Ad gentes divinitus,* II, 11; my emphasis). Furthermore, the decree argues for the value of full formation of catechists, appropriate education for missionaries according to their state and their intended functions, and, most of all, a sympathy for the culture towards which they wish to preach the Gospel. If at all possible, that education should take place in the place where they will work so that they "might more fully understand the history, social structures and customs of the people, that they might have insight into their moral outlook, their religious precepts, and the intimate ideas which they form of God, the world and humanity, according to their own sacred traditions" (*Ad gentes divinitus*, IV.26).

That last point tacitly acknowledged that the attempts made by the sixteenth- and seventeenth-century Jesuit missionaries such as Matteo Ricci and Philip De Nobili had been prophetic voices not recognized in their own time. Furthermore, the ideals implicit in that same observation gave wider warrant for those in the Church who raised the critical question of how to balance the expression of the Gospel in terms understandable to peoples whose cultures had a quite different philosophical, cultural, and intellectual set of presuppositions to those derived from the Western cultural milieu. What did an Indian Christ look like? How to express the biblical concept of God in terms even imaginable to a Buddhist culture? In other words, the adaptation of the missionary to culture involved many more profound issues, which are, in our own time, critical issues holding the attention of those who are competent to do comparative theology. This is the deep issue which Karl Rahner made in his famous essay on the World Church he saw emerging at Vatican II. He said that the Early Church had to make the transition from its Jewish roots in the law and, then again, in its place in the culture embodied in the period after its emergence as a powerful presence in Western society. Now, after Vatican II, it had to confront the reality of becoming a world Church.

AFTER VATICAN II

One of the most paradoxical things about our contemporary situation is that in the West we see a decline in the number of religious and ordained priests both in Europe and in North America. In response to the lack of religious and priests, there is a significant number of personnel coming to the West taking on parochial and other offices from what were formerly mission countries. In the English-speaking world, on both sides of the Atlantic, priests and religious from India and Africa are coming as missionaries to, rather than from, the West. That shift, of course, is one sign that Rahner's observation about the coming World Church is, in fact, true.

It would seem that under the impetus of demographics alone, the primacy of European and North American Catholicism will give way to new realities. Africa is a good test case. It is estimated that in the year 1900 there were just a little fewer than 9 million African Christians. That number grew to 346 million in 2000 and is projected to increase to 600 million by the year 2025. By 2025, it is judged that there will be roughly 768 million Christians in Europe and North America, but, leaving aside that population, in 2025 there will be 1.85 billion Christians in the other parts of the world.[4]

The other point is that the missionary character of the Church is not only *ad extra,* that is, to the traditional missionary lands as seen from the West. Mission is also *ad intra* – shaping the Church from within and always calling it back to its Gospel roots. This kind of mission is intimately tied to reform (to be considered in the next chapter), but it does at least need to be acknowledged that evangelization is both local and universal. In the early 1940s, a provocative book was published in France whose English title was *Is France Pagan?* Written by a French priest (Abbé Henri Godin), it posed the question about the loss of any sense of being Christian in France, which prided itself as being the Eldest Daughter of the Church. From that book was sparked a whole movement to think about the evangelization of one's country (and the pertinent strategies for undertaking such a task) which have reverberated in many self-described Christian countries down to the present day. That discussion, of course, only underscores what the Church has always taught, and especially so at Vatican II, namely, that missionary work cannot look only outside the land of the missionary but must look inside as well. That is as true of the whole Church as it is of every believer individually.

In the period after Vatican II, two different popes added to the rich documentation on missionary activity. In 1975, Pope Paul VI issued an apostolic exhortation called *Evangelii nuntiandi,* which is still regarded as a model for evangelization. The pope called on the Church to evangelize not only peoples but also cultures. He rightly pointed out that such activity not only took in foreign cultures but also those of the historic Christian ones. He also advanced words of praise for small Christian communities as seedbeds for Christian witness. Most commentators still see that document as foundational contemporary thinking on mission activity.

Pope John Paul II issued his encyclical on missions in 1991 under the title *Redemptoris missio* in which he called on the primacy of proclaiming the Gospel as the preferred means of evangelization. It was also he who called for a "new evangelization" of traditionally Christian countries where the fervor for the faith might be on the wane as, for example, in Western Europe and parts of Latin America. It was this same pope who first used the word "inculturation" in a papal document (on catechesis in 1979), which is merely a technical term for something already suggested

---

[4] These figures are taken from Sanneh's *Disciples of All Nations,* pp. 276–7.

in the documents of the Second Vatican Council and the subsequent papal documents mentioned above.

Both the word itself and the process by which inculturation might best be achieved are burning subjects in contemporary theological discourse. Those engaged in the discussion are not unaware of the problems involved – problems which involve but are not restricted to the authentic meaning of doctrinal beliefs, the balance between the particular and the universal, say, in liturgical rites, the degree to which metaphysical realities involving the notion of God or the Trinity or the Incarnation can be adapted, and so on. Everyone agrees that Western styles of architecture, art, cultural customs, and so on can be adapted to particular settings (or should not even be thought of as models in the first instance!), but deeper matters of belief and morality are far more delicate and require cautious reflection.

This problem is not a new one in the history of the Church. In the patristic period, the Church had to balance its belief against the inherited wisdom of pagan culture just as in the Middle Ages Thomas Aquinas and others learned to absorb the newly recovered works of Aristotle into the worldview of Christian theology. In neither case was this done without trial and error, but it was done. The Church today is faced with a similar challenge and must be prepared to face up to it. Not to do so runs the risk of making the Church a museum of the past rather than a living tradition which draws forth old things and new.

THE NEW EVANGELIZATION

We have already noted that the late Pope John Paul II used the term "new evangelization" in his encyclical letters, but he also used the term often in his homilies and speeches. According to his long-time secretary, the pope was greatly disturbed by the tepid state of Christian practice as he made his many visits to the countries of the world especially his pastoral visits in Europe itself. The pope thus became convinced that the Continent was "gradually drifting further and further from its roots and so from its history and its culture."[5] The secularization of Western Europe is perhaps best exemplified by the fact that, despite the concerted effort of Christian thinkers, the new constitution for the European Union resisted acknowledging the Christian roots of Europe.

[5] Cardinal Stanislaw Dziwisz. *My Life with Karol* (New York, N.Y.: Doubleday, 2008), p. 159. The issue of Europe's de-Christianization has also been a concern of the recent popes relative to the formation of the new charter and constitution of the European Union.

What the pope called for was a proclamation of the person and message of Jesus Christ in a new, urgent, and compelling way. The term "new evangelization" is not to be identified simply as foreign missionary work (even though such missionary activity is subsumed under the call), but a radical reminder that all Christians, by virtue of their baptism, are called upon to witness and proclaim the faith. That call targets not only individuals but also, as the pope often said, whole cultures. In his encyclical *Redemptoris homo,* he said that it is part of the Christian call to inculcate Christian values into society and to encourage the Christian message into the world of culture.

It is not difficult to see why this notion of the "new evangelization" would be of paramount interest to the pope (and to his successor Benedict XVI). They were acutely aware of the slide into secularism in Europe; they understood the flagging energy of the old missionary movement after Vatican II; they realized that the traditional religious orders were in crisis but that there was new energy in the new ecclesial movements. Most of all, the papal exhortations were a recalling-to-mind of the essential missionary character of Catholic Christianity in the face of terrible injustices and the looming area of violence in the world. John Paul II was famous for his plea to "build a civilization of love," which he thought only possible by a re-energized commitment to the person of Jesus Christ and his message. John Paul saw this call as a recommitment to the call first made by the late Paul VI in his apostolic exhortation *Evangelli nuntiandi* (1975) and reiterated it in his messages as he celebrated the coming of the new millennium. Thus, the new evangelization had roots in both the earlier teaching of the papacy and in anticipation of what was the future of the Church in the new millennium.[6]

FINAL CONSIDERATIONS

At the beginning of the twentieth century, scholars began to study the missionary work of the Church in a systematic fashion by founding a new academic discipline known as *missiology.* Those studies continue apace today, enlarged by the light shed on missions from the researches of history and the whole spectrum of the social sciences. Thanks to the theological insights brought to bear on the formulations of the documents of

---

[6] The problem of secularization is not peculiar to Western Europe; see the essays on the erosion of traditional Catholicism in Leslie Tentler, ed., *The Church Confronts Modernity: Catholicism Since 1950 in the United States, Ireland, and Quebec* (Washington, D.C.: The Catholic University of America Press, 2007).

Vatican II, the Church has put a new theological emphasis not on missions understood as outreach to those who are not Christian, but to the richer concept of *mission* itself – that is, the fundamental dynamic by which the whole Church and the individual members in it are "sent" by Christ under the impulse of the Holy Spirit to express the message of Christ locally and universally. Recalling that the word "mission" is from the Latin word "to send," it is of the essence of Catholic Christianity that as the Father sent the Son, so the Son sends the Apostles and their successors to preach the Gospel to all creatures. In that sense, "mission" is a core concept and cannot be reduced to the narrow meaning of sending professionals out to plant the Church in alien lands. Such missionary expansion, of course, is a critical part of the Church's activity, but it occurs under the impulse of the far more fundamental notion imposed on all baptized Catholics to be missionaries in the broadest sense of the term.

It is that universal sense of mission that most likely prompted Pope Pius XI in 1927 to name Saint Thérèse of Lisieux (1873–97) as the patroness of missions along with Saint Francis Xavier. Francis, of course, as we have seen, traveled incessantly as a missionary in the Far East. Thérèse, by contrast, never left her Carmelite convent after she entered at the age of fifteen. Her "mission" was to identify herself with those who were actively engaged in the apostolate, to pray in union with them, and to encourage them to live out their lives as fully as possible. In a wonderful passage in her autobiography, she noted that while she had "adopted" two priests, as on the foreign missions, she did not neglect those whose mission was elsewhere:

I could not fail to pray for all [missionaries] without ceasing and I could not forget to pray for all without casting aside simple priests whose mission at times is as difficult to carry out as that of apostles preaching to infidels. Finally, I want to be a loyal daughter of the Church.

Box 8   Papal encyclicals

In this book, we have often made mention of papal encyclicals, but it should be noted that documents from the popes appear under any number of rubrics. In fact, papal encyclicals are a relatively modern form of communication for the papacy. They were first introduced by Pope Benedict XIV (1740–58) as a kind of circular letter of the pope addressed to the entire episcopate or a portion of it or to laypeople or all persons of good will. Their subject can and historically has covered a whole range of topics either on economics or social doctrine or pertinent teachings of the Church and so on. They are an instrument of the ordinary teaching role (magisterium) of the pope.

Box 8 (cont.)

Other forms of papal address should be noted, even though, obviously, there are many unofficial ways in which the popes can communicate (for example, today, via the mass media or through weekly audiences, and so on). The papacy, given the realities of our new electronic world, maintains a website for instant communication; this new medium adds to the newspaper published by the Vatican since the nineteenth century (*L'Osseravore Romano*) and the twentieth-century establishment of Vatican Radio. The more important forms of papal documents would include the following:

Papal bulls. These official pronouncements of the papacy from the twelfth century on carried a (usually) leaden seal (Latin *bullarium*), which carried an impression of the pope on one side and the images of Saints Peter and Paul on the other.

Apostolic constitutions. These are specific documents which carry legislative weight and may deal with doctrinal, moral or disciplinary matters. One excellent example of a doctrinal text would be the apostolic constitution issued by Pope John Paul II in 1996 which regulates the procedures for the election of a new pope upon the death of the current one. That document was a refinement of a similar one issued by Pope Paul VI in 1975. Today, this is the typical usage of the Church for what were known more commonly as papal bulls.

Motu proprio. Latin for "On his own initiative," this is a papal document addressing a particular kind of matter of interest to the pope. A number of such documents came from the popes to help give shape to the reforms of the Second Vatican Council.

Apostolic exhortations. Such documents are usually homiletic both in form and content urging greater piety or attention to a particular celebration in the Church.

It is important for Catholics to understand the distinctions implied in these varying forms of communication since doctrinal, moral, or disciplinary matters are weighted according to the form of the letters. Taken as a whole, they represent the ordinary teaching authority of the pope, but it is conceivable that one of these documents could be the vehicle for solemn definitive teaching.

More recently, during the papacies of John Paul II and Benedict XVI, we have seen these "scholar" popes publishing books under their own names without any claim to papal authority. Pope Benedict XVI wrote in his introduction to his *Jesus of Nazareth* that his book was open to any criticism that reasonable scholars wished to make.

FURTHER READING

Anderson, Carl, *A Civilization of Love* (New York, N.Y.: HarperOne, 2008). A popular plea for a reinvigoration of Christian values in society as proposed by Popes John Paul II and Benedict XVI.

Bevans, Stephen and Schroeder, Roger, *Constants in Context: A Theology for Mission Today* (Maryknoll, N.Y.: Orbis, 2004). A useful work for both mission history and a theology of mission.

Bosch, David, *Transforming Mission: Paradigm Shifts in Theology of Missions* (Maryknoll, N.Y.: Orbis, 1991). An irenic view of different theologies of mission by a Protestant authority. Important work.

Jenkins, Philip, *The Next Christendom: The Coming of Global Christianity* (Oxford: Oxford University Press, 2002). A large-scale study of the changing demographics of Christianity.

Moffett, Samuel H., *A History of Christianity in Asia* (2 vols., Maryknoll, N.Y.: Orbis, 2005). A comprehensive history of Christian expansion as it spread east.

Rahner, Karl, "Towards a Fundamental Theological Interpretation of Vatican II," *Theological Studies*, 40 (1979): 716–27. Seminal essay on the changing face of Catholicism into a world Church.

Sanneh, Lamin, ed., *The Changing Face of Christianity* (Oxford: Oxford University Press, 2005). Essays on the emergence of a world Christianity.

Sanneh, Lamin, *Disciples of All Nations: Pillars of World Christianity* (Oxford: Oxford University Press, 2008). Has a useful bibliography on mission.

Schreiter, Robert, ed., *Mission in the Third Millennium* (Maryknoll, N.Y.: Orbis, 2001). Prospective work on mission by a noted Catholic authority.

Stark, Rodney, *The Rise of Christianity* (San Francisco, Calif.: Harper, 1996). A somewhat contested account of how early Christianity grew.

Yates, Timothy, *Christian Mission in the Twentieth Century* (Cambridge: Cambridge University Press, 1994). Valuable for historical view and critical analysis of challenges.

CHAPTER 9

Catholic reformation(s)

INTRODUCTION

Catholic Christianity has always been aware that only the Church in Heaven will live in perfect harmony and in a state of predestined perfection. It knows that in this life, from its beginnings, the early followers of Jesus showed themselves imperfect and even, at moments, craven. It knows that in the life of the Church reflected in the early New Testament writings there were moral lapses, dissensions, and party strife. Catholicism has never understood itself as a perfectionist sect; it takes seriously the images left by Jesus to the effect that only at the Last Judgment would the Judge of all separate the sheep from the goats and the wheat from the weeds.

All that being said, the history of Catholicism also shows that in the recognition of the imperfect nature of the Church in this life, despite its equal conviction that the Church, as the rule of faith has it, is one, holy, catholic and universal, there was an equal determination to re-form the life of the Church, to cleanse it of its most conspicuous failings, and to call it back to its mandate to be the visible presence of Christ on this earth. It saw this as a duty given by its apostolic teaching. One way to say it is that the Church is one, holy, catholic and apostolic, but it can always be more unified, more holy, more universal, and more faithful to the apostolic preaching.

Thus, when the Catholic Church describes itself as holy, it means that it has the means of holiness, and, ultimately, its holiness is connected to its divine origins. Thus, when the Second Vatican Council asserts (in *Lumen gentium,* No. 39) that it is part of our faith that the Church is "indefectibly holy" or, in other translations "unfailingly holy," it is making a very precise claim, namely, that the Church will not lose its essential holiness; it does not mean that it is without defect.

This determination to remedy its defects has been often summed up by a little Latin tag: *ecclesia semper reformanda* – the Church is always in need of reform. As the Dogmatic Constitution on the Church at the Second

Vatican Council said, the Church has faith that "by the power of the Gospel, he [i.e. the Holy Spirit] rejuvenates the Church, constantly renewing it" (*Lumen gentium,* I, 4). This chapter will investigate in broad lines the various moments in its history when the need for reform most clearly manifested itself and what shaping consequences derived from those reform efforts. It will become clear that a number of practices which have shaped modern Catholic life entered its tradition through the reform undertaken at different periods of the Church's history.

THE LEGACY OF CONSTANTINE

When Constantine granted toleration to the Christians with an edict he issued in Milan in the early fourth century, he offered both an opportunity and a potential problem for the Church. That opportunity and danger became magnified in the late fourth century when, in 381, Emperor Theodosius decreed that Christianity would be the official religion of the Roman Empire. The opportunity, of course, appeared as the Christians were no longer under the threat of persecution. They were able to practice their faith openly and, more importantly, to preach it with impunity. That opportunity was enhanced by the patronage of the imperial office which built churches, endowed works of the Church, and ever more closely aligned the policies of the Empire with that of the ever-growing Church.

The danger came, of course, from that very same largesse of the Empire. Church officials could call on the power and the purse of the imperial government to subsidize its building program and to use its political and coercive power to enforce Christianity's claims and privileges. One result of this was that the local bishops took on the power and privilege afforded by the imperial largesse. For those not so dutifully inclined but ready to seize the main chance, participation in the clergy (and, more especially, the episcopacy) was a sure route to upward mobility, wealth, and civil prestige. It is not unimportant to note that the great defender of Catholic orthodoxy, Saint Athanasius of Alexandria, came in conflict with the political powers of the time and ended up exiled from his episcopal home more than a few times. Later in the century, the same thing happened to Saint John Chrysostom in Constantinople. More compliant bishops suffered no such inconveniences.

Between 325 and 451, there were four great ecumenical councils (Nicaea, Constantinople, Ephesus, and Chalcedon), which were convened to discuss and formulate doctrines about the nature of the Trinity and the person of Jesus Christ in the face of powerful heretical movements. We have discussed these issues in the chapter on the rule of faith. At some of the same councils, the participants also issued "canons" or rules dealing with Church matters of discipline. When those canons are read, it is clear that a number of them were written in response to abuses, especially abuses with respect to the performance of bishops. Behind those canons, it is clear that what the councils wanted to do was to insure that bishops were worthy men and not careerists of dubious character.

Such canons reflect abuses in the Church which were conspicuous enough to come to the attention of the entire episcopate. Newly baptized Christians were not to be admitted to the clergy in undue haste (Nicaea, Canon 2). At least three bishops should be present to lay hands on a new bishop (Nicaea, Canon 4). Priests are not to be ordained unless previously examined to be sure of their probity (Nicaea, Canon 9). Neither priests nor bishops should transfer from one city to another, and, if they do move themselves, they are not to be received by a new place (Nicaea, Canons 15–16). Clerics are strictly forbidden to loan money at interest (Nicaea, Canon 17). Ordaining anyone to any office by payment of money is absolutely forbidden because grace is "unsaleable" (Chalcedon, Canon 2). No cleric is to engage in economic business (Chalcedon, Canon 3). All priests and deacons are to be ordained for a specific title (a church or a shrine) (Chalcedon, Canon 6). No cleric is to have a title in two different churches (Chalcedon, Canon 10).

When one compares the canons of Nicaea and Chalcedon, it is abundantly clear that the number of canons against abuses of the clergy, bishops, and monks rises exponentially in the latter council indicating, on the face of it, that there were tendencies which required the attention of the bishops of the whole Church. The examples we provided in the previous paragraph could be replicated in the writings of the fathers of the day. In the canons themselves (and we have not even considered the canons of provincial councils or local synods of this or that area), we see a concern for the reformation of the Church or, more precisely, those who were ordained to teach, sanctify, and rule over the Church – i.e. the bishops. The very fact that it was necessary to call local synods to deal with disciplinary matters, such as that of Elvira in the fourth century, is reason enough to prove that the Church was not in a state of perfection.

A far more ambitious attempt at reform can be seen in the rise of monasticism. There is a way in which one could see the flight to the desert, which began in the late third century and became conspicuous in the fourth, to be a countercultural form of Christianity, mainly by laypersons, to live a Christian life different to that lived in the urban centers of the Empire. With their emphasis on humility, solitude, prayer, work, and hospitality, they lived out a rejection of the Church as worldly power. It is interesting that there is a strain in ancient monasticism that does not welcome the idea of monks becoming priests or, at a minimum, they desired only that number of priests sufficient for the weekly celebration of the eucharist. In this regard, the *Rule of Benedict* is illuminating. *Rule of Benedict,* Chapter 60 allows for the reception of priests in the monastic community "but not too quickly." If they do enter, they are to "observe the full discipline of the rule." Because they are priests, they may stand next to the abbot out of honor for their ordination, but they are not to seek exceptions to the discipline of the Rule, and they are to give everyone "an example of humility."

The practice recommended by Benedict is a cautious and careful one, but the entire body of early monastic literature makes it clear that the vocation to be a monk is distinct from that of being called to the priesthood. Early monastic literature also has many stories about how monks fled and hid themselves when there was a suspicion that the Church wished to make them bishops. This is not to say that all bishops or priests were corrupt, but it is clear, from the monastic witness, that such offices were seen clearly to be a temptation.

In the period of late antiquity and moving into the early Middle Ages, monks were an important source of missionary expansion, and, with the decline of city life in the West, they were a conspicuous presence in the Church. Bishops and their parish priests became part of the social landscape of Europe but often received little or no instruction or even a particular calling to the spiritual life of a priest. Lords of the manor often controlled the benefices that supported the clergy, and some ecclesiastical offices became a source of income for which not always worthy persons were appointed as incumbents. Indeed, some Church offices became, as it were, the property of families in which said offices were handed down through the generations by a family or fell under the control of civil authorities. That situation became so noxious in the Church that it had to be brought under control by a reformation in its own right. Various attempts to do that over the centuries met with mixed success, but the real reformation in these matters most conspicuously crystallized in the eleventh century.

THE GREGORIAN REFORM

The great renovation of the Church in the eleventh century is called the Gregorian Reform after Pope Gregory VII (reigned 1073–85) who was himself a monk. He had a strong sense of the papacy and made the reform of the Church central to his reign. He set out a number of reform principles and used his legates throughout Europe to apply them. He attempted to halt the practice of simony, which was the terrible abuse of buying and selling of Church offices.[1] He also tried to enforce clerical celibacy, which was not then the general norm in the Church except for monks. Too often a priest would pass on his office to a son without reference to the son's capacity for the priesthood. His greatest struggle was against the practice of lay lords naming bishops and abbots of dioceses or monasteries to their office – a practice fraught with abuse or the potential of abuse. Gregory had a titanic struggle over this matter with the Holy Roman Emperor, Henry IV. The Emperor tried to depose the pope, but, in the end, Henry had to stand outside the papal residence at Canossa in northern Italy to show his penitence and to have his excommunication lifted. Despite that gesture, the Emperor later connived to remove Gregory and, for a time, engineered the election of rival popes. Unfortunately, the Emperor misunderstood the tenacity of the pope's will to stop the practice of lay investiture.

Gregory's successors, impelled by his example, tried to continue the reforming movement. Two elements characterize their work, one directly attributable to the popes and the other bubbling up below. Each deserves consideration.

First, between 1123 and 1512 – a span of roughly 400 years – the popes called ten general councils whose collective aim was almost exclusively concerned with Church reform. Five of these councils met at the Lateran palace in Rome (Saint John Lateran was the cathedral of the bishop of Rome) with the last of these occurring just on the eve of the Protestant Reformation. If one looks at the canons at just one of these councils, it is easy to see the problems facing those who wished to reform the life and mores of the Church. Lateran IV in 1215 is a good example because it was called when the power of the Church was at its temporal apex. It issued seventy-one canons of which all but the first two were directly disciplinary in nature. The canons make sad reading, for example, in their condemnation of clerical sexual incontinence, drunkenness among the clergy, clerical duels, profane objects being housed in churches, misuse of the church and civil courts, punishments for those who wield the power of excommunication unjustly, misuse of abbatial or episcopal power, etc.

---

[1] The word "simony" was coined from the name of Simon Magus who attempted to buy the power of the Holy Spirit; see Acts 8.

Reading the documents which came out of Lateran V (1512–17), such reforms are still mentioned, but Lateran V even made a tentative effort at reforming the papal curia and the College of Cardinals. There was, however, a gap between stipulating reform and putting it into practice. Lateran V finished its work in March 1517; about six months later, a friar named Martin Luther posted his ninety-five theses on the door of the collegiate church at Wittenberg in Germany.

Lateran V on the eve of the Reformation

The lengthy documents that form the dossier of the Fifth Lateran Council are instructive to read. The Council attended to a number of political concerns, but much of its energies were concerned with the internal reform of the Church on issues ranging from the reform of the Curia and the College of Cardinals to more practical concerns such as the printing of books, the state of preaching in the Church, and abuses concerning the administration of the *montes pietatis* – loan offices established to check the problem of usury. It is ironical that a number of these reform documents were written under the signature of the Medici Pope Leo X, who shortly after the close of the Council, and no paragon of virtue in his own right, would sign the bull of excommunication directed to Martin Luther. Here is Leo on the reform of the Roman Curia:

When we notice, out of solicitude for our said pastoral office, that church discipline and the pattern of sound and upright life are worsening, disappearing and going further astray from the right path throughout almost all of the ranks of Christ's faithful, with a disregard for law and with exemption of punishment, as a result of the troubles of the times and the malice of human beings, it must be feared that, unless checked by a well regarded improvement, there will be a daily falling into a variety of faults, a complete breakdown. (Tanner: I, 614)

The breakdown, of course, was only a few years away.

Second, just as monasticism can be seen at least in part as a reaction against the post-Constantine accommodation of Church and State, so, deriving from the energy coming from the Gregorian reform, there was a new desire to reform the Church from below. Modern scholars have pointed out that one of the most frequently asked questions of the eleventh and twelfth century was this: What constitutes the true Gospel life? How can someone lead a life which can be properly called the evangelical life? The answer to those questions was various. Some thought that the traditional monastic life of the Benedictines was the answer because they lived with the sharing of goods described in the primitive Church according to the Acts of the Apostles.

Others thought that traditional monastic life itself ought to be reformed, by going back to a new reading of Benedict in leading a life of contemplative simplicity based on manual work. It was that impulse that led to the founding of the "White Monks" or Cistercians. Others, more inspired by retirement from the world combined the monastic and hermit life as did the Carthusians, also a twelfth-century reform movement.

A third voice insisted that the active clergy could be reformed by giving them a rule of life that would combine pastoral service and a variation of monastic regularity. The Regular Canons of Premontre adopted this strategy.

Still others thought that evangelical poverty and preaching were the fitting way to lead the Gospel life and those who undertook such a life became the direct descendants of the followers of Saint Francis of Assisi (1181–1226) and Saint Dominic (1170–1221), whose movements took their names: The Franciscans and the Dominicans were a predominant force in the religious revival of the thirteenth century. One interesting facet of these two movements is that they made space for laypersons who did not formally join their orders with canonical vows but who were affiliated in what were called "Third Orders" – laypeople who attempted to follow the ideals of the religious orders while still living in the world. Saint Francis of Assisi actually wrote a rule for such persons. Some people, especially women, adopted a version of the Dominican way of life but did not enter into the world of the cloister. Saint Catherine of Siena (1347?–1380) is a conspicuous example of someone who adopted the Dominican way of life without becoming a cloistered religious.

Finally, there were lay movements such as the Patarines in Milan and the Poor Men of Lyon, inspired by the layman Peter Waldo, and women who joined informal groups of piety such as the Beguines in the Low Countries and small sororities of women who added care of the poor to their life of prayer. Some of these, such as the Poor Men and the Patarines, ran foul of Church authority by their drumbeat criticism and rejection of a sinful clergy and by their demand for their right to preach free from episcopal oversight.

What is most interesting about these various impulses of reform is that they derived quite frequently from the desires of ordinary men and women who thirsted for a more authentic religious life rather than in response to some hierarchical authority. Just as monasticism came from the desires and experiences of ordinary people so these new evangelical movements, taking on various hues, were part of the larger hierarchical call for reform. Nonetheless, despite these efforts, the Church, for reasons both external and internal, was weakened and ripe for something truly momentous to happen. The fourteenth century saw the emergence of the Black Death, the Hundred Years' War, the retreat of the papacy to France, and the great schism that at one time saw three papal claimants. The fifteenth-century rebirth in the form of the Renaissance in the arts and learning, as well as newer technologies such as the invention of moveable type, combined with the inner dynamic to radically reform the Church – these all were the antecedents for what was to happen early in the sixteenth century. In fact, it could be said that the Renaissance, especially that of the north, with its emphasis on getting back to the Patristic sources, its emphasis on biblical study, and its focus on moral growth and religious experience were all elements that make the Protestant Reformation more understandable.

REFORMATIONS PROTESTANT AND CATHOLIC

It is not possible to even sketch out the history of the Protestant Reformation without the worst kind of superficiality, but suffice it to say that by the end of the sixteenth century various forms of Protestant Christianity had taken firm hold in large parts of Germany, Switzerland, in parts of the Low Countries, Scandinavia, the British Isles, and as far east as the Baltic countries. Europe, not to put too fine a point on the matter, was divided between Catholic and Protestant countries.

The causes of the Protestant Reformation have been the subject of much scholarly discussion for a very long time, but surely one of the triggers was the persistent abuses orbiting the behavior of the clergy and the members of religious orders as well as the real or perceived misuses of the sacramental and popular practices of the people deriving in part from the ignorance or rapacity of the same clergy. Although the degree of such abuses may have been exaggerated in polemical arguments, no serious student of the period disagrees that there were real and conspicuous abuses.[2]

It should also be pointed out that, as we have seen, any number of reforms had been launched long before the Reformation, but those

---

[2] Eamon Duffy's *The Stripping of the Altars, 1400–1550* (London and New Haven, Conn.: Yale University Press, 1992) has argued that Catholic life in England on the eve of the Reformation was robust and hardly decadent while, at the same time, collapsing under the pressure of the Henrician reform – raising the question of why that collapse occurred.

reforming impulses did not seem to answer adequately the full demand for reform. The latent energies of reform found their full power with the rise of Luther and everything triggered by his resistance to Rome in the early sixteenth century. As many scholars have pointed out, the Reformation cannot be fully understood apart from the impulses for reform that were alive long before the Protestant Reformation.[3]

What is of interest to us is how Catholicism responded to the indubitable fact of the Protestant Reformation. The broad answer to that question is that the Catholic response, once called the Counter-Reformation, but now more familiarly the Catholic Reformation, was various. It should come as no surprise that the dynamic we have seen before – the official response in the form of conciliar reform and the movements from below – was again characteristic of the Catholic reform. Along with those two standard impulses also came a desire to define and enhance sharply the place of the bishop of Rome, the pope, as the center of Catholic orthodoxy since it was the papal office that was the one nodal point of Protestant reaction upon which all the various stripes of pro-testing parties could agree.

The Council of Trent in northern Italy met between 1545 and 1548, again in 1551–2, and for a third time in 1562–3. Those who attended varied in number, and, in the latest sittings from 1551 on, Protestants were invited to attend, but the hardening of positions made that gesture a futile one. In retrospect, it is hard to overestimate the shaping force of the Council of Trent. Indeed, the period after it closed has often been called the Tridentine Church, alluding to the Latin name for Trent (*Tridentinus*). The Council issued some doctrinal statements after it adopted the tradi-tional creed of Nicaea and Constantinople to show its continuity with the ancient Church. It set out its belief that Christ's revelation comes to us in both the scriptures and unwritten traditions against the Protestant insistence of scripture alone. It articulated a nuanced decree on justifi-cation, which, the Council claimed, came from grace alone but allowed for human cooperation. It codified its belief in the seven sacraments and insisted on the real presence of Christ in the eucharist. All of these doctrinal pronouncements were in reaction to the various Protestant articulations.

In reaction to the iconoclastic tendencies of the Reformation and its jettisoning of devotions to Mary and the Saints, it reaffirmed the

---

[3] Clear evidence of the truth of this assertion may be seen in the very title of Steven Ozment's fine survey: *The Age of Reform, 1250–1550* (London and New Haven, Conn.: Yale University Press, 1980).

legitimate use of images and devotions to Mary and the saints while warning against superstitious practices, and it defended the pious practices of the tradition including praying for the souls in Purgatory and the use of indulgences as remittance of punishment due for sins already forgiven. It reiterated its condemnation of the misuse of Church offices and, for the first time, stipulated that all those who wished to be priests had to attend a seminary prior to ordination. That latter piece of law had a profound effect on the formation of the clergy, and its effects are still felt today in that the obligation of having men trained in seminaries prior to ordination is still very much in effect.

It was left to the papal office to oversee the implementation of the decrees of Trent, and a series of popes were not timid in doing so. The books used in the liturgy were corrected and made uniform. The *Roman Catechism,* designed for the use of parish clergy, was published to insure uniformity of teaching. Rome began to issue a list of forbidden books (the infamous *Index*) and books dealing with religious matters were required to have authorization from appropriate religious authorities.

At the very opening of the Council of Trent in 1545, it was stated that the purpose of the convocation was the uprooting of heresies, for peace and unity in the Church, for the reform of the clergy and the Christian people, and for the crushing of the enemies of the Church. It has been debated among scholars whether Trent exacerbated the split between Rome and the Reformers, but one thing is clear: Within Catholicism itself, Trent clearly enunciated what the Catholic Church believes, what traditions it holds on to and cherishes, and what reforms need to be made to repristinate the Church from within.

A second element in the Catholic reform was the energy supplied by religious orders of men and women who were either newly founded to carry on the work of Church reform or which were renewed through reform. In the latter case, we have, in this period, the rise of the Capuchin Franciscans who led lives of simplicity and poverty reaching out to the poor in both cities and countryside and, in Spain, the reformed movement within the Carmelite family. Spain had not been touched directly by the Reformation but was the home of both Saint Teresa of Avila (1515–82) and Saint John of the Cross (1542–90), who called the Carmelites back to their roots in the tradition of contemplative prayer. The outreach of the reformed Carmelites into France in the early seventeenth century provided a spiritual wellspring for the rise of the so-called French School of Spirituality which so shaped the religious life of seventeenth-century France and its burgeoning religious communities of men and women. Other religious communities of men and women were also founded to serve specific needs and possible challenges hitherto unmet in the Church thanks to the growth of piety in the period of the Catholic Reformation.

It is generally acknowledged that the strong arm of Catholic reform came from the founding of a new religious order known as the Jesuits. Founded by Ignatius of Loyola (1491–1556), a Basque soldier who underwent a series of profound religious experiences while recuperating from war wounds, the Jesuits were formed in a spirituality laid out by Ignatius in a little handbook known as the *Spiritual Exercises.* Ignatius had a small cadre of followers who vowed to live a poor life and serve others while living in Paris. Thwarted in their original plan to go to the Holy Land, Ignatius settled in Rome where the religious community took shape and found approval in 1540.

The Jesuits had certain novel characteristics: They wore no distinctive habit; they were not bound to the choral recital of the Office; they refused any promotion to the hierarchy unless directly ordered to do so by the pope; and they vowed to undertake any work asked of them by the pope. The very flexibility of their rule of life as well as their rigorous spiritual and intellectual formation made them highly mobile and well adapted to various apostolates. Very quickly they became the principal agents of the Catholic Reformation throughout Europe, adept at missionary work and famous for the schools they planted throughout Europe and later in various mission lands both in Asia and in the Americas. Their growth was quite phenomenal. At the death of Ignatius, there were 1,000 members of the society and, by 1600, almost 9,000. Their works included everything from catechetical work to the giving of missions and retreats using the methods enshrined in the *Spiritual Exercises* first developed by Ignatius himself. Some of their members, such as Peter Canisius (1521–97) in Germany and Robert Bellarmine (1542–1621) in Italy, both later canonized as saints, were almost synonymous with the apologetic response of Catholic theology to the challenges of the Reformers. In fact, they were famous for their use of *apologetics,* a form of theology that both defended the faith and impugned the positions of their adversaries.

The reforming movement within Catholicism in the sixteenth century would evolve in the seventeenth century into what is commonly called "baroque Catholicism." Its most characteristic way of expressing Catholic values, practices, and beliefs was based less in theology than in the various aesthetic expression of religious piety as reflected in sacred music, art, architecture, and literature. Sometimes the fusion of these various aesthetic modes would find a synthesis in the baroque *concetto* – an ensemble expressing an artistic whole. One might see that baroque concetto at work in watching a papal liturgy in the finished basilica of Saint Peter's in Rome with its Michelangelo dome covering the famous *baldacchino* done by Bernini over the papal altar while the split Vatican choir sang – a rather theatrical but deeply spiritual expression of papal self-confidence done in the service of the Church. Perhaps an even better example might be found in the Cornaro Chapel honoring Saint Teresa of Avila in the Church of Santa Maria della Vittoria, done by Gianlorenzo Bernini between 1645 and 1652. Teresa lies recumbent in ecstasy as an angel pierces her heart with an arrow representing divine love. In side tribunals, the donor families watch the scene as if looking at a sacred drama. The scene recalls a passage in Teresa's autobiography where the saint described being pierced by the love of Christ so that Bernini transforms a literary text into stone – a fitting tribute to a saint who had been canonized in 1622 along with other luminaries of the Catholic reform: Saint Ignatius of Loyola and his early companion, the missionary, Saint Francis Xavier (1506–51), and Saint Philip Neri (1515–95), who was a zealous missionary in Rome itself.

The spirit of the baroque not only influenced all of Europe but also was exported as part of the missionary spirit of the Catholic reform. One finds exuberant Catholic churches done in the baroque style in places as different as Goa in India and the major cities of Central and Latin America. The spirit of the baroque characterized both Catholic Europe and, in different ways, Protestantism itself. The supreme example of Protestant baroque can easily be seen in the music of Johann Sebastian Bach and in the oratorios of Handel in Great Britain, but it is useful to remember that the Oratorio was an invention of Philip Neri who used such choral music for Christian apologetic purposes in Rome just as the Jesuits used stage plays for the same purpose.

One last development in the time of the Catholic reform deserves mention: the emergence of active orders of religious women who, freed from the restrictions of the cloister, were able to involve themselves in the active works of education, care of the sick, and other forms of charity. We have already mentioned this important part of modern Catholic life, but it is worth underscoring a crucial point. By giving women alternatives to cloistered seclusion or the traditional path of marriage and motherhood, women were able to use their intelligence, skills, and energy in a wide range of activities earlier closed off to them. This new form of religious life, detached from the cloister, was so innovative that the first to attempt it were treated with grave suspicion. Mary Ward (1585–1645) founded a religious institute modeled on the Jesuits. She had houses in Belgium, France, Rome, and elsewhere, but, desiring that her order be subject directly to the pope and free from episcopal oversight, the order was suppressed, and she was actually imprisoned in a Poor Clare monastery in Cologne for a period. It was only after an appeal to Pope Urban VIII that she resumed her labors with mixed success, only to die back in England. Her Institute of the Blessed Virgin Mary exists to this day.[4]

Pioneered by seventeenth-century innovators such as Saint Vincent de Paul (1581–1660) and Saint Louise de Marillac (1591–1660) in Paris, the Daughters of Charity were first a community of like-minded women who banded together informally only eventually becoming a religious order with vows of poverty, chastity, and obedience, but, in a singular act, were free from the enclosure. Not only did they thrive but they also provided the inspiration for many other similar congregations with most founded after the French Revolution. Those congregations not only provided elementary forms of charity, but also, in time, a path for technical training, academic administration, and higher learning. The story of these congregations is one of the most conspicuous examples of energizing the role of women in the Church before the rise of movements to liberate women for the professions in our own time.

REACTION AND REFORM

It has been wittily but perhaps uncharitably said that the Catholic Church marched towards the Enlightenment and the French Revolution and took a hard right turn. There is no doubt that the French Revolution encompassed within it a revolt against the Church in France, unleashing an attempt both to erase whatever power the Church had in that country and to domesticate it to its own civil purposes. It is equally true that the philosophical ideas of the Enlightenment and the rise of the empirical sciences were seen as a deep threat to the integrity of Catholic doctrine, both theological and moral. The restless desire to overthrow the old regal regimes of Europe (or to herd all power under their auspices) was seen, and rightly so, to put the authority of the Church under the jurisdiction of civil powers. The overthrow of the Papal States in the mid-nineteenth century brought the Church's worst fears to a real conclusion. Papal power

---

[4] The members of the Institute of the Blessed Virgin Mary are also known as the Loreto Sisters; their motherhouse is in Rome, and they work in twenty-four different countries.

was erased, and the old Papal States were absorbed into the emerging unified Italy, with the pope becoming a prisoner in the Vatican.

The reaction of the Catholic Church to these rapidly unfolding social and political realities was clear: throwing up the barriers against the tide of history and condemnation of the new ideas abroad. This reactive mode was implemented by two strategies: condemnation of the perceived errors of the age and highlighting the authority of the teaching office of the pope. A word about each is in order.

The great "No" of the Roman Catholic Church to the pretensions of the modern world was most clearly expressed in a collection of errors issued by the papacy in tandem with Pope Pius IX's 1864 encyclical *Quanta cura*. The so-called "Syllabus of Errors" summarized ideas and movements condemned in a whole series of papal documents. Some of these errors were of an intellectual character in which a whole series of "isms" were ruled out of court: pantheism, naturalism, rationalism, indifferentism, latitudinarianism, socialism, etc. Other condemnations had in their sights mistaken views about the power of the Church, but the set dealing with civil society most clearly was in reaction to the rising power of the State:

- Civil law can overturn Church law.
- State authority can oversee the educational curriculum of seminaries.
- Civil authorities can nominate and hold veto power over episcopal appointments.
- The State has the ultimate right to legislate law for marriages.
- The State can accept freedom of religion to all groups.

The capstone error that concluded the Syllabus was this: That the pope should reconcile himself to "progress, liberalism, and modern civilization." At the First Vatican Council held less than a decade later (in 1870), the canons expressed a rejection of the regnant philosophical and theological errors implicit in the errors of the Syllabus by condemning philosophical materialism, pantheism, and any attempt to limit religious knowledge to those matters which derive from human philosophy (fideism).

The other strategy against the errors of the day was to insist on the powers of the papacy. It was at the same Vatican Council, as we have seen in an earlier chapter, that the Council proclaimed the doctrine of the infallibility of the pope. Apart from the theological issues concerning the nature of this doctrine, it is easy to understand why the Council was interested in highlighting the power of the pope. Among other things, it was a way to highlight the spiritual power of the pope when his temporal power was in precipitous decline. In fairness, it should also be noted that many bishops, especially in Europe, saw the emphasis on the spiritual power of the pope as a way to check the increasing meddling of the State in the affairs of the Church. To be able to call on a person, possessed of supreme moral and spiritual authority, beyond the demands of the State in favor of the internal needs of the Church was a check on the presumptions of civil power.

Even though the official Church was in a state of theological stasis, there were signs that some very creative theology was being done in the nineteenth century, but the fruits of that theology would not become apparent until well into the next century. Johann Adam Mohler (1796–1838) was one of the more famous German theologians associated with the University of Tubingen. In a series of influential works, he attempted to understand the Church not only as a visible hierarchical institution with the pope as the apex of an ecclesiastical pyramid but also as a living breathing organic community kept vibrant by the power of the Holy Spirit. This theological angle would point to the crucial work done in the twentieth century to find a deeper model of the Church described, retrieving very Christian language, as the body of Christ and the pilgrim people of God.

Perhaps the most fecund thinker of the nineteenth century was the Anglican convert and priest, John Henry Newman (1801–90), who made seminal contributions on topics as diverse as how doctrine develops to subtle treatises on the character of religious faith as knowledge and the role of laypeople in the Church. His ideas, for the most part, were viewed suspiciously in his own lifetime (although he was named a cardinal in the twilight years of his life), but his thinking would have such an impact in the next century that some have called the Second Vatican Council "Newman's Council."

Both Mohler and Newman were theologians of retrieval; they looked back to the earliest sources of Catholic theology to escape from the somewhat sterile theological manuals of the time. They illustrated by their work the typical Catholic movement of looking back in order to move forward – to draw on the tradition in order to restate the faith. Such efforts were not always seen in a good light. At the end of the nineteenth century, scholars in various European countries began to confront the newer historical studies of the Bible and more critical attitudes towards Christian origins. Known collectively as the *modernists,* they appeared to the Catholic authorities as undermining the foundations of the faith. A fierce reaction against these newer approaches was unleashed by Pope Pius X, who assumed the papacy in 1903, who called modernism the "synthesis of all heresies" even though the movement itself was amorphous and took many forms.

In 1907, in two separate documents, the pope condemned modernism in the encyclical *Pascendi* and in a companion papal decree entitled *Lamentabili*. To enforce the condemnation, in 1910, the pope ordered that all clerics prior to ordination, every recipient of a degree at a papal university, and every bishop had to take an antimodernist oath. What was more troubling was the erection of a semisecret agency that actively sought out suspected modernists, with denunciations sent to the Vatican. This small group, the so-called Sodalitium Pianum, was not suppressed until Benedict XV succeeded Pius X to the papacy. The ill-effects of the antimodernist movement were felt right down to the middle of the twentieth century by retarding scholarship done in the Catholic Church and, in large part, ossifying the education of priests while giving scant regard for scholarship.

TOWARDS THE SECOND VATICAN COUNCIL

In the twentieth century, the Catholic Church underwent an unprecedented growth outside of Europe itself. The Church in English-speaking countries such as the USA and the UK, thanks to both conversions and immigration, entered a period often called the "brick and mortar" era: Churches, schools, hospitals, colleges, and other institutions were built to aid in this growth. The Church in Africa also saw a steady increase in population and self-confidence. Nonetheless, the toll taken by the modernist suppression, the effects of the worldwide economic depression of the 1930s, and, especially, the rise in antireligious totalitarian governments such as the Soviet system in Eastern Europe and fascism in the West created insufferable problems for large populations.

It was widely felt within Catholic circles that a more vigorous and open intellectual and spiritual life was required if the Church was to be at all relevant. New openings were sought in Europe, mainly for a new understanding of the liturgy (the so-called Liturgical Movement had its roots in nineteenth-century Germany); a greater openness to Christians of other faiths led to a small but influential ecumenical set of thinkers; from the time of Leo XIII there was a strong interest in social problems especially the rights of workers; and a renewed interest in the history of theology was preparing a new generation of Catholic thinkers to engage with its historic past. Finally, thanks to the encouragement of Leo XIII, there was a vigorous flowering of interest in the ideas of Thomas Aquinas, not only as a philosopher but also as a theologian. The rise of a new Thomism (a lot of it spearheaded by lay thinkers such as Jacques Maritain and Etienne Gilson in France) gave promise of a new humanism based on the interrelationship of reason and revealed truth.

One sees the result of this foment in some of the encyclicals of Pope Pius XII, who assumed the papal office in 1939, just at the outbreak of hostilities that led to the world war. While those encyclicals seem a bit timid today, they were, in fact, momentous in the life of the Church as starting points for what would happen when his successor, John XXIII, at the end of the 1950s, announced his intention of calling another Vatican Council. From the vantage point of history, we can see that certain of Pius's writings anticipated many of the reforms that would come in the latter half of the century. In 1943, Pius published *Mystici corporis* on the nature of the Church, which gave impetus to those who wished to think more organically about the nature of the Church as something beyond its structural character. In the same year, he published *Divino afflante spiritu* – an encyclical on biblical scholarship, which is regarded as the beginning of a deeper understanding of scripture with its admission that the study of the literary forms of the Bible would give a greater entry into an understanding of that book. Biblical scholars regard the publication of that encyclical as the beginning of serious Catholic scholarship on the Bible. Third, the encyclical *Mediator dei* (1947) was a landmark document giving encouragement to the burgeoning ecumenical movement. Finally, an instruction from the Holy Office in 1949 (*Ecclesia catholica*) saw the work of those who engaged in ecumenical work as doing a Spirit-inspired work and, however gingerly, encouraged Roman Catholic experts to have serious conversations with other Christians on matters of faith and morals. Such exchanges would come to fuller advances when Vatican II was convened.

Pope Pius XII was not by instinct a progressive person. A Roman aristocrat who was aloof by temperament and upbringing, he knew that it is part of the papal portfolio to "conserve the faith." His 1950 encyclical *Humani generis* expressed his distaste for the then-fashionable philosophy of existentialism, for what was called *la nouvelle theologie* whose major figures were, in fact, under a cloud in his pontificate (the Dominicans Marie-Dominique Chenu and Yves Congar; the Jesuits Jean Danielou and Henri De Lubac, and other thinkers who would be the architects of Vatican II), and he suppressed the Priest Worker movement – an experiment in France to have priests actually live in the milieu of the largely de-Christianized culture of the French working class.

One sees, then, in the pontificate of Pius XII, a kind of dualism, with one side of his thinking giving encouragement of certain reforms while, on the other hand, reacting negatively to what he saw as the reforming avant-garde. That tension in Pius would also characterize the sessions of the Second Vatican Council.

VATICAN II

The Second Vatican Council held its sessions between 1962 and 1965. Pope John XXIII, who called the Council into session, desired that its work should pay particular attention to internal reforms within the Church (the term in Italian was *aggiornamento* or "bringing up to date"), Christian unity, and a willingness to address an audience beyond that of the Catholic Church itself. Before the Council was called to a close, the participants issued a series of documents ranging from dogmatic constitutions to a series of declarations. In all, the documents were sixteen in number, covering a wide variety of topics. What was singular about the finished documents was that they were written in a pastoral style without the rigorous articulation that one normally found in earlier Councils, and none of the documents had "canons" appended to them, which, in shorthand, crisply defined Catholic belief and practice with a condemnation of those who would not accept the canon in question.

Within the pages of this book, we have had many occasions to quote from the documents of the Council, but, in this place, we do not intend either to give a history of the Council or to summarize all of its work. There is a veritable mountain of literature attempting to do one or other of those tasks. With our idea on "reform" in mind, it will be sufficient to give account of some of the decisions made at that time to show how they changed or re-formed the lives of Catholics. In other places, we have discussed the particular points the documents made relative to theology. The more salient reforms of Vatican II would surely include the following:

1. A reversal of the tendency to enclose the Church in some kind of spiritual and intellectual fortress. The pastoral constitution on the Church in the modern world (*Gaudium et spes*) was not only addressed to all persons of good will but charged the Church itself to take its place in the needs and aspirations of all humanity.
2. A ringing endorsement of the idea of ecumenical and interreligious engagement and, where possible, cooperation. The declaration *Nostra aetate* was the premier document among others that fostered that ideal.

3. A radical reform of the liturgy including an openness to a vernacular liturgy and the adaptation of the liturgy to the cultural needs of the worldwide Church.
4. A reversal of the older notion that the Church should be privileged in social society and an affirmation of the right of religious liberty.
5. A partial attempt to balance the rights and duties of bishops in relation to the papacy so as to right an imbalance between papal and episcopal authority that developed after the proclamation of papal infallibility at the First Vatican Council.
6. A demand that the antiquated customs and usages in religious life be examined in the light of the original intentions of their founders and an *aggiornamento* in the light of current pastoral needs.
7. A description of the Church to right the undue emphasis on the Church as rigid hierarchy by underscoring the common membership of all baptized persons as part of the pilgrim people of God.

The irenic tone of the Council and its shifting emphases away from some of the more rigid formulations deriving from the reactive forces of Catholicism springing from the Catholic Reformation and the twin traumas of the Enlightenment and the French Revolutions was a breath of fresh air but also in the documents was an uneasy compromise between those older formulations and the need for reform and *aggiornamento*. The reception of the changes at Vatican II was not an easy one. There were those who insisted that the conciliar formulations changed nothing, and others who felt that the shifts in thinking were radical. This diverse way of reading the Council led to the simplistic divisions which we still see today, decades after the Council closed, described in polarizing language: Orthodox Catholics versus Dissident Catholics; Conservatives versus Progressives, etc. Indeed, at the fringes of Catholic life were schisms, with some departing from communion with the Church because they thought the Council heretical (for example, the followers of the late Archbishop Marcel Lefebvre, who formed a dissident schismatic Church) and those on the Left who started various schismatic groups such as, for example, the American Catholic Church.

It is a truism in Catholic Church history that after every Council there is a period in which the Church needs to "receive" what the Council taught and to absorb what new realities it demanded in the way of reform. There were schisms after Vatican I, triggered by those who could not accept the doctrine of papal infallibility, as there were attempts to accommodate the Church's perceived conservative picture to the needs of culture as was the case with the modernists. Interestingly enough, some contemporary progressives are today charged, by their opponents, with "modernism."

Some have seen the period after Vatican II as having had a debilitating effect on Catholicism. They point to the precipitous decline in vocations to the priesthood and the religious life, the falloff in mass attendance, the increased secularization of society, the rise in divorce, etc., as evidence of their claim. Of course, such evidence may have little to do with the Council and much to do with profound shifts in Western culture since there are countersigns to such statistics in Africa, Latin America, and Eastern Europe. One thing is clear, however, and that is the most vigorous growth of Catholic Christianity is happening outside the West, and more particularly in Africa.

It is also true that the impact of the Council has led to new forms of thinking within the Church. Liberation theology is a post-conciliar reality. With its origins in Latin America, liberation theology is an attempt to give a local cast to framing the faith by, in the case of Latin America, starting theological reflection from the vantage point of the poor to make the Gospel truly "Good News" for the teeming masses of disadvantaged peoples. Similar attempts have been made in other contexts: What does a theology from the perspective of women or Asians or Native Americans or Africans look like? The Roman authorities have had their suspicions about these theological enterprises (especially when they draw on Marxist sources for their social analysis) but whatever the long-term strength of these contextual theologies they most assuredly indicate that the theological enterprise itself is alive and well.

The very decline in candidates for the priesthood inevitably led to discussions about the possibility of ordaining married men to the priesthood and, equally inevitably, women. While the Western Church (of the Roman Rite) has had a celibate clergy for at least a millennium,[5] it is a disciplinary matter and is possible to change since Eastern Rite Catholics have a married clergy. The issue of women as priests is more complex; the fact that the Anglican Church has ordained women has been seen – at least at this point – as an insuperable ecumenical problem. Pope John Paul II was on record as saying that the issue was beyond discussion.

[5] The Catholic Church has permitted married clergy who convert to Catholicism to exercise priestly ministry; the majority of such clergy come from the Anglican Church.

The ecumenical thrust of Vatican II has not lost its vigor. Bilateral discussions between Catholics and a spectrum of other Christian denominations have carried on its work over the decades with some genuine breakthroughs (for example, Catholic-Lutheran agreements on the doctrine of justification). Popes Paul VI, John Paul II, and Benedict XVI have strongly favored ecumenical exchange with the Orthodox Churches of the East with whom they share close understandings in both doctrine and liturgy although the long centuries of suspicion between the two Churches will only slowly dissipate. The breakup of the old Soviet Union has brought both opportunity and challenge to this exchange.

One vigorous element in the contemporary Church is the rising number of laypersons who have taken on greater roles in Church activities. There is an increasing number of lay missionaries; laypersons are largely supplanting religious in classrooms of Catholic schools; almost all parishes now have lay lectors, eucharistic ministers, etc. Other forms of lay ministry, especially in outreach to the poor and disadvantaged, are more than common; they are ubiquitous in ministries as diverse as feeding the hungry at parish-sponsored soup kitchens to ministering in hospitals, homes for the dying, etc.

Finally, we have seen the enormous growth of what are called "new ecclesial movements" in the contemporary Church. Some of them, like the Spanish organization Opus Dei, predate the Council but, despite their various ranks of membership, do put a high priority on the part laypeople should play in the sanctification of the world. Other groups, such as Communion and Liberation, Focolare, and the Neocatechumenal Way, were founded after the Council. Collectively, they are regarded as "conservative" in their theological orientation, but all of them, while allowing for priest members, are oriented toward laypeople. Other groups, such as Cursillo, Marriage Encounter, the Sant Egidio Community, and L'Arche tend to be more flexible, with all of them heavily committed to the lay vocation. Some of these groups have been motivated by the development of the charismatic movement, which has emphasized the movement of the Holy Spirit both as the agent of conversion, the point at which God touches and changes human lives, and as the way in which the New Testament charisms are made real in people's lives.

These movements may be the first signs of new ways of conceptualizing the Gospel life, not unlike the rise of the mendicants in the thirteenth century and the new religious congregations after the Council of Trent in the sixteenth century. Speaking to representatives of the new ecclesial movements in Rome in 1998, Cardinal Joseph Ratzinger (now Pope

Benedict XVI) acknowledged that in their development these new communities had their "growing pains" (i.e. their tendency to authoritarianism,
rigidity, secrecy, etc.), but these pains would be overcome as they reached
maturity. Ratzinger saw in such movements (and many other ones that
grew up after the Council) hope-filled signs of renewal and reform.
History, of course, will decide if that is the case.

THE DYNAMICS OF REFORM

The word "reform" derives from a Latin word meaning to reshape. When
we speak of reform in the context of the Catholic Church, the term must
be understood in a number of different directions. First, and most obviously, there is that internal reform in which abuses are corrected, procedures are streamlined for greater clarity and efficiency, and ways of
doing things are changed in order to better reflect the changing situations
in which the Church finds itself.

Such internal reform, as we have noted in a number of places, has two
components illustrated by two neologisms that have become part of the
currency of Church language. The first is *ressourcement* – that effort to go
back to the sources of the Catholic tradition to reappropriate the best
insights and the most authentic witness to the essentials of belief and
practice. The second component is *aggiornamento* which recognizes the
need to speak to the contemporary world. These two components need to
operate in some sort of dynamic relationship. To rely on *ressourcement*
alone is to risk the condition of antiquarianism, while focus solely on
aggiornamento is to be allured by faddism. The Church, like the good
householder, should strive to bring forth both the old and the new.

Reform *ad extra* means that the Church must "reshape" itself by paying
attention to the fact that it lives in a larger world, and, if it is not to be
sealed off to that world, it must present itself as being intelligible to that
world. Here again, the dynamics of reform demand that the Church must
balance its role as teacher and *as learner*. The foundation for that kind
of subtle relationship to the larger world was set out programmatically
in the opening paragraph of *Gaudium et spes*:

> Nothing that is genuinely human fails to find an echo in their hearts. For theirs is
> a community of people united in Christ and guided by the Holy Spirit in their
> pilgrimage towards the Father's Kingdom bearers of a message of salvation for
> all of humanity. That is why they cherish a feeling of deep solidarity with the
> human race and its history. (*Gaudium et spes*, No. 1)

The question of reform must always be seen in the light of the relationship of the
people of God to the entire human race.

Box 9   The signs of the time

Vatican II's Pastoral Constitution on the Church in the Modern World (*Lumen gentium*) says in its preface that "In every age, the Church carries the responsibility of reading the signs of the times and of interpreting them in the light of the Gospel, if it is to carry out its task" (No. 4). The phrase "signs of the times" was a new coinage in a Church document, but behind it is the very old idea that the Church is both a teacher and a learner. Since the Church unfolds in human history, it is shaped by the history in which it lives and, in turn, shapes that history. There is a dialectical tension in that notion. The Church sees itself responsible of being faithful to its message while at the same time preaching that message, which is the Gospel, in terms that make it understandable in each moment of that very history.

It is that very tension between the immutable truth of the Gospel and the contingencies and changes of history and culture that drives reform in the Church. The history of theological expression is an excellent example of the need to re-form its reflection on the faith in the light of the signs of the time. When Thomas Aquinas, writing in the thirteenth century, adapted the newly discovered ideas of Aristotle, which came to the Christian West via Islamic sources, in order to express the truths of the faith using those categories, he was not changing the doctrines of the faith but, rather, expressing them in terms that could be best grasped by the intellectual world of his time. Similarly, when, in the sixteenth century, Catholic theology was cast in a more apologetic (and, at times, polemical) fashion, it was a response to the signs of the times made urgent by the rise of the challenges brought about by the Protestant Reformation. In our own day, the prodigious task, still a work to be accomplished, of stating Catholic teaching in a way that makes it comprehensible, just to cite two audiences, for modern secular society or the parts of the world with quite different worldviews, such as the vast worlds of Hindu, Buddhist or Islamic culture, the theologians who undertake that task are doing so in obedience to recognizing the signs of the times.

Apart from the more technical tasks of doing theology, the Church must also be alert to broad advances in the world of culture. How does one assess the vast revolution that has taken place in the world of communications today? What are we to make of some of the advances in genetics, bioengineering, neonatal strategies, and the other life and cognitive sciences in the light of the Church's fundamental conviction that all people are made in the image and likeness of God? Are the traditional vehicles of the works of charity sufficient to confront the requirements of the world's poor? How does the Church respond to contemporary warfare? Terrorism? Can the Church speak to the ecological crisis? And so on.

Reform in the Church is never simply a matter of tidying up our own house but is also a task of the Church in conversation with other faiths and with the world at large. Every time, as this chapter has attempted to show, that the Church pulled in on itself, trumpeting its own certainties, and resisting the world beyond it, there has been a need for reform – a reformation that almost always comes from below. At the same time, the Church

Box 9 (cont.)

has had to struggle not to cave in to the pretensions of the age since the Church is a countersign to the world and, at its best, says "no" to the world. That is what the martyrs did both in antiquity and today; it was the "no" of the desert fathers and mothers who fled the corruption of late antique society; it was the "no" of the barefoot friars who protested the smugly rich hierarchs of the medieval Church.

Reformation, in the final analysis, is the impulse of the Spirit which prays in, through, and for the Church because, as Saint Paul said a long time ago, "We know that the whole creation has been groaning in labor pains until now and not only creation but we ourselves, who have the first fruits of the creation" (Rom. 22–3).

FURTHER READING

Bellitto, Christopher, *Renewing Christianity: A History of Church Reform from Day One to Vatican Two* (New York, N.Y.: Paulist, 2001). A reliable short survey.

Congar, Yves, *Tradition and Traditions* (Basingstoke and New York: Macmillan, 1967). A classic study of the unchangeable and changeable elements in the Church.

Dulles, Avery, *The Reshaping of Catholicism* (San Francisco, Calif.: Harper, 1988). A study of how models of the Church have changed over the centuries.

Hanna, Tony, *New Ecclesial Movements* (Staten Island, N.Y.: Alba, 2006). A survey of new movements in the Catholic Church since Vatican II.

Kung, Hans, *The Council, Reform, and Reunion* (London and New York, N.Y.: Sheed & Ward, 1961). A clarion call for reform on the eve of Vatican Council II by the noted Swiss theologian.

Ladner, Gerhard, *The Idea of Reform* (New York, N.Y.: Harper, 1967). A somewhat older but classic study of Church reform.

Lakeland, Paul, *Catholicism at the Crossroads* (London and New York, N.Y.: Continuum, 2007). On the role of the laity as reformers in the Church.

Olin, John, ed., *Catholic Reform: From Cardinal Ximenes to the Council of Trent* (New York, N.Y.: Fordham University Press, 1990). Anthology of primary sources.

Prusak, Bernard, *The Church Unfinished* (New York, N.Y.: Paulist, 2004). A succinct historical study of the changing formulation of ecclesiology.

Sullivan, Francis A., *The Church We Believe In* (New York, N.Y.: Paulist, 1988). A very good discussion of the meaning of the creedal affirmation "One, Holy, Catholic, and Apostolic."

Rausch, Thomas, *Toward a Truly Catholic Church* (Collegeville, Minn.: Liturgical/Glazier, 2005). A perspective on needed reforms in the contemporary Catholic Church.

The moral life

INTRODUCTION

As a long-time university professor of theology, I have found that it is not infrequently the case that students will express their unhappiness with religion in general or express resistance to the required courses in theology demanded of all undergraduates at our university, because, they aver, it is so preoccupied with "You shall" and "You shall not." In the thinking of these young critics, Catholic Christianity is too concerned with rules and regulations concerning moral behavior. There is no doubt that Catholicism does preach a moral code, but what is not often emphasized is that the moral or ethical life, according to Catholic teaching, flows out of faith, which is to say that Christian morality derives its strength from the prior conversion of a person to the Way of Jesus. The "shall" and the "shall not" are subsequent to the embrace of faith itself.

According to a dictum attributed to Saint Augustine of Hippo, the correct relationship between faith and morality is this: "Love God and do what you please." That aphorism assumes that a right relationship with God will lead, inevitably, to a moral way of being. Cardinal John Henry Newman caught this truth perfectly when, in a sermon, he said this: "You need not attempt to draw any precise line between what is sinful and what is only allowable: Look up to Christ, and deny yourself everything, whatever its character, which you think He would have you relinquish. You need not calculate and measure; if you love much."

When viewed more generally, there is a religious conviction that requires a certain way of living pertinent to all of the great historical religious traditions. Hinduism, Buddhism, and the other religions that emphasize liberation from the iron rules of karma, all insist that if one knows deeply the reality in which a person is here and now, a path of righteous living will flow from it. That perception of knowing deeply about what religious commitment entails is certainly true of the Jewish tradition from which Christianity springs and from which it draws many of the foundational concepts of its morality. Thus, in the Hebrew scriptures, if one is faithful to the Covenant of Sinai between God and the People of Israel, one will obey the Commandments. The Ten Commandments do not exist as free-floating laws but as a guide to those who embrace the way of God. Moses, who was the mediator of both the covenant and the law (of which the Ten Commandments were a part) put the matter to his people in this fashion: "So now, O Israel, what does the Lord Your God require of you? Only to fear the Lord, to walk in his ways, to love him, to serve the Lord your God with all your heart and soul and to keep the commandments of the Lord your God" (Deut. 10:12–13). Pious Jews to this day recite the prayer called the *Shema* which Jesus would call the summary of the law: "Hear [*Shema*], O Israel, the Lord is our God, the Lord alone. You shall the Lord your God with all your heart and with all your soul and with all your might" (Deut. 6:4–5).

The Hebrew prophets had a profound interest in the relationship of Israel's faith to its moral behavior. They often pointed out that the social and political problems of the Chosen People had roots in their lack of fidelity to the demands of the Sinai covenant. They insisted that the cult of Israel was worthless in the eyes of God unless that worship was rooted in obedience to the ethical demands of the law. Typical of this insistence is the voice of Jeremiah:

Thus says the Lord of Hosts, the God of Israel [. . .] for on the day that I brought your ancestors out of the land of Egypt, I did not speak to them or command them concerning burnt-offerings and sacrifices. But this command I gave them, 'Obey my voice and I will be your God and you shall be my people; and walk only in the way that I command you, so that it will be well with you. (Jer. 21–3)

Such observations in the literature of the prophets are so common and so insistently repeated that it would be otiose to cite more instances.

The wisdom literature of the Bible is even more thoroughly ethical in its orientation. In fact, books such as Proverbs and Ecclesiastes are the closest thing we have in the biblical canon to a moral philosophy. It is in those books that the wise and foolish are contrasted, with the wise being those who have learned how to live in "the fear of the Lord." In fact, the wisdom literature, often encapsulated in the aphorisms, exempla, and proverbs, was an educational form handed down in families, tribes, courts, and generations, with the best of it produced by Israel's "sages" to be a kind of formation, especially of the young.

The early Christian community inherited the moral code of Judaism. Jesus himself was formed in this tradition, and, more frequently than not, his preaching must be seen against the background of that inherited past. The Christian community, as reflected in the writings of Paul, accepted as a given that those who followed the way of Christ would behave in a certain fashion and would eschew forms of behavior which were seen as incommensurate with being a follower of Jesus. There were disputes about how much, if any, of the Jewish laws of purity with respect to foods and so on were to be observed, but of the larger moral issues the norms established in the Old Covenant still held. These norms (exemplified, for instance, in the Ten Commandments) were a given.

The observance of the moral law, however, flowed from living the Christian life. In a famous passage, Paul contrasts living in the Spirit from living in the flesh. For Paul, the fleshly or carnal person is one who has not been vivified by the Spirit. From the fleshly or carnal life (note that Paul distinguishes "flesh" from "body") comes fornication, impurity, licentiousness, idolatry, sorcery, enmities, factions, envy, drunkenness, carousing, and things like these (Gal. 5:19–20) but, by sharp contrast, the gifts of the Spirit are love, joy, peace, patience, kindness, generosity, faithfulness, gentleness and self-control" (Gal. 5:22–3).

Paul's emphasis on the fruits of the Spirit as well as the beatitudes enunciated by Jesus in the Sermon on the Mount (see Matt. 5:3–12) are core texts appealed to when Catholics have attempted a positive articulation of a Christian moral life. Those texts, of course, are put into play along with the more fundamental demands that Christians be followers of the Way of Jesus. Of course, the "putting into play" is never done in the abstract but, rather, in concrete situations according to concrete ways of life.

The early Christians had to confront the demands of their faith in Jesus in relationship to the culture in which they lived. Certain moral expectations within paganism could be accepted easily enough; after all, Roman ethics and the law that enforced them demanded that a person should not steal, rape, murder, commit perjury, and so on. Nonetheless, there were tension points. It could be argued that those who died for their faith did so because they could not observe the demands of Roman civil society, which they saw as immoral. Beyond their refusal to worship the Roman gods, there were other annexed moral problems they had to confront: Could they swear by the Roman deities in a court of law or as part of their enrollment in the military? Was it legitimate to buy meats from temple butcher shops when the carcasses had first been offered to the gods in sacrifice? Was it legitimate to attend the games in the circus with the inevitable violence and bloodshed? What about attendance at the notoriously lewd plays in the popular theaters of the time? Each of these questions inevitably demanded a specific moral response to specific circumstances.

A kind of moral theology derived from the very exigencies of living in a concrete social setting. In all these settings, however, moral codes derived from the previous acceptance of life in the Christian *ekklesia*. In other words, the development of a religious code of ethics derived from the acceptance of some fundamental principles which were then tested against regular situations. If the Commandments say, "Thou shall not kill," the question then immediately becomes: In self-defense? In legitimate war? Does this command cover suicide? And so on.

Christianity grew mainly by conversion, and every conversion carries with it an aversion: One turns to something or someone by turning away from something. The early Christian handbook, perhaps as old as the latest books of New Testament, is prefaced by what most regard as a baptismal homily, which preaches two ways – the way of death and the way of life – and, between those two, the *Didache* says, there is a vast gulf. The text goes on to describe the way of death, borrowing mainly from the Bible, the usual catalog of sins ending with a warning against those who "have no heart for the poor, are not concerned with the oppressed, do not know their maker, murderers of children, destroyers of God's image, of men who turn away from the needy, oppress the afflicted, unjust judges of the poor – in a word, those who are steeped in sin." The text also inveighs against the mores of the pagan world: the practice of magic and sorcery; those who abort a fetus and those who practice infanticide. "The Way of Life," the prologue to the *Didache,* by contrast, begins with love of God and one's neighbor, praying for one's enemies, and so on. "The Way of Life" is, in effect, a catena of scriptural passages underwriting those demands of the Christian way. "The Way of Death" is garnered from, mainly, biblical prohibitions.

By the fourth century, with echoes that go back much earlier, those who presented themselves to the Church to enroll for baptism were queried by the bishop of the place about their behavior. Witnesses come before the bishop, Egeria says in her description of practices in Jerusalem in the fourth century, to attest that a person respects his or her family, is not a drunkard, and lives beyond reproach. If persistent faults are found in candidates, they are sent away from the font until they amend their lives. It is further of interest to note that as part of their catechetical instruction prayers of exorcism are pronounced over the candidate, and, as part of their lessons, they must learn the Ten Commandments. Finally, to add ritual to instruction, at the time of their baptism the candidates faced west and renounced Satan, his works, and rituals (pomps) and then east to profess their faith.

It is obvious that the conversion to the believing community and the symbolic rejection of the Way of Death were part of an elaborate ritual to establish the boundaries of the Christian community. Hence, what we would call today the ethical demands of Christianity were understood not as an atomized code of behavior but as a way of right acting that established what it meant to be in a community. The ancient *Apostolic Constitutions* put it this way: When unbelievers wish to repent we bring them into the Church to hear the Word, but we do not have communion with them until they have received the seal of baptism (Chapter 2, Section 39). As a well-known contemporary biblical scholar (Wayne Meeks) has put it: The making of morals and the making of community are a dialectical process.[1]

But what of those who had come into the fellowship of the Christian community and then turned out to be sinners? Apart from a few fanatical sectarians, the Great Church was not a perfectionist sect. It knew that people sinned; it prayed for conversion during its liturgy; it recommended practices such as prayer, alms, and fasting as a remedy for sin; it stipulated in its literature corrections for abuse; and so on. Beyond that, however, was the question of those who fell into grave public sin. What those sins were is variously described in early Christian literature, but apostasy in time of persecution, murder, notorious adultery or fornication and participation in public false witness were frequently mentioned. For such persons, the remedy was extreme: excommunication. Excommunication meant not damnation but being refused the right to participate in the liturgy – the loss of the right to communicate at the celebration of the eucharist. It is hard to generalize about this practice; such excommunications were, perhaps, for a time or for life or symbolic (being made to kneel in the back of the church while others stood for the liturgy) or ritualized as a time of penance and fasting during the period of Lent. That this form of penance was a serious one explains, since it was only open to one once in life, that many waited to be baptized only late in their lives.

---

[1] Wayne A. Meeks. *The Origins of Christian Morality: The First Two Centuries* (New Haven, Conn.: Yale University Press, 1993).

In a Lenten sermon preached in 398, Saint Augustine spoke of "penitents of the Church" in a grave tone of voice describing those

who are barred from sharing in the sacrament of the altar, in case by receiving it unworthily they should drink judgment upon themselves [see 1 Cor. 11]. Theirs is a serious wound: perhaps adultery has been committed; perhaps murder; perhaps some sacrilege, a grave matter, a grave wound, lethal, deadly. However, the Doctor is almighty [. . .] Lazarus was raised up, he came forth from the burial mound; and he was bound, as people are who do penance when they confess their sins. (*Sermon* 352)

The complex of confession, satisfaction, and reentry into the communion of the Church was known by the Greek term *exomologesis*, elements of which were known by the second century; such a practice, in the striking image of Tertullian, was a plank thrown to one who had been shipwrecked. Elements of that ancient practice find an echo in the opening moments of the present-day Catholic eucharistic liturgy when the congregation is invited by the celebrant to pause to remember their sins with the priest ending the moment with the short prayer "May almighty God have mercy on us / forgive us our sins, and bring us to everlasting life."

THE PENITENTIALS AND THEIR INFLUENCE

Although there was no distinct field of theology known as "moral theology" or "Catholic ethics" until the early modern period, there was much reflection on the nature of sin and virtue from various points of view – pastoral, ascetic, theological reflection, and biblical commentary – from the earliest period of the Church's history. One influential development (which would profoundly influence the sacrament of penance) was the custom, originating in the Celtic Church in the sixth century, of making compilations or lists of sins and the corresponding acts of penance which would be expected of sinners as a sign of amending their wayward behavior. It seems that this practice first arose within the then highly influential circles of Celtic monasticism but would in time extend to laypersons who were bent on a serious Christian life.

These catalogs, known as *penitentials,* would list the sins of persons according to both the gravity of the sin and the social status of the person (for example, fornication was considered more serious for the monk than for the layperson). The person who confessed had the right of choosing a confessor (not always a priest in this period), and the penance, which typically consisted of fasts and the assignment of prayers from the psalter, was to be of a given duration. For especially grievous sins such as incest, the penance might involve a stay in a monastery or even perpetual exile. It was possible to mitigate the length of a penance by intensifying a more austere choice of activity. No person was exempt from the demands of a penitential life. The ninth-century (?) *Rule of the Celi De* says that any bishop who ordains a man who cannot instruct the people or who is ignorant of scripture or who does not understand the law of the Church is to do penance for six years and to pay a fine to the Church of a certain quantity of gold which was the equivalent of the purchase price of three milk cows.

The use of these penitentials in the Celtic Church spread from Ireland and Wales to the Anglo-Saxon Church and eventually to the Continent. The Irish monks frequently took it upon themselves to go into self-exile as a form of ascetic behavior and, in that activity, spread their customs and practices to the Continent, including their penitential practices. The famous Saint Columbanus (d.615) left Ireland for Gaul and set up monasteries there. The bishops of Gaul found his insistence on Celtic penitential practices too severe, so he went on to the area of Lake Constance where one of his companions settled into what would become the famous abbey of Saint Gall. He and some of his companions went on to Italy and founded the monastery of Bobbio near Genoa, which had an enormous influence on monastic life in Italy. Among his writings is a penitential ascribed to his pen.

It is hard to overestimate the influence of these penitentials. They had a shaping influence on the development of the sacrament of penance and are the forerunner of the medieval books of penance and the actual practice of auricular confession of sins. The shift from public penance gradually changed into the practice we know today of private confession of sins to a priest and a light (almost token) penance. Around 1200 we see the emergence of handbooks for confessors, and, at the Fourth Lateran Council in 1215, it was decreed that every Catholic was to make such a confession at least once a year and to receive holy communion during the Easter season. This demand, known subsequently as the "Easter Duty," came to be seen as the norm distinguishing the practicing from the non-practicing Catholic. This codification of penance was the foundation of what would become the shape of the sacrament of penance or, as it is known today, the sacrament of reconciliation as practiced in the Catholic Church.

MORALITY AND THEOLOGY: THE CASE OF
THOMAS AQUINAS

From the New Testament and beyond, as we have seen, Christian authors have dealt with moral issues. One finds discussions of what is ethical or virtuous and what is sinful or immoral in monastic literature, canons of regional and ecumenical councils, in sermons, letters, treatises, and spiritual books. With the rise of the universities, however, there now emerged academic texts, generated by professors and lecturers, on every branch of theology. It would be impossible to even sketch out this literature so this chapter will limit itself to a consideration of the moral teaching of Saint Thomas Aquinas (d.1274) and further narrow the case by asking how Thomas treated moral questions in his justly famous *Summa Theologiae.* We single out Aquinas's work because it became the source and model for most of the later manuals of moral theology.

The *Summa,* as Thomas indicated in some prefatory words, was written as a textbook for beginning students in theology. It was never finished in his own lifetime. The *Summa* was divided into three parts with the second part subdivided into two parts. Part I discussed the nature of theology, the doctrine of God, and what comes out from creation. Part II. I focuses on the human movement to God with an investigation of human acts, how the habits of virtue and vice are developed, and how law relates to the human pilgrimage to God. Part II.II discusses human acts in particular, especially the three virtues of faith, hope, and charity, which are pure gifts of grace from God, and the four cardinal virtues of prudence, justice, fortitude, and temperance, along with the gifts that come from the cultivation of these cardinal virtues and their opposite vices. In Part III of the *Summa,* Aquinas speaks of the central mystery of the Catholic faith, namely, the Incarnation of Jesus Christ; he then takes up the sacraments but never finishes: The text abruptly ends as he discussed the sacrament of penance. As many know, Thomas had some kind of a breakdown and simply set down his pen and wrote no more.

Obviously, as this brief outline shows, Thomas Aquinas thinks of the moral life within the larger context of the human destiny to go back to God in order to complete the trajectory of human life as coming out from and returning to God. That is why he takes up the subject of virtue, vice, law, and the specific theological and cardinal virtues in the first and second half of Part II. The brilliance of Thomas's treatment of morality is that he sets his discussion in the large framework of the relationship of men and women as creatures who have an end willed by God: to enjoy God's company for all eternity at the end of the earthly sojourn.

For Aquinas, ethics and morality are not free-floating inquiries but are framed within the larger theological context of God's relationship to creation. This becomes clear when we consider how in the first part of Part II, in eighteen questions, Aquinas discusses law. He distinguishes various kinds of law beginning with what he calls "divine law," which, for him, is intimately tied to the doctrine of divine providence and to God's predestinating will. Second, he speaks of "natural law" by which he means what is particular to the end of rational human beings. Despite a lot of discussion about natural law today, for Aquinas natural law meant, at its most fundamental, the doing of good and the avoidance of evil (which is not as easy as it sounds because Aquinas was a Catholic who believed in original sin). Third, he talks about "human law," i.e. those codes of behavior stipulated by lawful authority for the practical end of making individual and social life possible. The external criterion that judges human law is whether it engenders and supports justice; nobody is held to observe an immoral human law. Finally, Aquinas speaks of "revealed law" – that which God spoke, first, to the Children of Israel and, second, the revelation which comes to us through the Word made flesh, Jesus Christ.

Thomas had prefaced his discussion on law by a consideration of human acts, and the habit of virtue as well as opposing vices. In the second part of Part II, he takes up the theological virtues of faith, hope, and charity (those virtues which are a free gift from God through Christ to which we respond) and the four fundamental virtues, called the cardinal virtues, of prudence, justice, fortitude, and temperance. Under the discussion of each of these virtues he finds space to discuss their opposites. Just to cite one example from his consideration of the theological virtues: The twin opposites of hope are presumption and despair.

We mention the moral doctrine as found in the two parts of Part II of the *Summa* because it was upon that intellectual platform that later moralists, either by commenting on Thomas or by using his distinctions as the writers of the moral manuals would do, that the discipline of moral theology would develop. The emergence of moral theology as a distinct discipline found its inspiration in the need for confessors to have an education to adjudicate sin and to apply appropriate remedies. It is in the setting of the training of priests as potential confessors that one must see the beginnings of what today is called "moral theology." Thus, the classic scholastic manuals of moral theology would take up, in the first place,

some basic foundational issues such as the nature of the moral law and
its attendant problems and then move on to a more practical level of the
nature and gravity of sins, which were the opposite of the virtue in
question, and end, finally, with an expanded commentary of the various
kinds of sin discussed, commonly, under the umbrella consideration of
the biblical decalogue.

Oftentimes, these textbooks (or at least the teaching based on them)
would use hypothetical case studies to test the abstract moral principles.
This rise of casuistry would result, inevitably, in turning moral discussion
into a kind of legalistic cheese-paring exercise with little anchor in the
biblical tradition. It had become too easy to forget that for Thomas, the
discussion of morality was intimately connected to what he envisioned for
Part III of the *Summa,* namely, the person of Jesus Christ who in his
incarnation oriented all human activity towards God.

THE MODERN PERIOD

The obligation first issued at the Fourth Lateran Council in the early
thirteenth century and reiterated at the Council of Trent in the sixteenth
century, that every Catholic was to go to confession to a priest at least
once a year, put an undue obligation on both the penitent and the priest.
Every Catholic was expected to examine his or her conscience to see
to what degree he or she had sinned, how many times, and with what
awareness before going to confession. Catechisms stipulated that there
were stages necessary in order to make a "good" confession: One had to
examine one's consciences; one was obliged to confess in detail the types
and frequency of sin; one had to express true sorrow for those sins and
resolve, with the help of God, not to repeat the sin; and, finally, one was
obligated to perform the penitential act adjudicated by the confessor.

These steps inevitably put emphasis on a certain number of realities.
Confession was focused not only on sin but also on the number of sins
and their gravity. Sin was conceived of in highly personal terms; it was
the sin of an individual person making an individual confession. Finally,
the person confessing had to take into account their interior dispositions:
were they truly sorrowful? Were they authentically motivated to resist
the same sin in the future? Did the penitent conscientiously perform the
penance assigned?

From the perspective of the priest, there was also a certain set of
expectations. Was the priest mature enough to hear the confession of a
person and understand what was being said, and did the confessor

understand the shadings of gravity involved in the acts of sins being confessed? Did the confessor have the prudence to assign a correct penance for the person having been assured that the person was sorrowful for sin? The confessor, in short, was put into the position of being a judge – assessing the gravity of sin and disposition of sorrow and resolution as well as assigning an appropriate penance.

For the training of the priest, then, at least two things were absolutely necessary. First, the priest needed to be educated sufficiently to make judgments about the morality of acts brought forth in the confessional. In order to assure that this was the case, the moral-theology books used in seminary education (and seminary education for priests was mandated by the Council of Trent) became, almost exclusively, manuals to prepare confessors to hear confessions. Second, how did the Church know that the confessor was well prepared? After being instructed in the seminary? The general answer to that latter question was that priests had to be examined by the local bishop or his surrogates in order to see if he was so trained.

Without passing the examination, even though by virtue of his ordination a priest had the power to be a confessor, his right to hear confessions was limited until he gave evidence that he had a sufficient training in moral theology to do so adequately. As a general rule, priests do not have the right to hear confessions anywhere; they possess that right of exercise under the authority of some governing Church authority even though by their ordination they have the power to hear confessions. A bishop grants priests the right to hear confessions in his diocese; such a right is known as possessing the *faculty* of being a confessor.

The inadequacy of such a narrow focus in moral theology, oriented almost solely to preparing confessors, slowly came to the attention of the more forward thinkers in the Church for the reasons already alluded to above. The focus on modern moral theology was judged to be too narrowly restricted to sin, the number and gravity of sins, and was considered again too narrowly on the individual in the confessional. The consequence of such a restricted consideration inevitably made moral theology, as commonly taught in seminaries, legalistic, preoccupied with sin, and inattentive to the larger Christian life. The common criticisms of auricular confession were not without justification. On the one hand, participation in the sacrament of penance could become routine and mechanical (one confesses, hopes to do better, fails and goes to confession again), while, on the other hand, it could lead more sensitive persons to a state of anxiety (Did I confess everything?) or a scrupulosity that borders on the obsessive compulsive. Finally, the narrowing of attention to the sinful acts of the individual

seems to have lost one fundamental emphasis of penance as it was understood in the Early Church, namely, that the whole process of penance was
not only a way of being forgiven of one's sins but also a way of expressing
reconciliation as something that involved being within the believing
community. In other words, the focus on the individual had somewhat
submerged the idea of penance as a communal act of reconciliation.

In its Decree on the Training of Priests (*Optatam Totius*), the Second
Vatican Council, fully aware of the need for reform of moral theology,
said this: "Special care is to be taken for the improvement of moral
theology. Its scientific presentation, drawing more fully on the teaching of
holy scripture, should highlight the vocation of the Christian faithful and
their obligation to bring forth fruit in charity for the life of the world"
(No. 16). Behind that rather laconic encouragement to improve moral
theology was a whole literature published in the decades before the
Council to insist that moral theology should be better understood in the
light of the theological virtue of charity, the law of Christ, and the relational theology flowing naturally from the life of the Trinity. It is
worthwhile noting that even in the brief statement quoted above the
emphases were on scripture, the human vocation, the requirements of
charity, and the relationship of the individual to the larger world. Nothing
in that exhortation drew undue emphasis on sin and guilt.

The good confessor

Saint Alphonsus de Liguori (1696–1787) was one of the most influential
moral theologians of the modern period. Here is part of his exhortation to
confessors in his work on moral theology written in 1755:

The confessor, to be a kind father, should be full of charity. This charity
should be shown, in the first place, in the way everyone is welcomed: It does
not matter whether they are poor or rough mannered or sinners [. . .]

That is why confessors, clothed with compassion as the Apostle Paul urges,
should act in this way: The deeper they find that a person has sunk into the
mire of sin, the greater the love they will show in order to draw the soul back to
God. These or similar words should be used: Come on, now, Be happy! Make a
good confession. Say everything with a sense of freedom; don't be embarrassed
about anything. It doesn't matter if you haven't fully examined your conscience; it is enough to answer whatever questions I put to you. Say thanks to
God who has been waiting for you to come. Now your life is to be changed. Be
happy; God certainly forgives you if you have the proper intention. Indeed,
God has been waiting just to be able to forgive you.

(From: *Alphonsus de Liguori: Selected Writings*, ed. Frederick Jones, C.S.S.R.
[New York, N.Y.: Paulist, 1999], pp. 318–19)

THE PRESENT SITUATION

Writing a generation after the close of the Second Vatican Council, the Jesuit moral theologian Richard McCormick (1922–2000) looked at the shifting emphases of moral thinking and indicated some trajectories that would move away from the old approach of the manuals. They would include among others:

1. The increasing specialization of moral theology. The day when one professor could "cover" all of moral theology is over. Moral issues arising from the fields of medicine, technology, and science as well as the complex world of social policy, both national and international, are so varied that no single person can hope to understand them all with any sense of adequacy.

2. The shift from thinking about ethics and morality only in terms of the individual to the larger questions of social justice brings its own challenges for moral theologians. The late Pope John Paul II, in his social encyclical *Sollicitudo rei socialis,* spoke of "structures of sin," which leads moralists to think about morality or immorality of a whole range of realities: governments, financial institutions, corporations, etc.

3. The consideration of personal and social experience as we learn more about human behavior thanks to the insights of everything from psychiatry to the cognitive and social sciences. If, in the past, it was thought that Catholic moral theology shapes and educates for moral living, the new question is how has our ethical thinking been shaped by experience?

4. Cultural diversity brings with it its own challenges to the ethicist. While Catholic morality has always taught that there is an embedded law of nature that underpins fundamental standards of behavior, the differences in culture also indicate that there are no universal ways of thinking about how a person relates to the family, to society, and so on.

5. A shift away from thinking about morality only in terms of law and sin towards a deeper appreciation of the cultivation of virtue, the exemplary witness of saints and holy people, the following of Jesus Christ as model and paradigm, and so on. This emphasis also brings up a demanding issue: Is there a distinctive Christian ethics, or is there a more general ethics to which the Christian witness gives nuance and depth?

6. Moral thinking, under the impulse of the clear teaching of the Second Vatican Council, must be in conversation with other Christians and with those outside the Christian family altogether. In fact, in recent

decades, the Catholic Church has sought actively to cooperate with other religious (and, for that matter, nonreligious) bodies to give witness to and cooperate in the needs of the world both material and spiritual.

7. There has been a shift in both who studies and teaches moral theology and what consequences flow from that shift. Up until the period immediately after Vatican II, moral theologians were almost exclusively ordained priests who taught largely in seminaries. With the explosive interest in all fields of theology – and moral theology was no exception – it is more commonly the case that those who both study and teach moral theology are laypeople and especially laywomen. The result of that shifting demographic is that laypeople bring different questions to the table and from quite different perspectives. It was one thing for a priest to discuss, say, the moral questions concerning sexuality with regard for family planning and quite another thing for married men and women, themselves raising families, to frame questions. This is not to argue that a person must have an experience to judge its morality, but it is to say that the questions become contextualized when experience helps frame the question. This shift in emphasis also comes when those thinking and writing about morality reflect voices that speak from different cultural milieus in which the very language is different from that of the inherited past of Roman law and Western customs.

8. The perennial task of moral theology in particular and the Church's task more generally is to teach and learn how to live after the manner of Jesus Christ by recalling the great themes of love understood as self-giving, the claims of justice, the cultivation of deep reverence for the self and the other by a full realization of what is meant by saying that we are made in "the image and likeness of God," and how our common fidelity to the person and Gospel of Jesus flows out from our own appropriation of faith to help bring about the coming kingdom.

THE MORAL TEACHING OF THE CHURCH

It is a small sign of the contemporary turn in Catholic moral theology that the third "pillar" of the *Catechism of the Catholic Church* outlining the moral teaching of Catholicism is called simply "Life in Christ." That part is then divided into three large sections which treat, in order, the dignity of the human person, the human person in society, and the nature of the moral life organized under an extended excursus on the decalogue (the Ten Commandments). Each of these three large sections deserves some detailed consideration.

The dignity of the human person

The fundamental text of Catholic morality roots itself in the affirmation of the Book of Genesis that all humans are "made in the image and likeness of God," and that affirmation emphasizes the stipulation "all humans" because it is from that fundamental fact that moral theology goes on to insist that every human being has inalienable rights and privileges as somehow sharing the divine life. It is from this datum that the Catholic Church goes on to insist that the end – the *telos* – for every person who comes out from God has, as his or her finality, to go back to God to share in beatitude. Furthermore, every human being is, by nature, free and gifted with the capacity to choose as a free person.

Drawing on this fundamental principle, Catholic morality teaches the central fact of human *solidarity*, which insists that because all humans are interdependent it is a moral obligation for each individual to act responsibly and morally to all others. This is both an individual obligation and a social one; thus, for example, political entities are morally bound to act towards each other with this sense of human solidarity in mind.

Human solidarity demands that there be a recognition that individuals have certain fundamental rights. These non-negotiable rights spring from the fact that all humans are created in the image and likeness of God (a biblical way of speaking of solidarity). From this foundation, Catholic social teaching attests to rights such as life, security, work, sustainable income, educations, and so on.[2] It is easy to see that from these foundational principles other moral imperatives can be drawn, ranging from such large issues as war and peace to the powers and limitations of the nation-state.

It is the very freedom of a human being that makes that person also a moral actor who chooses what is right or what is wrong depending on how the person judges the morality of his or her actions. Catholic morality resolutely resists the idea that people are programmed, fated or driven under compulsion to act, even though it recognizes that some human actions may be deficient by reason either through pathology or social coercion. A person chooses the good and resists what is evil through the judgment exercised by that person when confronted by alternatives:

---

[2] All of these human rights are spelled out in detail in the authoritative *Compendium of the Social Doctrine of the Church* published by the Pontifical Council for Justice and Peace in 2005.

That judgment is called, traditionally, a moral conscience. Catholic morality insists on the necessity to follow one's conscience even in those circumstances when conscience may lead a person to make a bad moral judgment. Catholic morality goes on to insist that every human person has an obligation to form a good conscience based on education, adequate models of behavior, and the cultivation of virtue, by, of course, listening to the word of God and the teaching of the Tradition, and by asking for the light of prayer.

The *Catechism* goes on to argue that the truly moral person is the one who cultivates the traditional "natural" virtues of prudence, justice, temperance, and fortitude and, more importantly, by the assiduous cultivation and cooperation with those graces God has given us in the theological virtues of faith, hope, and charity. At the heart of this education in virtue is the grace of charity (love), which, in the words of the *Catechism*, "gives to the Christian the spiritual freedom of the children of God. He no longer stands before God as a slave, in servile fear, or as a mercenary who is looking for wages, but as a son responding to the love of Him who first loved us" (No. 1828). It is that life in virtue that helps us, in our weakness, to resist the tendency to sin and to sin itself.

The human community

While Catholic morality begins with the unique character of every created human being "made in the image and likeness of God," it is not a moral theology of individualism. On the contrary, Catholic morality insists that all human being are, by nature, relational – borrowing from the Old Testament insight that the two fundamental laws of our relation to God involve love of God and love of neighbor. Just as Christianity argues that God is a relational trinity of persons, so it sees all humans as radically relational.

It is on the basis of the above belief that Catholic morality insists that people must take seriously duties as members of the human community and, in addition, must give due recognition to human rights of all people while, at the same time, resisting the notion that certain classes, races, or other human cultural characteristics that differentiate by the fact of that difference have the right to discriminate or denigrate or lessen fundamental human rights due to every person. The entire spectrum of Catholic social teaching, the articulation of all Catholic thinking on human rights, and the active work for both charity and justice rest on the right of the individual who is also part of the human community.

The Catholic tradition has never accepted the notion that all human law is merely established by human genius but reflects a deeper law which is found in the very nature of being human. Hence, if human law is not oriented towards the common good, if it seeks to erase fundamental rights of a person, or if its aims are immoral, it must be resisted. Catholic morality insists that all human endeavors must be obedient to the deep structures of both the natural law and the divinely revealed law which God has given us in Jesus Christ. It is for that reason that, as the late John Paul II insisted in his 1995 encyclical letter *Veritatis splendor*, the greatest witness to the moral law may be, in certain circumstances, martyrdom, because the martyrs, by their willingness to give up life, say, in effect, that certain moral principles are beyond change.

Jesus also urges us to live a life that goes beyond the observance of law narrowly understood. Some, for the sake of the kingdom of God, will assume freely a life of poverty and chastity while all are called to press forward to live out the beatitudes uttered by Jesus in his famous sermon on the mount – to become pure of heart, peace makers, and so on – as well as undertaking those "ordinances of religion" such as prayer, fasting, and almsgiving.

The Decalogue

There is a very old tradition in Catholicism to use the Ten Commandments as a scaffolding upon which to erect a whole structure of obligations, virtues, and sins related to the moral life of Christians. Indeed, the older manuals of moral theology structured their teaching by an expanded meditation on these Commandments. The *Catechism of the Catholic Church* uses that same template, dividing the second section of its teaching on morality into ten sections based on the biblical decalogue.

The first three Commandments – worship of God alone, keeping holy the Lord's name and the observance of the Sabbath – command reverence for God and the prohibition of polytheism and idolatry, while ordering the worship of God. Honoring God's holy name obviously forbids activities such as blasphemy.

The Fourth Commandment, to honor one's parents, is the entry way for a discussion of the place of the family, its rights and duties, its place in civil society, the obligation of educating children, as well as the vexatious topic of the question of divorce and the place of the sacrament of matrimony in the life of the Catholic.

The Fifth Commandment against murder involves a discussion of the dignity of human life, life as sacred, and the general Catholic insistence that all life must be protected – from human conception to death. Obviously, under this broad rubric, there ramified out Catholic teaching on everything from the prohibition of abortion, direct euthanasia, when and under what conditions life may be taken in self-defense, in times of war, and whether it is legitimate for the State to inflict death as a punishment.

The Sixth and Ninth Commandments are the places where the Catholic teaching on human sexuality occurs. Put basically, the Catholic Church teaches that human sexuality is a good given by God to be exercised responsibly for the purposes of human procreation and as a sign of love within marriage itself. The misuse of sexuality would range from extramarital abuse of sex – as in adultery, fornication – to sexual activities alone or with others that are not licit since they are acts outside the ends for which sex is intended by both natural and divine law.

The Seventh and Tenth Commandments involve fundamentally the prohibition of taking another's property ("Thou shall not steal"), but, by extension, the moral use of personal goods and property in light of our social relationship with others. This Commandment is often the basis for reflections on social and economic justice, the solidarity required between groups and nations who are wealthy vis-à-vis the just claims of the poor, and the Gospel requirement to love and succor the poor.

The Eighth Commandment, which forbids "bearing false witness against thy neighbor" may have had, as its original intention, truth-telling in judicial proceedings – the prohibition against perjury – but has always been more broadly interpreted by the Catholic tradition as concerned with truth-telling more generally. Truth-telling, of course, covers a wide swathe of human behavior ranging from the simple sin of lying through to the more serious issues of perjury, fraud, character assassination by innuendo, and all of those instances where truth is subverted for gain (for example, cheating on tax forms) or to destroy another's good name or personal standing.

MORALITY AND THE CHRISTIAN LIFE

It would be the conviction of the Catholic tradition that the moral life is rooted in and nourished by the life of faith. Catholic theology holds as a fundamental conviction that we are all flawed and imperfect through the effects of original sin, and, further, the healing remedy of that flawed state is a pure gift of grace freely given by God through Christ.

Seen through the eyes of faith, however, there are certain fundamental truths about our lives, both as individuals and as social beings, which form the basic theological anthropology of Catholic Christianity and from which moral behavior derives.

First, the conviction that all human life comes from God and that every individual person, class, gender, human capacities notwithstanding, are made in the image and likeness of God. From this fundamental datum flows any number of moral imperatives: Every person is made in the image of God; to harm any person or to degrade or oppress them, or in any way erase their humanity, is to somehow besmirch the image and likeness of God which is their mark.

Second, Christian morality insists that all human beings are by their nature social: They live in relationship to others. Drawing on the Christian doctrine that God is trinitarian, Christian moralists insists that every human has a right to a place in society and that the social bonds which make up humanity, whether they be communitarian or familial bonds, bring with that right, obligations. From this first insight derives a panoply of ethical assertions ranging from the right to a living wage for workers to animadversions about the education of children, the rights of the poor, etc. Obviously, behind these assertions are long periods of ethical reflection. One could scarcely argue that the Church before the modern era condemned human slavery (in fact, it did not), and one could confidently assert, as Pope Benedict XVI himself did in his first encyclical *Deus caritas est* (2006) that the Church was slow to take up the question of social justice, satisfying itself, for the main part, in urging the obligation of charity for those who required it.

Third, just as there was a development in doctrinal understanding so there was also a development in ethical understanding, as John Noonan has recently argued in a recent influential work (see Further Reading). For a long time, the Church condemned the taking of interest on monetary loans, arguing that such practices, already condemned in the Bible, were usurious and against the natural order. It was not until money became understood as a dynamic source rather than a simple possessed commodity that the use of interest-taking became less objectionable. Contemporary discussions about the ethical character of various new reproductive technologies, genetic testing, and a whole range of such issues draw Catholic moralists into highly technical discussions as ethical thinking comes into contact with current scientific advances.

Fourth, Catholic ethics has to be done in the context of a truly spectacular revolution in mass communications as monumental as the period in the late fifteenth century when moveable type was invented, making books accessible to a hitherto ill-instructed general population. This new capacity to communicate almost instantaneously also brings with it a deluge of advertising, political rhetoric, alternative forms of suggested behavior, and so on. With that also comes a wide variety of moral claims and challenges which ethicists must consider. How is the Catholic Church to respond to the excesses of consumerism? To the rampant sexuality so easily available in the media? To the persuasive power of mass entertainment? How, positively, does one acquire a place in the media marketplace?

Perhaps no place is the role of media so powerful as in the marketplace of public policy and governmental activity. One of the greatest challenges of the present time is to use the media to present an alternative to public-policy issues which seem, in the face of it, inimical to the moral standards proposed by Catholicism. Raging debates, to cite just a few examples, over questions such as same-sex marriage, accessibility of abortion, policy over immigration, care for the poor, and end of life – all of these and other burning contemporary questions bring Christian moral issues to the fore. The most difficult problem, of course, is to show, via the mass media, that these issues are not simply reactionary moral standards but are deeply rooted in the fundamental convictions the Church holds about the meaning and end of creation, the meaning of the incarnation, and the social dynamics derived from a trinitarian understanding of God's own self.

In the bitter contemporary debates over abortion and euthanasia, it is too often the case that the arguments get simplified down to "liberals" versus "conservatives," when, in fact, the deeper issues concern the very significance of what it means to say what makes a human a human and to what degree is human life valued and worthy of protection. It is for that reason alone that the moral understandings of the Catholic tradition can never be seen as a set of "rules" but as a natural consequence of a very few radical assertions which are at the heart of biblical teaching about the intimate nexus between the creator God and the human beings who are not only from the hand of God but who are also sustained by God. That radical truth is underscored more foundationally by the equal conviction that God "became flesh and dwelt among us" (John 1:14).

Box 10   The question of contraception

If there is one topic that non-Catholics find curious about Catholic moral teaching it is the prohibition of the use of artificial forms of birth control within marriage. It is also a moral teaching which is widely resisted by many married people within the Catholic Church.

It is very difficult to understand this prohibition without putting it into the larger context of the Catholic understanding of marriage as a sacrament within the Church. Catholics believe that the stable and indissoluble union of a man and woman is a sign of grace. It further believes that God is the author of marriage and that marriage's precise purpose is to allow a man and a woman to be for each other a mutual support, a mutual source of love, and a relationship which is oriented towards the raising of a family and the education of the children who are born to the couple. It is common within Catholic circles to describe marriage as the "domestic church."

Catholicism also teaches that sexual intercourse is only legitimate within marriage and that such sexual activity must be "open" to the possibility of children. It argues that the very nature of the sexual act itself is procreative even though at times no procreation will occur. Because of this understanding of sexuality and its intrinsic orientation towards procreation, it does not find "recreational sex" (alone or with others) or homosexual sex acts as legitimate; on the contrary, it sees such acts as disordered and sinful.

Interestingly enough, this view of sexual activity derives from the resolute resistance of the Early Church to those groups, such as the Manichees or, later, the Albigensians, who argued that bringing forth children was itself sinful because it trapped more "souls" into the bondage of flesh. Until the twentieth century, artificial means of birth control were forbidden or frowned upon by almost all Christian bodies. Pius XI's encyclical on Christian marriage (*Casti connubii*) in 1930 and Pope Paul VI's *Humanae vitae* in 1968 reiterated the Catholic Church's condemnation of contraception. That latter encyclical brought about a crisis in Catholicism which has not yet subsided because it was widely believed that a commission, organized by Popes John XXIII and Paul VI to study the issue, would admit some mitigation of the traditional doctrine due to the invention, in the 1950s, of the so-called "birth control" pill. While the Church encourages "natural family planning," it still resists artificial contraception.

Critics of this prohibition within the Church argue that the ethical doctrine upon which it is based is rooted in a defective understanding of both human physiology and human sexuality, but the Catholic Church has stood firm on this point both in its papal teaching and in such semi-authoritative sources as the *Catechism of the Catholic Church* and in the encyclical *Veritatis splendor* (1993) of John Paul II. That the general Catholic population has not "received" this teaching in its fullness has been a source of dismay for Church authorities. It is a conspicuous social reality that some very traditional Catholic countries as Spain and Italy have some of the lowest birth rates in Europe – a situation so parlous that governments now worry about the population deficit in those areas in the future.

FURTHER READING

Curran, Charles E. and McCormick, Richard A., eds., *Readings in Moral Theology* (London and New York, N.Y.: Paulist, 1979). Many volumes of collected essays that reflect current thinking in Catholic moral theology.

Groody, Daniel, *Globalization, Spirituality, and Justice* (Maryknoll, N.Y.: Orbis, 2007). An excellent synthesis of social ethics from the perspective of liberation theology.

Häring, Bernard, *The Law of Christ: Moral Theology for Priests and Laity* (Paramus, N.J.: Newman Press, 1961). A crucial text triggering a shift in Catholic moral theology to a more biblical basis.

Mahoney, John, *The Making of Moral Theology* (Oxford: Clarendon, 1997). The standard account of the development of moral theology as a discipline.

MacIntyre, Alasdair, *After Virtue*, (2nd edn, Notre Dame, Ind.: University of Notre Dame Press, 1984). A classic philosophical study of ethics in the Catholic tradition.

Meeks, Wayne, *The Origins of Christian Morality: The First Two Centuries* (New Haven, Conn.: Yale University Press, 1993). Excellent study of the development of early Christian moral thinking.

Meilander, Gilbert and Werpehowski, William, eds. *The Oxford Handbook of Theological Ethics* (Oxford: Oxford University Press, 2005). Topical set of essays from an ecumenical perspective.

Noonan, John T., *A Church that Can and Cannot Change* (Notre Dame, Ind.: University of Notre Dame Press, 2005). Study of changes in Catholic understanding of moral issues such as slavery, usury, etc.

O'Connell, Timothy, *Principles of a Catholic Morality* (New York, N.Y.: Harper, 1998). A foundational study of Catholic moral theology.

Osborne, Kenan, *Reconciliation and Justification: The Sacrament and its Theology* (New York, N.Y.: London, 1990). A good survey of development of the sacrament of penance and reconciliation.

Pinkaers, Servais, *The Sources of Christian Ethics*, Washington, D.C.: Catholic University of America Press, 1995). A study by a noted Thomist scholar.

Porter Jean, *The Recovery of Virtue: The Relevance of Aquinas for Christian Ethics* (Louisville, Ky.: Westminster/John Knox, 1990). An excellent study about the shift to virtue ethics.

Wawrykow, Joseph, ed., *The Westminster Handbook to Thomas Aquinas* (Louisville, Ky.: Westminster/John Knox, 2005). Excellent articles on the work of Aquinas with good bibliographies for other sources.

Woods, W. J., *Walking with Faith: New Perspectives on the Sources and Shaping of the Catholic Moral Life* (Collegeville, Minn.: Glazier/Liturgical Press, 1998). Explorations of new approaches to integrating moral theology into the larger world of Catholic belief.

Walsh, M. and Davies. B., eds., *Proclaiming Justice and Peace* (London: Harper Flame, 1991). An excellent anthology of papal documents on social justice from Leo XIII to John Paul II.

CHAPTER II

The contemporary Catholic Church

INTRODUCTION

One of the persistent threads running through this book is the tension which may erupt between Catholicism's past and its present. It is always a challenge to rise up to the challenges of the legitimate need for reform while attempting to balance that need against the task of fidelity to the past. There is no doubt that the Catholic Church attempts to be faithful to its ancient Tradition; of fidelity to the apostolic teaching of which it claims to be a guardian just as it treasures many parts of its lesser traditions as they have come down to us over the centuries. The constant risk inherent in any ancient historical religious tradition is either to turn its reverence for Tradition and traditions into an ossified set of articulated beliefs and practices in the name of that tradition or, contrariwise, to quickly jettison the past in the name of some putative "relevance" for the present exigencies of life. In the former temptation, a religion runs the risk of becoming a museum in which practice and idea are trapped in amber or held onto because of nostalgia. Giving in to the latter temptation runs the risk of modishness by not remembering that today's relevance may be tomorrow's fading faddism.

As we have seen in detail when thinking about reform within the Catholic Church, the Catholic Church is always conscious of the fact that, until the end of time, the Church in this world is never at a state of perfection. It must continually engage in the process of both looking back at its roots (a process called in French *ressourcement*) and making itself relevant to the age (known in Italian as *aggiornamento*) without straying from its rule of faith, its sacramental wholeness, and its episcopal unity anchored in fidelity to the successor of Peter, the bishop of Rome.

Since the Church lives in time and history, each age presents its own challenges. The Church had to learn to live in an adversarial world in the age of persecution just as it had to learn how to meet the challenges of

Islam in the early Middle Ages, the discovery of the New World in the late fifteenth century, the age of revolution in the eighteenth century, and the rise of modernity and postmodernity today. History shows that it responded to those challenges with mixed success.

After recognizing that each age brings its challenges, Catholicism is then led to ask what the challenges might be as the Church has now entered into the new millennium today. In other words, this chapter is a tentative look into the future prospects of Catholicism. Even as Catholics pose that question, they are aware that our age is conspicuous for any number of issues that indirectly (the communications revolution, the phenomenon of mass immigration and migrations of people) or directly (the rise of fundamentalisms both Islamic and otherwise, the secular impulses in Western society, the emergence of terrorism on a world scale, etc.) challenge the Church. The issues are so complex and the challenges so multiform that this chapter will only try to outline the thinking of Catholicism as it enters the third millennium of its existence.

THE NEW MILLENNIUM

At the conclusion of the celebrations held to mark the year 2000, the late Pope John Paul II wrote an apostolic letter (*Novo millenio ineunte*) to the entire Catholic Church in which he highlighted the events that were emphasized during those celebrations leading up to the millennial year using them as a starting point for his vision about the direction the Church ought to take as it entered the new century and the beginning of a new millennium. While the document was very much directed to the Catholic faithful, it did offer some hints about the direction the pope wished the Church to go relative to the larger world and the areas to which he felt it necessary to give special emphasis. In the back of his mind, as always, he saw these remarks as part of his plan to bring to authentic fulfillment the reforms called for by the Second Vatican Council at which he had been an active participant. It was very much his own vision so we will have to wait and observe if the new pope, Benedict XVI, will have the same priorities.

Among other things, the pope encouraged the Church to continue what he had already begun in his own papacy, namely, that the Church examine its conscience, "to purify its memory," as he said, and to ask forgiveness for the sins of its past. In contrast to that penitential task, he further recalled some great positive moments of ecumenical openness when, for example, for the first time in the history of the Roman Church, both the Anglican Primate and a metropolitan of the Patriarch of Constantinople joined him in opening the holy doors at the basilica of Saint Paul's Outside the Walls on January 18, 2000. The pope expressed the hope that such symbolic gestures might encourage continuing opportunities for Christian reconciliation. He recalled his trip to the Holy Land and urged further initiatives for peace in the Middle East; he urged the Church not to forget the poor of the world and took consolation that many of the creditor nations reduced international debt in favor of the poorest of the debtor nations. He ended the first part of his letter by reminding his readers that such initiatives were no cause for complacency.

In the final part of *Novo millenio ineunte,* the pope highlighted some urgent tasks for the future such as a new creativity in international charity not only insuring that charity is put to effective use but also "by getting close to those who suffer." He singled out his concern for the ecological crisis facing the world, for the increasing contempt by many for fundamental human rights, an erosion in the respect for the life of every human being, challenges for those involved in new forms of bioscience and biotechnology – not to disregard fundamental ethical norms by ignoring the dignity of every human being. It is clear that the pope was reacting to issues which are of intense interest to a large part of the world's population.

He further urged attention to openness and dialogue with the followers of other religions while warning that dialogue should never reduce itself to religious indifferentism. On that last point, the pope reiterated the fundamental point that Catholicism is a missionary religion with a right and duty to proclaim the Gospel while insisting that this missionary activity be linked to a dialogue "with an attitude of profound willingness to listen." He ended, as a reminder that would naturally come from a pope who had once been a philosophy professor, that the Church's dialogue should also involve open discussion with other philosophies and cultures.

John Paul's letter was a relatively brief one and rather schematic in terms of coverage. However, a close reading of his text reveals that he marks off certain themes as critical for the Church itself (with the need not to lose sight of the need for internal renewal) and others regarding the Church in relation to those outside the Church (the suffering poor of the world). We will use those two directions, of internal needs and needs of the larger world, as markers for our own divisions in this chapter as we move beyond what the pope saw in the year 2000.

Each Catholic community faces its own particular challenges, whether it be the fallout of the sexual-abuse scandal in North America, the challenges from Pentecostal and Protestant fundamentalist Churches in Latin America, the erosion of Church participation in many countries of Western Europe or the challenge of Islam confronting the African Churches and those in Southeast Asia. Those challenges and possible approaches to the challenges look differently depending on the perspective from which they are viewed as well as the cultural matrix in which they are located. The challenges facing the Irish Church may be and, indeed, are quite different from those of the Church in Pakistan. When viewed more globally, however, some of the major issues facing the Church as a whole, which may have resonances for particular parts of the Church, include the following.

The reform of the Roman curia

While some restructuring of the offices of the Vatican took place in modern times, the deeper issue of reform has not been faced even though it has been widely discussed for a long time. The question is, namely, what is the correct relationship of the local church under its bishop in relationship to the power and authority of the papacy? When the doctrine of papal infallibility was defined at the First Vatican Council in 1869, the Council broke up, under the threat of the Franco-Prussian war, before it could describe adequately the nexus between papal and episcopal authority. As a consequence, there arose a common perception (an incorrect perception but a real one nevertheless) that the bishops were merely the spokesmen for the wishes of the pope and delegates to fulfill his intentions. Vatican II attempted to right the imbalance by asserting the rightful authority of the bishop as the pastor and authentic teacher/ guardian of the Catholic faith in his area of competence. However, episcopal authority has been largely circumscribed by the accumulation of authority in Rome. It is Rome, alone, that names new bishops (this practice of naming bishops by the pope is itself a modern innovation), exercises oversight over liturgical practices, determines what or what is not to be discussed when synods are called in Rome, and takes over issues which could or should be handled at a more local level.

In one way, this centralizing of authority has resulted in a level of uniformity within the Church. It is an open question whether uniformity is a good thing absolutely since, in other ways, such centralized uniformity has not been for the good of the local church especially when pressing topics in need of clarification are "off the table" by Roman fiat. One emerging challenge for the Church is to determine ways to strike a balance so that the local church has more of a say in handling its own needs without breaking the essential unity of the Church with the bishop of Rome.

When the 1917 Code of Canon Law was in the process of being updated after Vatican II, it was generally agreed that the principle of subsidiarity, recognized as a fundamental principle of social justice in Catholic thought, should be more widely implemented within the Church itself: "While canon law must remain a unified system for the universal church, greater weight should be given to particular legislation, even at the national and regional level, so that the unique characteristics of individual churches should become apparent."[1] That desire echoes the fundamental social principle of subsidiarity, namely, that the best institutions responding to a particular task are those most proximate to it. For example: Catholic social doctrine teaches that the family has the first right to educate its children prior to any claims of the State.

When the new Code of Canon Law for the Latin Church was published, with the approval of Pope John Paul II in 1983, commentators did agree that one of the better features of the new code was a certain "promotion of the value of subsidiarity in the hierarchical communion and an acceptance of the resultant structural pluralism,"[2] but that fact notwithstanding, there is a broad feeling in the Church that too many decisions and too much legal oversight resides in Rome to the detriment of the Church as a whole. How to implement fully a sense of both subsidiarity and a fuller recognition of the rightful power of the local bishops to articulate the needs of the local Church has not yet been fully articulated. That issue becomes all the more important as the sheer demographics of the Catholic world shift more preponderantly towards the non-European world.

What has resulted after Vatican II finished its work in 1965 is that we have ended up, and one suspects that this is a transitional situation, with a view of the Church blending a model of the Church as communion (of all bishops with the bishop of Rome) and, simultaneously, as an hierarchical

---

[1] Introduction to *The Code of Canon Law: Text and Commentary* (New York, N.Y.: Paulist, 1986), p. 6.
[2] *Code of Canon Law*, p. 21.

pyramid with, in this understanding of the model, the papacy as apex. This compromise of two views of the Church, never fully realized at Vatican II, has resulted in what the noted German theologian (and Cardinal) Walter Kasper has called, using a Latin term, *communio-hierarchia*.[3] Communion and hierarchy are not mutually exclusive, but they do create tension points, and, from the perspective of Church administration, hierarchy seems too often to trump communion. It is important to note, finally, that the "reform of the curia," while an administrative task in itself, is also an issue that has roots in the theology of the Church.

The crisis in ministry

The Second Vatican Council issued a decree on the role of the laity in the Catholic Church and had much to say about the subject in its pastoral constitution on the Church in the modern world (*Gaudium et spes*). Its basic assertion was that everyone in the Church has a role in building up and expending the Kingdom of God by reason of their baptism. It is likewise true that the same Council, echoing a very long doctrinal truth of Catholicism, makes a sharp distinction between the sacramental role of bishop, priest, and deacon by reason of their sacramental ordination from the ministry of laypeople. That being said, we are a long way away from the day when, as a nineteenth-century cleric would put it, the duty of the laity was to "pay, pray, and obey." The Council laid out quite explicit areas where it is the precise role of the laity in the Church to exercise their ministry by reason of their competency and their place in society.

Laypersons of both genders have active roles in many ministries of the Church. Indeed, they have enhanced roles at least in part for the very reason that there is a crisis in most parts of the Catholic Church today: The diminishing number of people of both genders who are entering religious life and the declining number of candidates for the priesthood. While laypeople can take on many roles that once were the near total provenance of the consecrated religious (in education, healthcare ministry, parish and even diocesan administration, large charitable institutions, etc.), there is no role for laity at this moment in the history of the Church to replace the declining number of priests, especially priests who are the pastors of local parishes and other places that make the liturgy available to ordinary Catholics.

---

[3] Walter Kasper, *Theology and the Church* (New York, N.Y. and London: Crossroad, 1989).

The increasing phenomenon of "priestless parishes" or large geographical areas that rarely see a priest (common in South America, parts of Africa, and increasingly in other parts of the world) is not only a crisis in ministry but, more fundamentally, threatens the core of Catholic life. Put simply: Where there is no Eucharist, there is no Catholic Church. The shortage of priests is so acute that the ritual books of the Catholic Church today have an established rite for holy communion to be celebrated where no priest is available. It is called, simply, "Sunday Celebration in the Absence of a Priest." There has been considerable discussion about whether it is opportune to have such celebrations on weekdays. Always present in such discussions is the (tacit) fear that Catholics will confuse or, better, could confuse such services for the full eucharistic liturgy which does require a priest celebrant.

The clerical and religious shortage is happening at precisely the same time when, in certain parts of the world, the Catholic population is exploding both by reason of population increase and, especially in Africa, through conversion. While some of these areas are also seeing an increase in ordinations, it is also clear that the relationship between ordinations to the priesthood and the increase in the Catholic population is not in conspicuous balance. These demographic facts have almost inevitably raised the larger issue, much discussed today, about the nature of the qualities required for priestly ordination: Is it to be restricted to celibate males? Is it thinkable that women should be admitted to priestly orders? Should priests who have been released from their obligations in order to be married be allowed to resume their priestly duties?

Large among the reasons proffered for the shortage of priests is the Western discipline, common in the Early Church, obligatory from the twelfth, that all priests must be celibate. Without arguing the merits of that judgment (there may well be other compelling reasons why more men do not enter the priestly ranks today), the point here is that the question of ordaining non-celibate males (the issue of women being ordained priests is a whole other and highly contested question[4]) is an issue where we can see the problem of universal versus local coincide in the manner described above when discussing the principle of subsidiarity. More than one bishop, indeed more than one conference of bishops, has argued,

---

[4] One sign that the issue is openly discussed can be judged by the fact that Rome has intervened twice with authoritative statements declaring that such an option is beyond the competency of the Church: Under Paul VI with the declaration *Inter insigniores* (1976) and more forcefully by the late John Paul II in *Ordinatio sacerdotalis* (1994).

out of desperate need in their own area, that the question of ordaining *viri probati* (well-qualified and mature men) should at least be discussed.[5] The only exception to this general rule of celibacy has been the permission afforded a small number of ordained married clergy from other Christian denominations who have entered the Catholic Church. Such ordinations actually highlight an anomaly: Why should converts but not born Catholics be allowed to marry and still function as priests?

For a variety of reasons, it has been forbidden to have formal discussions about the rule of celibacy either at regional or Roman synods. In fact, it is a commonly known but a rarely expressed truth that any priest who ever expressed in public a favorable inclination to having a married clergy much less calling women to the priesthood will never pass the Roman vetting process for ordination as a bishop. It has also been well known and widely reported that recent popes, especially the late John Paul II, stoutly rejected any discussion of the issue.

In the two generations since the end of the Second Vatican Council, there has been a veritable explosion of new lay movements within the Catholic world, which is a providential sign that the energies latent in the Church are far from exhausted. Within some of these communities men go on for ordination to the priesthood. Other married men are being ordained to the permanent deaconate in many parts of the world.[6] However, despite flourishing seminaries in a few parts of the world, the maldistribution or out-and-out shortage of priests is a looming challenge which must be addressed some time in the Church.

Secularization

While the term "secularization" is a protean one, its broad contours are well understood. Generations ago, French sociologists studied the phenomenon of French peasants leaving their native Brittany in order to seek employment in the large urban areas of France. It was as if the move to the city was an act that caused them to give up the practice of their faith. The city somehow did not make it possible to find a rhythm of life compatible with their traditional faith. Other students have noted

[5] For details, see: Thomas C. Fox, *Pentecost in Asia: A New Way of Being Church* (Maryknoll, N.Y.: Orbis, 2002).
[6] On the issue of the ordination of women as deacons and how that relates to women in the priesthood, see John Wijngaards. *Women Deacons in the Early Church: Historical Texts and Contemporary Debates* (New York, N.Y.: Crossroad, 2006).

the same phenomenon as people moved up into higher economic classes, received more education, and so on. The fact is that the older forms of rural folk Catholicism could not be sustained in the face of an aggressive urban culture. The sharp decline in mass attendance in historically Catholic countries has been partially, but only partially, explained by this radical social transformation – a transformation going on now for some generations. In Europe, the problem is exacerbated by a declining birth rate such that current statistics indicate that there is now a situation in which births do not provide replacement for an aging population. This imbalance, interestingly enough, is most conspicuous in traditionally Catholic countries such as Italy and Spain.

Demographic shifts, of course, do not tell the whole story. Culture after the Enlightenment, with its emphasis on rationality, scientific models of the cosmos, and newer forms of understanding relative to authority, had both a corroding influence on the authority of the Church over people and a demand, often half-articulated, for more autonomy. The State itself also took over more jurisdiction of the activities of the Church and, from at least the time of the late eighteenth century, more juridical control over such matters as marriage. Many parts of Europe still have religious houses, monasteries, churches, and other former church buildings which were simply taken over by the State and put to secular uses – with most of these confiscations taking place in the early nineteenth century (as in Germany) or in the early twentieth century (France).

The degree to which secularization in the contemporary life of people intrudes upon or impedes religious life is a very subtle subject. It is clear, however, that the voice of the Church is only one voice in the public arena speaking about the destiny and purposes of life. There was a time when a person's religious and moral life was pretty much shaped by family, church, local mores, and the limited exposure one got in schooling. Today, at almost any hour, one can hear "experts" or pundits speaking about morality, belief, and so on, while holding forth on the public airwaves.

One of the great challenges to the Church today is the massive impact of the mass media on the shaping of the contemporary consciousness. Even a pope such as the late John Paul II, who had a keen awareness of the power of the media and exploited it to its fullest could not hold back the power of those who compete in the media. He thundered against consumerism in a world where advertising is everywhere. He urged the young to live chaste lives in a culture where pornography is a keystroke away on the computer and erotic imagery is the stock in trade of mass advertising. He asked people for self-sacrifice when the media urged self-indulgence. He cried out on behalf of the poor and destitute of the world, but they only got their minute – if that – on the evening news.

It has often been remarked that one of the agents of the Protestant Reformation's vast success was the invention of moveable type by Johannes Gutenberg in the mid-fifteenth century. The printed book made access to the teachings of the reformers instantly accessible to the many. It is not an exaggeration to say that the new electronic media mark a revolution as great as that of the invention of printing; perhaps even greater because now these media penetrate most of the world, making the world, to borrow a phrase, a "global village," at least as far as information is concerned.

The net result of that revolution, only dimly seen at the Second Vatican Council and responded to in the weakest of the conciliar documents (that on social communications), now presents the Catholic Church with a tremendous challenge: How does it carry out its mission to evangelize the world and to instruct its own people in the media world of today? Every failure in answering this question either increases secularization or drives people into either fundamentalisms of various stripes or into indifferentism or, more commonly in the Western world, into an attenuated identification with their faith which is more cultural than vigorous.

The communications revolution will force the Church, accustomed to an older and bookish way of teaching, to take into account this new phenomenon. Ponderous encyclicals, many pages in length, or voluminous catechisms with thousands of numbered paragraphs, seem to be oddly out of place in a world of sound bites, instant messaging, and the proliferation of blogs and podcasts.

Polarization

It is a historical truth that in every period after a particularly vigorous and effective ecumenical council, there is a period in which the Church is unsettled. It is during this period that the teachings of a particular council are "received" or not received by the Church at large, not in the assent to doctrinal propositions alone but as an absorption of the spirit articulated by a given council.[7] The process of reception has not always been a

---

[7] "Reception" is used as a technical term in theology to cover a number of situations; see Thomas Rausch. "Reception" in Joseph A. Komonchak, M. Collins, and Dermot A. Lane, eds, *The New Dictionary of Theology* (Wilmington, Del.: Glazier, 1987), pp. 828–30. In an ecumenical sense, it can refer to the acceptance of the theological consensus of one Church by another.

seamless one in Church history. Some turmoil was evident both after the Council of Trent in the sixteenth century and the First Vatican Council in the nineteenth. Even the first Council of Nicaea in the fourth century, which seemingly saw the end of the Arian heresy, had to confront the fact that Arianism was stronger in the period after the Council of Nicaea than it was before that council until Arianism finally lost the confidence of the Church after bitter and contracted struggles.

In the two generations after Vatican II, there was also a period of unease in the Church which was reflected most strongly in a certain polarization. At one end of the spectrum, a small but loud minority would not accept the reforms of the Council, and some few of them ended up in schism. Led by the French archbishop and former African missionary, Marcel Lefebvre (1905–91), these dissidents ended up in formal schism when the dissident archbishop ordained four men as bishops outside the unity of the Church;[8] some of these still have not been reconciled to the Church. Lefebvre himself was excommunicated by Pope John Paul II as a formal schismatic. This extremist group is small in numbers and of marginal significance, but it is a sign of fissures within the Church after Vatican II.

At the other extreme were groups who felt that the reforms had not gone far enough, and these ended up on the fringes of Church unity arguing for a "people's church" or even going so far as having congregations led by married priests or, for a smaller group, "ordaining" women to the priesthood. A number of these dissident movements have been found at the edges of Catholic life over the past few decades in many countries.

Within the larger body of the Church, counting the extremes of right and left as merely peripheral, it is fashionable to speak of "liberals" and "conservatives" within the body of the Church. Such terms are part and parcel of the vocabulary of the media who calibrate every appointment of every bishop and every argument about Church policy along these lines. Those descriptive tags are notoriously slippery because within the Church one can find persons who have radical social ideas while being religiously quite traditional so that when one speaks of liberal versus conservative it is not always clear where the tag is being placed. Thus, the late Pope John Paul II was socially and politically to the left of the political consensus of most North Americans (he was against the death penalty; he favored the social engagement of the State and the reduction of Third World

---

[8] A similar schism also happened after Vatican I when some would not accept the doctrine of papal infallibility and broke union with the Catholic Church to found the "Old Catholic Church."

debt; he was opposed to the American intervention in Iraq; etc.) but doctrinally and morally he was very traditional.

It has been suggested by more than one scholar that the fault line that separates the liberal from the conservative in the Church is the attitude the party takes concerning the prohibition of artificial contraception reiterated by Pope Paul VI's 1968 encyclical *Humanae vitae* and the vigorous defense of that teaching by subsequent popes.[9] While it is very clear that the teaching has not been received by the majority of lay Catholics, it could be argued that the issue of contraception masked a deeper fault line that may more clearly distinguish the polarity imperfectly described as liberal versus conservative. The deeper fault line involves the fundamental difference of understandings over the authority of non-infallible Church teaching versus individual conscience; the historical consciousness versus the classical consciousness; the degree to which certain Church teachings relative to ethics is or is not reflective of Catholic Tradition in the deepest sense of the term; the role of the lay witness in the development of doctrinal and ethical understandings; etc. These are very profound theological issues which require patient and prayerful attention, and, further, they need to be understood as being the deep background for the many more surface issues that are argued within the Catholic world.[10]

Apart from the issue of contraception, it is clear that at this stage of the Church's history there is a struggle within the Church about both how to understand its own life and how to express that life, and, further, the struggle orbits around the relationship of the past and the challenges of the future. It is beyond lamentable that this struggle gets reduced to stereotypical polarities such as orthodox versus dissident and progressive versus reactionary; such polarizing rhetoric – and history bears witness to this – while hardly edifying, is almost inevitable. It is a mirror image of the larger passions of public discourse today as well as a discourse founded in that tension between those who emphasize hierarchy over communion, and vice versa, in their understanding of the nature of the Church.

ISSUES EXTERNAL TO THE CHURCH

When, in a clear break with tradition, the Second Vatican Council, for the first time in Catholic history, addressed one of its conciliar documents

---

[9] The issues concerning contraception were discussed in Box 10.
[10] Leslie Tentler's *Catholics and Contraception: An American History* (Ithaca, N.Y.: Cornell University Press, 2004) is a brilliant study that sheds much light on both reception theory and the inadequate categories of liberal versus conservative.

(the pastoral constitution *Gaudium et spes*) to all people of good will, it marked a moment when the Catholic Church signaled that it was ready to engage in a dialogue with the large world outside of its own reality. It was the first time in the history of the Catholic Church that an ecumenical council addressed one of its documents to the world outside the visible bonds of Catholicism. The Church, obviously, has always had to deal with the larger world, but, in the wake of the loss of the Papal States, the fear of modernism, and the horrors of two world wars, Catholicism, for most of the twentieth century, lived in a fortress mentality. (I still remember, for some reason, from my youth, a cartoon depicting the Church as an impregnable bastion on an island with waves named secularism, Marxist ideology, etc., battering ineffectually at the base of the walls of the fortress church.)

The Council fathers somehow understood that the fortress mentality would no longer suffice in the modern world; indeed, they thought that it was a deficient way of looking at the world from a theological point of view. With the memory of World War II fresh in the memory of many bishops, they saw that the Church as a self-enclosed entity failed to rally Christian sentiments against the regnant virus of Nazism and fascism and worried about the Church's capacity to stand up to Communism. The Church as a defensive fortress did not adequately express even in metaphor its fundamental meaning. It was for that reason that the Church needed to be in conversation with the many voices outside its unity.

We can think of those needed conversations as a widening circle: First, with others who claimed the name Christian; then with the parent religion of Judaism; then with the other great tradition of Islam; and then the world's other great religious traditions; and, finally, with the still yet larger world, whether antagonistic to the Church, only curious about it, or even indifferent to it. About each, some observations need be made.

Christian ecumenism

"The restoration of unity, among all Christians, is one of the principal concerns of the Second Vatican Council." That bald assertion opens the Decree on Ecumenism (*Untitatis redintegratio*) adopted on November 21, 1964. The rest of that decree sets out a roadmap, from the Catholic perspective, of how such a unity might be attained. The Council was not so optimistic to think that a universal unity among all Christians was either an easy task to accomplish or that it would ever happen fully this side of the eschatological age. What it did accomplish, however, was the setting into place of a series of initiatives which proceed apace down to the present.

Of course, the term "Christian" is an abstraction, precisely because it is a blanket term that covers a huge of spectrum of doctrinal, ethical, and cultural differences among the various Christian Churches. Even the most optimistic ecumenist does not envision one huge "superchurch." Furthermore, the separation of Christians from an historical perspective did not happen purely as an intellectual choice; bitter clashes of culture, ideas, and deeply rooted sensibilities have more than just lingered in the historical consciousness of the traditions involved. Finally, as both the Council and later statements of the Roman magisterium have insisted, if true conversation is to take place, one must be ruthlessly honest about one's own beliefs and, as Pope John Paul II insisted in his 1995 ecumenical encyclical *Ut unum sint,* one's own failings and shortcomings. All authentic dialogue also implies an examination of conscience.

At the practical level, ecumenical relations are carried out in a diversity of ways. First, there are bilateral exchanges between Catholics and a wide spectrum of Christian denominations which are carried out at various levels ranging from national dialogues to international ones. These bilateral consultations are crucial since the issues between, say, Catholics and the Orthodox are quite different to the issues between Catholics and the various Churches of the Reformation. Second, where at all possible, common prayer has been a feature of ecumenism for the recent past and, where practical, common bible translations are encouraged. Finally, in the area of charity and social justice, Catholics and other Christians commonly cooperate "on the ground," in the alleviation of hunger, in times of natural disaster or during warfare.

While there are many setbacks in such cooperation – the decision of the Church of England to ordain women as priests and to consecrate women as bishops is a prime example of a grave setback for ecumenical exchange at the theological level – there is still a willingness to seek closer cooperation when and where it is possible. One sign of the concern of the Catholic Church for the continuation of such ecumenical relationships is that the Vatican maintains an official organ (the Pontifical Council for Promoting Christian Unity) to guide such activities with the full support of the pope, while, more locally, most Catholic dioceses of any size maintain ecumenical officers for such exchanges at the local level as well as various national ongoing dialogues between Catholics and other Christian denominations.

Interreligious dialogue

Judaism

The relationship between Catholicism and Judaism is a critical one for a number of different reasons. First, Catholic Christianity is unimaginable except against the background of Judaism. Jesus, his mother, all of the Apostles, and the early followers of Jesus were all Jewish. Pope Pius XI once put it famously: "Spiritually we are all Semites." Nonetheless, as Christianity began to define itself, it had to do so, of necessity, against its parent religion. Struggles already apparent in the writings of Paul (Romans and Galatians are prime examples) became exacerbated over time, and those struggles spilled over, in periods of the Church's history, into anti-Jewish legislation, social ostracism, and, intellectually speaking, a tendency to argue that Judaism had been superseded by Christianity. The history of Catholicism has been marked by various kinds of anti-Jewish acts, some of them ugly and violent ranging from anti-Jewish polemics to acts of social discrimination, exile, the building of ghettos, and, at times, violence fostered by anti-Jewish preaching. These dark moments of anti-Judaism have to be seen in the light of modern pogroms against the Jews in Europe, discrimination against them, and, of course, the attempt to exterminate the Jews during the period of National Socialism. When the Council met in the early 1960s, it did so with the awful memory of the Nazi Holocaust in mind.

In its *Declaration on Non-Christian Religions* (*Nostra aetate*) the Council spoke of its relationship to Judaism. In a crucial passage in the document (No. 4), it makes some very important assertions, including the following:

• that neither at the time of Jesus nor today are Jews to be indiscriminately charged with the death of Jesus – thus, in a stroke, disassociating the Catholic Church from the common charge, persistent in past history, that Jews were deicides or "Christ killers";
• that the Jews must not be spoken of as rejected or cursed by God as if this was found in scriptures – thus removing the Church as a place where old anti-Semitic canards like that could be taught;
• that in catechisms, preaching or teaching, anti-Jewish teachings must be avoided.

Finally, the Council explicitly condemns all forms of hatred, persecution, or displays of anti-Semitism leveled at any time or from any source against the Jews.

In the decades after the close of the Council, all kinds of efforts, both at the papal level and at the local level, have been encouraged to seek reconciliation and cooperation with the world of Judaism. These involved not only highly symbolic gestures such as those of John Paul II praying both at the Western Wall in Jerusalem and at Yad Vashem, Israel's Holocaust memorial, but also exchanges and, recently, diplomatic relations between the Holy See and Israel. The latter initiative was particularly daring because there were many pressures coming from the Catholic communities living in largely Muslim countries of the Middle East not to make such an arrangement for reasons of their need for security and tranquility.

While retaining the principle that the Church has the right of missionary activity towards all people, it has not aggressively evangelized in the Jewish world and has shown particular sensitivity when dealing with the huge pastoral problem of marriages between Jewish and Christian partners that occur with such frequency in the world today. One area where the Church has been explicit is in its readiness to condemn outbursts of anti-Semitism when they occur as, alas, is still too often the case, especially in parts of Western Europe. Finally, the most important part of the exchange of Catholics and Jews happens when, at whatever level, old stereotypes from both sides are diminished and new ways of cooperating for the common good are encouraged; these are small increments but vitally crucial ones.

At a theological level, the most important work in advancing a better understanding of Judaism has been discovered in the patient research being done to recover fully the Jewish roots of nascent Christianity on topics as different as the Jewishness of Jesus, the Jewish roots of Christian prayer and sacrament, the impact of Jewish exegesis on the formation of the New Testament, etc. At a more practical level, the most crucial efforts direct themselves to both an analysis and subsequent erasure of implicit anti-Jewish ideologies in intellectual discourse as well as an affirmative encounter with Jewish intellectual life and its very best expositors.

It is obvious that the Church cannot simply erase or ignore anti-Jewish acts from its own past. What it can do, and has made concrete actions to do, is to disallow such activities of the past from happening again today and, simultaneously, cutting off any practice or theory that allows such acts to be done in the name of the Church in the future.

Islam

The relationship between Catholicism and Islam has historically been a contentious one. Islam's sweep over largely Christian North Africa, its penetration into the Iberian Peninsula (until it was repelled during the expulsion of the Muslims (and Jews from Spain) in the late-fifteenth-century *Reconquista*), and the struggles of Christians with the Ottoman Empire, to say nothing of the attempts of the Crusaders to conquer the Holy Land, have not made for amicable relations between the two faiths. *Nostra aetate* praises the vigorous monotheism of Islam and the Qur'an's high regard for Jesus as a prophet and the praise of Mary (she is mentioned more times in the Qur'an than in the New Testament) in that same book. The document goes on to stipulate, as with all other faiths, that the Catholic Church recognizes what is true in Islam's teaching. Catholic historians also single out those ways in which Islam has been in fruitful dialogue with Christianity in certain periods of past history.

Today, Islam is in closer contact with the Christian world in two quite different ways. The Church is concerned with the historical Christian minorities in countries of the Middle East who are often the subject of harassment from the rising tide of militant Islamic fundamentalism. The increasing presence of Muslims in European countries such as Belgium, the Netherlands, France, Italy, and Germany has created its own set of problems. The Catholic response to the increased visibility of Islam on the world sociopolitical stage has been characterized both by a desire for greater dialogue and close study of the Muslim world as well as providing a conciliatory voice over the plight of immigrants in a sometimes hostile environment in traditionally Christian countries. The great clash of religious identities is being played out especially in Africa where both Muslims and Catholics compete for converts. Some voices in the Catholic world also call for a greater sense of reciprocity by insisting that as the Western world makes allowance for Muslim religious sensibilities in Europe so Muslims, in turn, need to give greater freedom to Christians in areas such as Saudi Arabia where the open practice of Christianity is forbidden by law. The current tensions between the West and Islam have been exacerbated because of political realities as well as Islamic terrorism, so the exchange between Christianity and Islam is both more urgent and more difficult; indeed, it is one of the signal issues of our day.

Hinduism and Buddhism

The Second Vatican Council's *Nostra aetate* has taken approving note of the yearning religious traditions represented by the great ancient traditions that sprang up in the Indian subcontinent before the birth of Christianity itself. Catholicism has been a minority presence both in largely Hindu India (although the Catholic presence is an ancient one) and in those countries where the different forms of Buddhism (for example, Thailand, Sri Lanka, etc.) have been prevalent. Catholic attempts at dialogue with both of these traditions have been most fruitful at the contemplative level since both traditions have a profound strand of ascetic and monastic observance within them. Although there have been tensions in places such as India where Christian missions have been seen as aggressive and "non-Indian," the Catholic Church has strong roots, with constant experiments in casting its practice in acculturated ways. There have also been serious interchanges with diverse Buddhist communities as Christian monastics have learned from Buddhists monks about their practices. For the past three generations, Catholic thinkers have made serious attempts to enter into "deep" dialogue with these ancient traditions (see "Contextual theology" below) through interchanges and mutual study. As is true with many diverse religious traditions, there is always the besetting problem of the identification of a given religious tradition with national identity. Aggressive political parties preaching a Hindu nationalism have shown signs of both anti-Christian and anti-Muslim tendencies in India just as parties given over to Buddhist nationalism have shown the same in countries such as Sri Lanka. To be fair, some of these tendencies derive from bad memories of Western colonial powers who once held sway over these countries.

CONTEXTUAL THEOLOGY

There is a sense is which all theology is contextual in that theologians work in specific settings addressing determined audiences for specific goals. Thus, to cite an obvious example, seminary professors write, teach, and tailor lectures towards the training of ministers in the Church. However, to speak of theology today is to speak of a theology responding to new publics – publics made available to them by the life of the Church after Vatican II.

The increasing openness of the Catholic Church reflected in the documents of the Second Vatican Council made it increasingly apparent that the Catholic theological tradition needed a language appropriate to enter into dialogue with world religions to say nothing of its desire to speak to the non-religious world of present-day secular society. This is not a new problem; indeed, it is a perennial one. The early Christian writers had to find a vocabulary intelligible to the pagan world of late antiquity just as the great medieval thinkers such as Thomas Aquinas had to develop thought patterns that took into account the new learning coming into the

West as the works of Aristotle (and later, more Plato) became more available to the theologians.

At a more practical level, as we have seen in earlier chapters dealing with the worship of the Church, it was crucial to provide a way for the liturgy to speak to new cultures as they became Christian. So, in the early Middle Ages, to cite one example, Saints Cyril and Methodius translated the liturgy into a language other than Latin for use in the European East. As the Church extended its missionary outreach to areas of the world that did not have roots in Western culture, both in the past and even today, cultural accommodation presents a persistent challenge to the Church.

Until a half a century ago, the study of theology was more or less similar all over the Catholic world. Theology was done in the traditional scholastic mode utilizing the traditional language and thought patterns derived from late medieval theology. The standard fare, both in dogmatic and moral theology, was the "manual," a predigested synthesis of scholastic thought presented in theses and their "proofs" set out in more or less argumentative fashion. Furthermore, theology was almost exclusively oriented towards the training of priests and was taught from those theological manuals using a dialectical form of theological propositions defended by an appeal to scripture, the Catholic thinkers of the past, and, negatively, as a rebuttal of alien (largely Protestant) "adversaries." While providing a compact way of "faith seeking understanding" (the traditional definition of theology coined by the medieval thinker Saint Anselm of Canterbury), it was clearly not an approach to theology that would be intelligible to those whose culture did not understand either the philosophical presuppositions of Greek metaphysics or the traditional language derived from the long commentary tradition on sacred scripture. What the manuals may have accomplished as intellectual modes of thinking was diminished by their austere bloodlessness. They were unremittingly cast in the form of syllogistic thinking and characterized by snippets of scripture and the writings of the theologians, with the whole written in the language of late scholasticism.

One break with this standard mode of theology[11] occurred around the time of the Council when a number of theologians began, within the

---

[11] There were exceptions to this model in the writings, for example of John Henry Newman in the nineteenth century as well as twentieth-century writers such as Romano Guardini, Erich Pryzwra, and others who, characteristically enough, were not thought of as "theologians" in the traditional sense.

Catholic context itself, to ask this simple question: What does theological reflection look like when it is done not in the lecture hall of the university or the seminary but amid the teeming quarters of the poor of Central and Latin America? Does traditional theology speak to this audience? This idea, magisterially advanced by a Peruvian priest, Gustavo Gutiérrez, in his book on liberation theology, was one of the first studies that spawned not only a cascade of books but also a movement soon to be called "liberation theology."[12]

Liberation theology is a contextual theology in the sense that instead of starting deductively from a set of doctrines it begins with specific cultural conditions and, from them, using an inductive track, asks what those conditions say to us about the faith and our responsibilities to person, society, and, ultimately, the transcendent order of things. While the methodologies used by theologians of this sort are sophisticated, the fundamental idea is simplicity itself. Here is a concrete example: We pray, in the Lord's Prayer, "give us this day our daily bread," and we ask, "What does this prayer mean when it is said in a refugee camp or a squatter's area outside a large city, and, further, what might we do in order for their prayer to be said with something approaching a realistic hope that the prayer might be answered?" It is not all that hard to see that once the questions are asked in that fashion, theology and its discourse ramify out into areas where theology meets sociology, politics, and profound areas of social justice.

What the liberation theologians first proposed lit a spark in the Catholic world as others began to see that theology took on a particular nuance when it started with the particular experiences and the particular cultural starting place of people. Thus, the rise of feminist theology still wrestles with the question of what theology looks like from the perspective of women who do not enjoy the privilege of priestly ordination but whose roles in the Church have either been idealized (think of the cult of Mary) or marginalized into stereotypical roles of *Kuche, Kinder und Kirche* (kitchen, children, and church). Other forms of such contextual theology soon followed in numbers that are hard to keep account of: Asian theologies of liberation; African ones; theologies from the perspective of indigenous peoples; and, latterly, gays and lesbians.

---

[12] The literature on liberation theology is vast; for a broad overview, see Ignacio Ellacuria, S.J. and Jon Sobrino, S.J., eds., *Mysterium Liberationis: Fundamental Concepts of Liberation Theology* (Maryknoll, N.Y.: Orbis, 1993). The foundational text is Gustavo Gutiérrez, *A Theology of Liberation* (Maryknoll, N.Y.: Orbis, 1973; rev. edn. 1988).

Such approaches have not been free from criticism from more mainstream theology, especially by those who see such constructions as either special pleading without limits or, as the officials within the Vatican have noted in several notifications, thinly disguised political agendas with only a patina of theological reflection. It is difficult to know, at this juncture in Church life, which of these many theologies will have staying power, but what is surely clear is this: Unlike the more austere forms of the older manuals of theology, these theological works take seriously the living experiences of people, and, once experience becomes a major factor in theological discourse (as we have seen in the chapter on Catholic ethics), the very way theology is done will have radically shifted.

The greatest challenge to all contextual theology for Catholics is, of course, maintaining the delicate balance between the rule of faith and its historic expressions while according latitude for the needs of diverse cultures. That balance requires a willing resistance to the reduction of the affirmations of faith to minimal cultural expressions. It is quite appropriate to understand Jesus as, for example, a *guru,* as that term is understood in India, as long as this is not to be understood that Jesus can be fully described as only a master teacher of religious wisdom and, in the process, ignore the reception of the teachings of the Council of Chalcedon regarding the person of Christ whose two natures (human and divine) subsist in one person as this is taught and enshrined in the liturgy of the Church.

The "Litany of Mary of Nazareth" composed by the peace organization Pax Christi is a telling blend of traditional Marian piety set into the context of contemporary life. Below is a sample of petitions that have biblical roots and contemporary concerns:
Model of the Liberator, *Pray for us.*
Mother of the Homeless.
Mother of the Dying.
Mother of the non-violent.
Widowed mother.
Unwed mother.
Mother of a political prisoner.
Mother of the condemned.
Mother of an executed prisoner.
Oppressed woman. *Lead us to life.*
Liberator of the oppressed.
Comforter of the afflicted.
Cause of our joy.

Sign of contradiction.
Breaker of bondage.
Political refugee.
Seeker of sanctuary.
First disciple.
Sharer in Christ's passion.
Seeker of God's will.
Witness to Christ's resurrection.

THEOLOGIES OF RELIGION

From the time of the ancient Christian fathers it has been common to see in the distant past certain hints and partial revelations culminating in the biblical revelation of Christ. Some early writers such as Clement of Alexandria (150?–215?) argued that ancient seeds of wisdom were sown which would only flourish later in the coming of the word. Indeed, some of the earliest apologists, such as Justin Martyr writing in the mid-second century, argued that the ancient philosophers such as Plato had been influenced by their knowledge of the Hebrew prophets. In the Middle Ages, there were stories about how the Roman poet Virgil had a certain obscure intuition of the coming of the Savior; hence his paradigmatic role in Dante's *Divine Comedy*.

In the contemporary world, fully aware of how large the world is, we now understand how disparate are the belief systems of the peoples of the world, as well as the sheer complexity of the world's cultures. This is a new issue that looms with intensity. A burning contemporary question within Catholic theological thinking is this: If Jesus Christ is the sole redeemer of the World, and, further, if only through Jesus Christ is a person saved, what happens to those who do not know Christ? This question, which had interested Christians for a long period, as, for example, after the fifteenth-century discovery of the New World, is especially of interest today as we begin to get a better grasp of the teeming millions who belong to other great religious traditions seemingly outside the salvific fold of Christian belief.

Some generations ago, the Jesuit theologian Karl Rahner made the term "anonymous Christian" rather famous. He argued that persons who respond to the overall salvific will of God which is planted in every person by the very nature of their humanity somehow respond to this primordial gift according to the lights they receive in life. His more daring contemporary, the Swiss theologian Hans Urs von Balthasar, put forth as a hypothesis the ancient opinion of Origen of Alexandria that we might hope that in the end everyone will be saved since the power of the mercy of God in Christ is greater than the power of evil.[13] Both writers made large claims (neither was condemned by the Church for doing so), but it has been a later generation of theologians, expert in the religious traditions of world religion, who have entered into a deeper discussion about this profound theological conundrum from the perspective of the other religions of the world.

Starting from the affirmation of the Second Vatican Council that whatever is objectively true in the many religions of the world is accepted as true by the Catholic Church, we can then see that there are at least four different "models" to respond to the question of the meaning of the centrality of Jesus Christ vis-à-vis other religions; the description of those models has been proposed by Paul Knitter from whom this model and language is borrowed:

1. The replacement model. When the significance of Jesus Christ is fully understood and his grace experienced, previous commitments and practices give way to the demands of the Gospel. Whatever the old religious tradition may have been, it is now "replaced" by the acceptance of faith in Jesus Christ.

2. The fulfillment model: The Gospel of Jesus Christ is so compelling that it fulfills the deep and honest strains of a different religion. In this understanding, the Gospel completes or deepens or enriches what has been hitherto accepted as good.

3. The mutuality model. In this approach, the Christian accepts and enters into dialogue with the other; conversion is not envisioned; and each exchanges honest religious "gifts" with the other. Christians become better Christians (and vice versa) by exchanging conversations with others.

4. The acceptance model. A variation of (3), this model explicitly says that their neighbor should be other than oneself and accept that fact as a given; that God loves and intends diversity as a consequence of this order of things.[14]

Some Catholic theologians find much in these various models to critique, but what comparative theologians commonly assert is that interreligious

[13] Hans Urs von Balthasar, *Dare We Hope?* (San Francisco, Calif.: Ignatius Press, 1988).
[14] Paul F. Knitter, *Introducing Theologies of Religion* (Maryknoll, N.Y.: Orbis, 2002). This survey has excellent bibliographies.

dialogue is a positive good, encouraged by the Church, and perhaps the very best strategy to follow in this enterprise is to be fully grounded in one's own faith, to express it as faithfully and non-polemically as possible, and to learn to listen to the other in an honest and open way. It is only in this fashion that the conversation partners can begin to grapple with the radical dissimilarities between traditions.

Such interreligious dialogues take place not only at the level of theological discourse. Catholic Christians can meet the others on the "ethical bridge" where common desires to help the helpless or to witness for human rights can be manifested to the world. Some Catholic missionaries have attempted to live a life of Christian presence in lands where it is forbidden by law or custom for any overt missionary effort (for example, in many Muslim countries) either by a simple contemplative life of prayer or by offering such services as schools or medical clinics to the neediest without any explicit attempt to preach except by the example of Christian charity.

THE CATHOLIC CHURCH AND THE CONTEMPORARY WORLD

The late Blessed Pope John XXIII (1881–1963) loved to describe the Church as being like the water fountain found in the main square of every village that allows everyone from peasants to grandees to refresh themselves. The image, undoubtedly drawn from his own experience as a son of peasant parents in the Bergamo area of northern Italy, has a certain charm so characteristic of that most loved of popes.

The problem, of course, with that image is that today people are hemorrhaging out of village life not only in Italy but also from villages all over the world. Both in the developed world and for others struggling to emerge from rural poverty, it is undeniable that cities are like an almost irresistible magnet luring people into urban space in search of some small entry into the cities' economic life. Increasingly, there are fewer people who take their evening ease in the traditional proverbial village square; they are more likely to be in their cars or using the underground to get home from where they work to where they live. The demographic facts are these: Center cities become less attractive as people move to the suburbs in developed nations or the urban centers become populated by the affluent young and in less developed countries the suburbs are, in fact, often dotted with crowded shanty towns, *favelas,* and squatter environments with all of the attendant problems that such migrations carry with them. Driving a good deal of this social displacement is the almost unparalleled movement of peoples as migrants, refugees, and other displaced people in response to political turmoil or economic necessity.

These vast shifts in populations carry with them enormous challenges for the Catholic Church. The traditional model of a clearly designated parish marked off as a discrete geographical area within the larger discrete geographical demarcation of a diocese reflected an older situation in which a stable population was envisioned. It assumed that people would be born, raised, spend their adulthood, and end their lives in a well-defined place. That still happens, but it is less and less the case for large numbers of people. One feature of big cities in the Christian West is that many churches within the city center no longer cater to the populations for which they were originally built. In the USA, one of the more painful duties of many bishops in not a few places has been the necessity of closing parishes who no longer have enough people to make them viable. In the city where my university is located, the once-thriving parishes catering to German, Irish, Polish, Hungarian, and Lithuanian communities are now either closed or consolidated to minister to the latest influx of immigrants, mainly, Mexican.[15] These closings are even more painful when the parishes had parochial schools that now serve the largely non-Catholic poor of the area but run such financial deficits that they become economically non-sustainable to keep open.

In such circumstances one can ask: What replaces the image of the village fountain in the new reality of an increasingly urbanized world? The answer to that question is all the more pressing when one factors in a shrinking number of ordained clergy, the truly enormous decline in the number of consecrated religious,[16] and the constant demographic shifts of the Catholic population.

Nobody, one suspects, has a clear answer to that question. Obviously, the traditional ministries of the Church will continue as they have in the past. The danger comes if the Church is not fully cognizant of the challenges arising from the conditions outlined above. How to react to those challenges will only emerge as the Church, as it has in the past, finds ways of ministry and evangelization. History teaches us great lessons about

---

[15] The influx of immigrants from Central and Latin America is having a dramatic impact on the contemporary North American Catholic Church; see David Badillo, *Latinos and the New Immigrant Church* (Baltimore, Md.: Johns Hopkins University Press, 2006).

[16] In 1965, in the USA, there were 185,000 religious sisters; in 2005 that number had dropped to just under 70,000 with 60 percent of those over the age of seventy. Those grim figures are not uniform throughout the Catholic world; some countries (for example, India) still have a vigorous number of religious sisters.

rising to new situations. The shift from rural to town life in the early Middle Ages brought forth the response of the mendicant orders to fulfill the needs of the newer urban realities. Similarly, new energies were unleashed in the period of the Reformation, both in newer forms of religious life and newer strategies of spirituality and theology. When, in the late nineteenth century, it was thought that with the loss of the Papal States the Church was finished as a world influence, a new energy slowly developed freed from the burdens of a temporal papacy.

At this moment in time, the Church, bruised by a decline of priests and religious, a loss of confidence in episcopal leadership due to the crisis brought about by the scandals connected to clergy abuse, and internal wrangling between factions, hopes to see the first signs of another new Pentecost. What would such signs be? The flourishing Church in the non-Western parts of the world? The impressive growth of new ecclesial movements? An increased willingness of lay Catholics to take up the challenges offered to them by the vision of the Second Vatican Council? Accepting the fact that the new reality is that of a Church as a minority force of dedicated Catholics in a largely secular and indifferent population? If the latter, then it is a new kind of evangelization that will confront the Catholic Church in the new millennium.

Box 11   The contemplative life today

One of the most characteristic features of Roman Catholicism is the persistence of the contemplative life, most commonly institutionalized in the various forms of monastic life for both men and women. The history of monasticism, as we have already noted, goes back at least as early as the third century. While few may be called to live a life of withdrawal, prayer, and work, the Catholic Church has always valued this form of life as one way of living out the Christian life.

It may well have been surmised that, given the impact of modernity, the contemplative life would have become very attenuated in the contemporary world. However, the fact is that interest in the contemplative life continues to attract the attention of Catholics today in one of three ways.

First, there has been an enormous appetite among lay Catholics for the literature that has been part of the contemplative tradition from its beginnings. Serious study of Catholic spirituality and the popularity of spiritual retreats, prayer groups, and other contemplative practices is noticeable among Catholics today as a way of deepening their lives as Catholics. This interest has been mirrored in the increasing demands in Catholic colleges and universities for courses and degrees in the area of Catholic spirituality.

Box 11 (cont.)
Second, the traditional religious orders of both men and women who emphasize the contemplative over the active life have had their own problems with declining numbers but, at the same time, there have been signs that as religious vocations increase they have tended to increase precisely in those orders that emphasize the contemplative life. Likewise, their retreat houses and outreach programs have attracted the attention of so many laypeople that in some areas there are long waiting lists for those who wish to make retreats or spend a period of time in quiet.

Third, since the beginning of the twentieth century, any number of newer communities have been founded to "experiment" in alternative forms of contemplative living whether by putting their monastic life within an urban setting (for example, the Jerusalem Community in Paris) or by living with the very poor in a contemplative setting (for example, the Little Brothers and Sisters of Jesus) or by rethinking monastic life as a predominantly lay endeavor such as the successful Bose community in northern Italy. Older religious orders have likewise experienced a kind of outreach to monastic traditions outside of Christianity such as the monastic dialogue being done by both Cistercians and Benedictines who have an interest in Buddhist monastic living or by founding simple monastic communities in non-Christian lands not as active missionary endeavors but as a sign of solidarity and "presence."

Monastic contemplative communities have always been a minority vocation within Catholicism but they have been at the same time a crucial part of the larger Catholic reality. The renovation of the contemplative life in the present story of Catholicism reflects the perennial faith that some Catholics will always feel a need to turn aside and pray.

FURTHER READING

Annuarium Statisticum Ecclesiae (Vatican City: Vatican City Press). Annual statistical survey from the Vatican; issued in English as *Statistical Yearbook of the Church.*

Barron, Robert, *The Priority of Christ* (Grand Rapids, Mich.: Brazos, 2007). An attempt to think through Catholic theology apart from the "conservative" and "liberal" categories.

Dulles, Avery, *The Reshaping of Catholicism* (San Francisco, Calif.: Harper, 1988). Treats theological issues concerning the Church.

Dupre, Louis, *Passage to Modernity* (New Haven, Conn.: Yale University Press, 1993). An excellent account of the rise of the modern and secular temper in the West.

Ellacuria, Ignacio and Sobrino, Jon, eds, *Mysterium Liberationis: Fundamental Concepts of Liberation Theology* (Maryknoll, N.Y.: Orbis, 1993). Survey of major themes in liberation theology.

Jenkins, Philip, *The Next Christendom* (Oxford: Oxford University Press, 2002). Studies of the shifting demographics of world Christianity.

Knitter, Paul, *Introducing Theologies of Religion* (Maryknoll, N.Y.: Orbis, 2002). Valuable for sketching out different contemporary approaches.

Oakley, Francis and Russett, Bruce, eds, *Governance, Accountability and the Future of the Catholic Church* (London and New York: Continuum, 2004). Essays addressing to the current difficulties in the Catholic Church responding to the clerical-abuse scandal.

O'Callaghan, Joseph, *Electing Our Bishops: How the Catholic Church Should Choose Its Leaders* (Landham, Md.: Rowan & Littlefield, 2007). A suggested model for a more democratic model of choosing Church leaders, by a noted medievalist.

Quinn, John R., *The Reform of the Papacy* (London and New York: Crossroad, 1999). The need for contemporary reform written by a retired archbishop.

Rausch, Thomas, *Towards a Truly Catholic Church* (Collegeville, Minn.: Liturgical/Glazier, 2003). Good for contemporary challenges facing Catholicism.

Schreiter, Robert, *The New Catholicity: Theology between Global and the Local* (Maryknoll, N.Y.: Orbis, 1997). The Roman Catholic Church in global perspective by a noted missiologist.

Ward, Graham, ed., *The Blackwell Companion to Postmodern Theology* (Oxford: Blackwell, 2001). Some contemporary approaches to the study of theology.

CHAPTER 12

Reading Catholicism: Bibliographical resources

INTRODUCTION

The English verb "to read" derives etymologically from the Middle English *reden,* which can mean, variously, to interpret, to inquire, as well as to read in the modern sense. We hearken back to the older senses of the word "read" when we "read the situation" or "read the look on her face," etc. Similarly, there are many ways in which we can "read" Catholicism as we have insisted in this work. We can "read" its architecture, art, worship, holy persons, popes, prayer life, its sacraments and sacramentals, and so on. Each time we attempt to get a "read" on such things, we are confronted with implicit intentions (Why do Catholics build cathedrals?); symbols (Why does that painting include a crown on the head of the Virgin Mary?); usages (What are holy-water founts for at the entrance of Catholic churches?); and sheer puzzlement (What do monks have to do with the teachings of Jesus?); etc. Such a range of topics may help to explain why it is that when a person writes the words "Roman Catholicism" into a search engine on a computer, the "hits" number in the millions.

It has been the conviction of this work that Catholicism is fundamentally both simple (a way of following Jesus Christ and his teachings) and bafflingly complex. The complexity, of course, at least in part, is due to its long history and its tendency to treasure its traditions. When an institution has been around for a long time, it tends to accrete material which it has found useful or meaningful and further tends to hold on to it until it no longer seems to make sense. The memory of the Church, as we have also insisted, tends to oscillate between looking back into its history to recover its best insights (*ressourcement*) and reinventing its practices for contemporary needs (*aggiornamento*) but always holding those two impulses in some kind of dynamic tension in order not to turn itself into a museum or, the opposite danger, giving way to faddism or current enthusiasms.

269

It is also the case that Catholicism has had a shaping force on many of the great achievements of Western culture. The current ubiquity of autobiographies has its roots in the *Confessions* of Saint Augustine – a book that some have argued is the fountain of all autobiography. Similarly, many of the great medieval literary classics – Dante's *Divine Comedy* and Geoffrey Chaucer's *The Canterbury Tales,* to name just two – are largely unintelligible except against the background of Catholic faith, practice, and popular piety. Even books which are highly critical of Catholicism require some background in Catholic practice to appreciate fully what they are all about. It is my judgment, for example, that no single person has been able to describe Catholic piety in modern Catholic life better than James Joyce in *The Portrait of the Artist as a Young Man.*

It would have been tempting to describe the vast panoply of "Catholic" belletristic writing, but space does not allow for such a catalog. Interested readers may wish to consult the work of Lucy Beckett whose *In the Light of Christ: Writings in the Western Tradition* (San Francisco: Ignatius, 2006) reads many of the works in the Western canon through the lens of her own Catholic sensibility.

WRITTEN RESOURCES

It is simply impossible to give any account of all the books written about Catholicism. For that reason, this bibliography will be highly selective and based on a number of useful criteria. First, even though the author has consulted a number of works in languages other than English, this bibliography will restrict itself to works in English. Second, every attempt will be made to highlight works that are serious reference works from which readers might find further bibliographical leads. Finally, even though there are excellent websites available to those who are computer-literate, they will not be included in this bibliography. On that point, however, as with many things, one must be careful to discriminate between the wheat and the chaff. There are many sites which are excellent, but others are tendentious, badly dated, argumentative, or just wrong.

There was a time when one marked distinction between Catholics and Protestants was in the use of Bibles: English-speaking Protestants read the Authorized Version (the King James Bible) and Catholics read the Douai-Rheims translation. If there is any place where ecumenism has advanced it is in the generous availability of good English translations usually done under the supervision of teams of scholars who are both Protestant and Catholic. This book has generally relied on the New Revised Standard

Version but has frequently checked translations against, among others, the New American Bible and the Jerusalem Bible, while making ample use of the excellent notes in the New Oxford Annotated Bible (my edition of the New Oxford is based on the Revised Standard Version). The proliferation of translations of the Bible, indeed, has created its own sorts of problems. Gone are the days when every Protestant "learned" the Bible in the Authorized Version known as the King James while every Catholic knew the Bible through the so-called Douai-Rheims version. The proliferation of translations has made it more difficult to cite the Bible in a version with which all are familiar.

In order to make this bibliography more "user-friendly," we will annotate some of the resources within brackets to signal their utility. Works that range beyond purely Catholic topics will be described as "ecumenical." Emphasis on the bibliography below will emphasize works that are survey or encyclopedic in nature; other works are cited at the end of each chapter.

BOOKS

Alberigo, Giuseppe and Komonchak, Joseph, eds., *History of Vatican II* (5 vols., Leuven: Peeters and Maryknoll, N.Y.: Orbis, 1999). A history of the Council compiled by an international committee of scholars.

Ante Nicene and Nicene and Post-Nicene Fathers (38 vols., Peabody, Mass.: Hendrickson, 1994). Reprint of classic translations of patristic literature.

Beinert, Wolfgang and Schüssler Fiorenza, Francis, eds., *Handbook of Catholic Theology* (New York, N.Y.: Crossroad, 1995).

Buckley, James, Bauerschmidt, Frederick Christian, and Pomplun, Trent, eds., *The Blackwell Companion to Catholicism* (Oxford: Blackwell, 2007).

Buhlmann, Walter, *The Coming of the Third Church* (Maryknoll, N.Y.: Orbis, 1978). A pioneering work on the shift away from a Eurocentric Church.

Bulman, Raymond and Parrella, Frederick, eds., *From Trent to Vatican II: Historical and Theological Investigations* (Oxford: Oxford University Press, 2006).

Burns, Paul, ed., *Butler's Lives of the Saints* (rev. edn, 12 vols., Tunbridge Wells: Burns & Oates and Collegeville, Minn.: Liturgical Press: 1998).

Cambridge History of Christianity (9 vols., Cambridge: Cambridge University Press, 2006). Ecumenical.

Catechism of the Catholic Church (Washington, D.C.: United States Catholic Conference, 1994).

Compendium of the Social Doctrine of the Church (Vatican City: Libreria Editrice Vaticana, 2004). Authoritative collection of official Church documents.

Coriden, James A., Green, Thomas J. and Heintschel, Donald E., eds., *The Code of Canon Law: A Text and Commentary* (New York, N.Y.: Paulist, 1985).

Cross, F. L. and Livingstone, E. A., eds., *The Oxford Dictionary of the Christian Church* (3rd edn, Oxford: Oxford University Press, 1997). Ecumenical.

Downey, Michael, ed., *The New Dictionary of Catholic Spirituality* (Collegeville, Minn.: Liturgical/Glazier, 1993).

Duffy, Eamon, *Saints and Sinners: A History of the Popes* (New Haven, Conn.: Yale University Press, 2001).

Dulles, Avery, *The Catholicity of the Church* (Oxford: Clarendon, 1985).

Dupuis, J. and Neuner, J., eds, *The Christian Faith: The Doctrinal Documents of the Catholic Church* (7th edn, New York, N.Y.: Alba, 2001). Translation of the Latin sourcebook *Enchiridion Symbolorum*.

Fink, Peter, ed., *The New Dictionary of Sacramental Worship* (Collegeville, Minn.: Liturgical/Glazier, 1990).

Fiorenza, Francis and Galvin, John, eds., *Systematic Theology: Roman Catholic Perspectives* (2 vols., Minneapolis: Fortress, 1991).

Brown, Raymond E., Fitzmyer, Joseph A., and Murphy, Roland E., eds., *The New Jerome Biblical Commentary* (Englewood Cliffs, N.J.: Prentice Hall, 1990). Standard one-volume Catholic commentary.

Flannery, Austin, ed., *Vatican Council II: Constitutions, Decrees, Declarations* (Dublin: Dominican Publications, 1996).

Froehle, Bryan T. and Gautier, Mary L., *Global Catholicism: Portrait of a World Church* (Maryknoll, N.Y.: Orbis, 2003). Statistical analysis on Catholicism based on 2000 data.

Gaillardetz, Richard, *Teaching with Authority: A Theology of the Magisterium of the Church* (Collegeville, Minn.: Liturgical Press, 1997). Excellent study of the Catholic understanding of the magisterium.

Glazier, Michael and Hellwig, Monika K., eds., *The Modern Catholic Encyclopedia* (rev. edn, Collegeville, Minn.: Liturgical/Glazier, 2004). Erratic but useful.

Haight, Roger, *Christian Community in History* (3 vols., London and New York, N.Y.: Continuum, 2004–8). An attempt to construct an ecclesiology from below.

Hastings, A., ed., *A World History of Christianity* (Grand Rapids, Mich.: Eerdmans, 1999).

Hillerbrand, H., ed., *The Oxford Encyclopedia of the Reformation* (Oxford: Oxford University Press, 1996). Ecumenical.

Jedin, Hubert, ed., *History of the Church* (10 vols., New York, N.Y.: Seabury/Crossroad, 1961–9).

Jones, Cheslyn, Wainwright, Geoffrey and Yarnold, Edward, eds., *The Study of Liturgy* (rev. edn, London: SPCK and New York, N.Y.: Oxford University Press, 1992). Ecumenical.

Komonchak, James, Collins, Mary, and Lane, Dermot A., eds., *The New Dictionary of Theology* (Collegeville, Minn.: Liturgical/Glazier, 1987).

Kazhdan, A., ed., *The Oxford Dictionary of Byzantium* (Oxford: Oxford University Press, 1990). Ecumenical.

Mannion, Gerard and Mudge, Lewis S., eds., *The Routledge Companion to the Christian Church* (London and New York, N.Y.: Routledge, 2007). Ecumenical.

Mcbrien, Richard, ed., *Encyclopedia of Catholicism* (San Francisco, Calif.: HarperCollins, 1995).

New Catholic Encyclopedia (rev. edn, 15 vols, Washington D.C.: Catholic University of America Press, 2003).

Norman, Edward, *The Roman Catholic Church: An Illustrated History* (Berkeley, Calif.: University of California Press, 2007).

O'Carroll, Michael, *Theotokos: A Theological Encyclopedia of the Blessed Virgin Mary* (rev. edn, Wilmington: Glazier, 1986). Idiosyncratic but of some use.

O'Collins, Gerald and Ferrugia, Mario, *Catholicism: The Story of Catholic Christianity* (Oxford: Oxford University Press, 2003).

O'Donnell, C., ed., *Ecclesia: A Theological Encyclopedia of the Church* (Collegeville, Minn.: Liturgial Press, 1985).

Pelikan, J., ed., *Creeds and Confessions of Faith in the Christian Tradition* (3 vols., New Haven, Conn.: Yale University Press, 2003). Ecumenical.

Quinn, John, *The Reform of the Papacy* (New York, N.Y.: Crossroad, 1999). A reformist plea from a retired Catholic bishop.

Rahner, Karl with Ernst, Cornelius and Smyth Kevin, eds., *Sacramentum Mundi: An Encyclopedia of Theology* (6 vols., New York, N.Y.: Herder & Herder and London: Burns & Oates, 1968).

Reese, Thomas, *Inside the Vatican: The Politic and Organization of the Catholic Church* (Cambridge, Mass.: Harvard University Press, 1996).

Schatz, Klaus, *Papal Primacy: From its Origin to the Present* (Collegeville, Minn.: Liturgical Press, 1996). Important historical study translated from the original German.

Schreiter, Robert, *Constructing Local Theologies* (Maryknoll, N.Y.: Orbis, 1985). Excellent introduction to contextual theologies.

Sheldrake, P., ed., *The New Westminster Dictionary of Christian Spirituality* (London: SCM and Louisville, Ky.: Westminster/John Knox, 2005). Ecumenical.

Steimer, B. and Parker, Michael G., eds., *Dictionary of Popes and Papacy* (New York, N.Y.: Herder & Herder, 2001). Translation of part of the *Lexicon für Theologie und Kirche*.

Sullivan, Francis A., *Magisterium: Teaching Authority in the Catholic Church* (New York, N.Y.: Paulist, 1983). Fundamental study by a noted Jesuit theologian.

Tanner, Norman, ed., *Decrees of the Ecumenical Councils* (2 vols., Washington, D.C.: Georgetown University Press, 1990).

Young, Frances, Ayres, Lewis, Louth, Andrew and Casiday, Augustine, *The Cambridge History of Early Christian Literature* (Cambridge: Cambridge University Press, 2004).

Vorgrimler, H., ed., *Commentary on the Documents of Vatican II* (5 vols., New York, N.Y.: Herder & Herder, 1967).

Wainwright, Geoffrey and Westerfield Tucker, Karen, eds., *The Oxford History of Christian Worship* (Oxford: Oxford University Press, 2006). Ecumenical.

CURRENT VATICAN DOCUMENTATION

Activities of the Holy See are easily retrieved from the Internet. The Zenit News Agency posts each day at www.zenit.org/english. There are also other sites easily accessed via a search engine, such as the English-language version of *L'Osservatore Romano,* which is an official organ of the Holy See. The Vatican itself maintains a useful website with links to the various offices and congregations. It is published in many modern languages.

For contemporary issues in the Catholic world, one can consult magazines and journals of opinion such as *The Tablet* in the United Kingdom or *The National Catholic Reporter, Commonweal, America,* etc., all of which come out on a weekly basis. The United States Conference of Catholic Bishops publishes, on a weekly basis, *Origins,* which prints current official statements both of the Holy See and the American hierarchy as well as important studies and reports germane to the Catholic world. The same Conference also sponsors the Catholic News Service which has its own website.

BOOK SERIES

There is any number of book series that treat various aspects of Catholicism. Paulist Press, for example, has a series called *101 Questions and Answers on . . .* that treats a single issue in a question-and-answer format ranging over a wide spectrum of topics from Vatican II to the papacy. Similarly, the journal *Concilium* reproduces its single issues as hard-cover books.

One of the more useful publishing ventures in the post-Vatican II Catholic world has been the proliferation of series of books to make the resources of the Catholic intellectual and spiritual tradition more accessible to both the professional and the interested non-expert. Beginning in 1978, for example, Paulist Press has published the series *The Classics of Western Spirituality,* which now numbers over sixty volumes in fresh translations with important introductions, notes, and bibliography by world-class scholars. The New City Press (under the aegis of the Focolare Movement) has been publishing a new series of volumes in which all of the works of Saint Augustine of Hippo are appearing in fresh translation. The same publisher is also publishing resources of other notable figures such as that of the three-volume work of everything written by and about Saint Francis of Assisi from his time and through the following century.

Religious orders have been very helpful in printing the works of their given spiritual schools. Noteworthy are the volumes published by the Institute of Carmelite Studies (Washington, D.C.), which has produced all of the works of Saint John of the Cross, Saint Teresa of Avila, Saint Elizabeth of the Trinity, Saint Thérèse of Lisieux, and is now issuing the complete works of Edith Stein. Cistercian Publications, started in the 1970s, produces works by the great Cistercian masters and mistresses of the medieval period along with other resources in monasticism.

Orbis Publishers (sponsored by the Maryknoll Society) is noted not only for its publication of works in the area of liberation theology but also for sponsoring two spiritual series: *Traditions of Christian Spirituality* focuses on schools of spirituality with tidy volumes weaving traditional resources and contemporary reflections while the *Modern Spiritual Masters* series now consists of nearly thirty titles discussing great writers of the twentieth century with a judicious blend of commentary and original texts. The *Spiritual Legacy* series from Crossroad Publishing Company produces rather brief volumes, usually less than 200 pages, on a major figure in the Catholic tradition in which both theologians and spiritual writers are represented.

Index

abortion, 236, 238
ad limina visits, 17, 36
adaptation, 11, 37, 65–6, 141, 182–3, 187–8,
  189–90, 213
Adrian VI, Pope, 35
aesthetic expression, 205–6
Africa
  growth of the Church in, 21–2, 25, 175,
    210, 214, 247
  Islam in, 29, 257
  missionary enterprise, 57, 65, 184–5,
    186, 188
Agatho, Pope, 29
aggiornamento, 43, 212, 213, 216
Alexander III, Pope, 47
Alexander VI, Pope, 34
Alexander VII, Pope, 37
almsgiving, 156–7
Alphonsus de Liguori, Saint, 230
altar, 17, 89, 108–9
ambo, 89
Anglicans, 16, 40
annulment of marriage, 118
anointing of the sick, 114–15, 119–20
anti-pope, 33–4
apologetics, 61, 144, 205, 217
Apostles' Creed, 127–8
apostolic constitutions, 193, 223
apostolic exhortations, 193
apostolic succession, 8–9, 12
Aquinas, Thomas, Saint
  faith, 142
  interest in, 210–11
  scholarship, 62, 180, 190, 217, 258–9
  sermons, 145
  Summa Theologiae, 117–18, 226–8
archbishops, 26
architecture
  additional functions, 87–8
  artistic decoration, 84–7
  baroque Catholicism, 205–6

evolution of, 76–81
focus of, 95–7
as guide to Catholicism, 75–6, 88
theological meaning of, 81–3
Armenia, 175
art, 84–7, 96, 97–8, 205–6
asceticism, 54–8, 154–7, 176–7
Athanasius of Alexandria, Saint, 196
Augustine of Canterbury, Saint (Apostle
  to the English), 28–9, 177
Augustine of Hippo, Saint
  confession, 224
  creeds, 132, 142, 167
  morality, 219
  mysticism, 67, 69
  sacraments, 102
  scriptures, 138

Balthasar, Hans Urs von, 262–3
baptism, 77, 87–8, 97, 102–5, 119–20, 126–8,
  142, 222–3
Baptists, 16
baroque Catholicism, 205–6
Basil, Saint, 55
basilicas, 77–8, 81
beatification, 73
Bede, Saint, the Venerable, 177
Bellarmine, Robert, Saint, 205
Benedict of Nursia, Saint, 55
Benedict XIV, Pope, 37–8, 192
Benedict XV, Pope, 41, 186, 210
Benedict XVI, Pope
  ecumenical work, 215
  life as a Catholic, 54, 148
  new ecclesial movements, 215–16
  publications, 135–6, 193
  reform, 45, 73, 104–5
  social justice, 237
Benedictines, 151, 200–1, 267
Bible, the, 137–9, 270–1
bibliography, 269–75